Husserl and Other Phenomenologists

Husserl and Other Phenomenologists addresses a fundamental question: what is it in the thinking of the founding father of phenomenology, Edmund Husserl (1859–1938), that on the one hand enables the huge variety in the phenomenological discourse and, at the same time, necessitates relying on his phenomenology as a point of departure and an object before which philosophizing is conducted?

The contributors to this book, each with his or her own focus on a specific figure in the phenomenological school vis-à-vis Husserl's thinking, demonstrate that every reference to Husserl is necessarily bound up with modifying his ideas and crossing the boundaries of his phenomenology. In this sense, and given the insight that Husserlian phenomenology is already imbued with the potential modifications and revisions, the post-Husserlian phenomenologies may be included together with Husserl in one so-called 'Phenomenological Movement'. The discussions in the book open for philosophers and intellectuals a window upon phenomenology, which has been one of the richest and most influential cultural phenomena since its very appearance at the beginning of the twentieth century. The book also conveys the complex interpretive dynamic within which a given framework of ideas becomes a sort of magnetic field, with attracting and repelling forces acting on its participants, and thanks to which the great ideas of modernity maintain their vitality and relevance a hundred years after their first appearance. This book was originally published as a special issue of *The European Legacy*.

Ronny Miron is a Professor of Philosophy at Bar Ilan University, Israel. Her research is focused on post-Kantian idealism, existentialism, phenomenology, and hermeneutics, as well as current Jewish thought. She employs an interdisciplinary perspective combining the aforementioned philosophical traditions. She is the author of *Karl Jaspers: From Selfhood to Being* (2012), *The Desire for Metaphysics: Selected Papers on Karl Jaspers* (2014), and *The Angel of Jewish History: The Image of the Jewish Past in Twentieth Century* (2014).

Husserl and Other Phenomenologists

Edited by
Ronny Miron

LONDON AND NEW YORK

First published 2018
by Routledge
2 Park Square, Milton Park, Abingdon, Oxon, OX14 4RN, UK

and by Routledge
711 Third Avenue, New York, NY 10017, USA

Routledge is an imprint of the Taylor & Francis Group, an informa business

© 2018 International Society for the Study of European Ideas

All rights reserved. No part of this book may be reprinted or reproduced or utilised in any form or by any electronic, mechanical, or other means, now known or hereafter invented, including photocopying and recording, or in any information storage or retrieval system, without permission in writing from the publishers.

Trademark notice: Product or corporate names may be trademarks or registered trademarks, and are used only for identification and explanation without intent to infringe.

British Library Cataloguing in Publication Data
A catalogue record for this book is available from the British Library

ISBN 13: 978-1-138-73999-4

Typeset in MinionPro
by diacriTech, Chennai

Publisher's Note
The publisher accepts responsibility for any inconsistencies that may have arisen during the conversion of this book from journal articles to book chapters, namely the possible inclusion of journal terminology.

Disclaimer
Every effort has been made to contact copyright holders for their permission to reprint material in this book. The publishers would be grateful to hear from any copyright holder who is not here acknowledged and will undertake to rectify any errors or omissions in future editions of this book.

Contents

Citation Information		vii
Notes on Contributors		ix
	Introduction	1
	Ronny Miron	
1	Husserl and Other Phenomenologists	3
	Ronny Miron	
2	Husserl and Levinas: The Ethical Structure of a Philosophical Debt	17
	Hagi Kenaan	
3	Husserl, Heidegger, and Sartre: Presence and the Performative Contradiction	29
	James Mensch	
4	Intentionality, Consciousness, and the Ego: The Influence of Husserl's *Logical Investigations* on Sartre's Early Work	47
	Lior Levy	
5	From Husserl to Merleau-Ponty: On the Metamorphosis of a Philosophical Example	61
	Meirav Almog	
6	Husserl and Jacob Klein	71
	Burt C. Hopkins	
7	A Tale of Two Schisms: Heidegger's Critique of Husserl's Move into Transcendental Idealism	92
	George Heffernan	
	Bibliography	112
	Index	121

Citation Information

The chapters in this book were originally published in *The European Legacy*, volume 21, issues 5–6 (August–September 2016). When citing this material, please use the original page numbering for each article, as follows:

Introduction
Introduction
Ronny Miron
The European Legacy, volume 21, issues 5–6 (August–September 2016) pp. 465–466

Chapter 1
Husserl and Other Phenomenologists
Ronny Miron
The European Legacy, volume 21, issues 5–6 (August–September 2016) pp. 467–480

Chapter 2
Husserl and Levinas: The Ethical Structure of a Philosophical Debt
Hagi Kenaan
The European Legacy, volume 21, issues 5–6 (August–September 2016) pp. 481–492

Chapter 3
Husserl, Heidegger, and Sartre: Presence and the Performative Contradiction
James Mensch
The European Legacy, volume 21, issues 5–6 (August–September 2016) pp. 493–510

Chapter 4
Intentionality, Consciousness, and the Ego: The Influence of Husserl's Logical Investigations *on Sartre's Early Work*
Lior Levy
The European Legacy, volume 21, issues 5–6 (August–September 2016) pp. 511–524

Chapter 5
From Husserl to Merleau-Ponty: On the Metamorphosis of a Philosophical Example
Meirav Almog
The European Legacy, volume 21, issues 5–6 (August–September 2016) pp. 525–534

CITATION INFORMATION

Chapter 6
Husserl and Jacob Klein
Burt C. Hopkins
The European Legacy, volume 21, issues 5–6 (August–September 2016) pp. 535–555

Chapter 7
A Tale of Two Schisms: Heidegger's Critique of Husserl's Move into Transcendental Idealism
George Heffernan
The European Legacy, volume 21, issues 5–6 (August–September 2016) pp. 556–575

For any permission-related enquiries please visit:
http://www.tandfonline.com/page/help/permissions

Notes on Contributors

Meirav Almog is based at the Kibbutzim College of Education, Technology and the Arts, Israel.

George Heffernan is a Professor at the Philosophy Department, Merrimack College, USA.

Burt C. Hopkins is a Professor of Philosophy at the Philosophy Department, Seattle University, USA. His main research interest is the philosophical foundation of the transformation of knowledge that began in the sixteenth century with the philosophical advent of modernity.

Hagi Kenaan is an Associate Professor at the Department of Philosophy, Tel Aviv University, Israel. His research specialises in continental philosophy, phenomenology, aesthetics, and philosophy of art.

Lior Levy is a Faculty Member at the Department of Philosophy, University of Haifa, Israel.

James Mensch is a Full Professor at the Faculty of Humanities at Charles University, Czech Republic, and a Sir Walter Murdoch Distinguished Collaborator in the School of Arts, Murdoch University, Western Australia. He is also a member of the Central European Institute of Philosophy.

Ronny Miron is a Professor of Philosophy at Bar Ilan University, Israel. Her research is focused on post-Kantian idealism, existentialism, phenomenology, and hermeneutics, as well as current Jewish thought.

Introduction

Ronny Miron

The Program for Hermeneutics and Cultural Studies, The Interdisciplinary Unit, Bar Ilan University, Ramat Gan, Israel

This special issue on "Husserl and Other Phenomenologists" addresses a fundamental question: what is it in the phenomenology of Edmund Husserl that on the one hand enables the huge variety in the phenomenological discourse and, at the same time, necessitates relying on his phenomenology as a point of departure and an object before which philosophizing is conducted? My answer to this question is that the very reference to Husserl is necessarily bound up with modifying his ideas and crossing the boundaries of his phenomenology. In this sense, and given the insight that Husserlian phenomenology is already imbued with potential modifications and revisions, allows us to include the post-Husserlian phenomenologies along with Husserl in the one so-called "phenomenological movement."

In the first of the seven articles included in this special issue, I analyze Husserl's idea of *givenness*, generally signifying what presents itself before the observing subject. I argue that this central idea of his entire philosophical work is a facilitating element that accounts for his influence on later phenomenologists. The different phenomenological perspectives that Husserl's writings invite are well represented in the selection of articles that follows. Hagi Kenaan, in "Husserl and Levinas: The Ethical Structure of a Philosophical Debt," examines Levinas's critical dialogue with Husserl's thought, specifically with Husserl's notion of "intentionality" and its impact on Levinas's ethical thinking. This is followed by "Husserl, Heidegger, and Sartre: Presence and the Performative Contradiction," in which James Mensch argues that Heidegger and Sartre attempted to avoid what they saw as Husserl's equation of being and presence. Mensch analyzes their claim of the essential nothingness that lies at the core of human experience that determines our pragmatic engagements with others and the world through which we disclose reality. The question he raises is whether their conception of being can be consistently carried through without undercutting its own evidence. Lior Levy, in "Intentionality, Consciousness, and the Ego: The Influence of Husserl's *Logical Investigations* on Sartre's Early Work," claims that Husserl's *Logical Investigations* both grounds and sheds light on central themes in Sartre's existential-phenomenological project. By analyzing Sartre's accounts of the structure of consciousness, its relationship to the world, and the nature of the self, Levy suggests that Sartre considered his work to be a direct continuation of Husserl's. His central debt to Husserl, she argues, lies in Sartre's account of freedom, which develops Husserl's early conception of the phenomenological method. In "From Husserl to Merleau-Ponty: On the Metamorphosis of a Philosophical Example," Meirav Almog sets out to show how the Husserlian example of two hands touching each other in *Ideas II* becomes a pivotal moment in Merleau-Ponty's late thought, inspiring his notion of a chiasm between the thing and the world that enables an ontological rehabilitation of the sensible and, thus, an ontology of a different order. In "Husserl and Jacob Klein," Burt C. Hopkins explains why Husserl's attempt to solve a problem concerning the essence of numbers failed. He argues that Jacob Klein showed that the problem Husserl was trying to solve was in fact insoluble because it followed from an untenable identification of symbols and concepts. Finally, in his historical-philosophical study, "A Tale of Two Schisms: Heidegger's Critique of Husserl's Move into Transcendental Idealism," George Heffernan examines the Great Phenomenological Schism and the Phenomenological-Existential Schism in the early history of the movement. Closely following the documentary evidence, he argues that Heidegger's critique of Husserl's move into transcendental idealism firmly establishes the linkage between the two schisms.

The range of this selection of articles shows that any serious engagement with Husserl holds the promise of further development of his ideas and thus the possibility of extending, if not crossing, the boundaries of his original phenomenology.

Finally, I wish to thank the editors of the *European Legacy* for inviting me to guest edit this special issue on Husserl and his followers, and especially the six contributors for their well-researched and original articles.

The Special Issue on "Husserl and Other Phenomenologists" is dedicated to the memory of the realist phenomenologist Hedwig Conrad-Martius (1888–1966) on the 50th anniversary of her death.

Husserl and Other Phenomenologists

Ronny Miron

The Program for Hermeneutic and Cultural Studies, The Interdisciplinary Unit, Bar Ilan University, Ramat Gan, Israel

ABSTRACT

This article addresses a basic question: what elements in Husserl's phenomenology can account for the variety of post-Husserlian phenomenologies? The answer, I suggest, is that Husserl's idea of reality, particularly his notion of givenness vis-à-vis self-givenness, facilitated the work of his followers by offering them at once a firm ground and a point of departure for their inquiries. However, adopting Husserl's phenomenology as their starting point did not prevent his followers from developing their own independent phenomenological theory. Moreover, despite the elusive particulars that shape one's individual experience of the world, so it transpires, Husserl's thinking which was different and beyond their own observations and actual experiences, namely, transcendent, appears to have been a genuine guide along their path to achieve meaning. This interpretation thus gives precedence to a metaphysical point of departure, that is, to Husserl's idea of reality as 'givenness', in launching phenomenological investigation—over any specific aspect of his work—as that which continues to sustain phenomenological discourse.

Introduction

The question of the relation of Husserl's theory of phenomenology and the various phenomenologies that followed it has long occupied scholars. Herbert Spiegelberg, for example, argues that phenomenology is an "elusive philosophy, hence there is no such thing "as a system or school called 'phenomenology' with a solid body of teachings." For Spiegelberg, "the common name of phenomenology, whether claimed from the inside or imposed from the outside" does not refer to "a common substance," which is why the "assumption of a unified philosophy subscribed to by all so-called phenomenologists is an illusion." Thus seeing the various phenomenologies as empirical expressions of Husserlian phenomenology and even as concretizations of its principles, Spiegelberg admits that it is difficult "to extricate the essential structure of phenomenology from its empirical expressions." However, since not all these expressions are "equally adequate manifestations of the underlying idea," but rather "the varieties exceed the common features," he concludes: "Phenomenology itself is given through various appearances."[1] Unlike Spiegelberg, Dorion Cairns argues that "the peculiar character of phenomenology lies not in its content but in the way the latter is attained" and describes that method as "phenomenological": "*No opinion is to be accepted as philosophical knowledge unless it is seen to be adequately established by observation of what is seen as itself given 'in person.' Any belief seen to be incompatible with what is seen to be itself given is to be rejected. Towards opinions that fall in neither class... one is to adopt an 'official' philosophical attitude of neutrality.*" [2] It appears that for Cairns the very participation in an agreed methodological procedure or even just "an understanding of what the one using the method sets up as the thing to be actualized by its means" suffices for including different phenomenologies in one general framework. Clearly, both approaches capture an important element in phenomenological thinking, yet they seem unable to discern the imprint of the common Husserlian infrastructure: while Spiegelberg overemphasizes the individuality of the phenomenologists, Cairns points to a more general element, which, however, does not constitute a distinctive method peculiar to phenomenologists alone.

The interpretation proposed in this article seeks to unveil the *facilitating element* in Husserl's thinking, which allowed his followers to draw on his theory without hindering them from establishing their own independent phenomenological observations. We can examine this element, which is a constant of phenomenological investigation, by means of the Husserlian "nucleus" (*Kernbestand*), which "*is not a concrete essence* in the constitution of the noema as a whole, but a kind of abstract *form* that dwells in it."[3] Husserl explains that the complete objective meaning around which the various intentional experiences "group themselves," the "*central 'nucleus*," is essentially the selfsame and persists in the various experiences that are "the '*object simpliciter*', namely, the identical element which is at one time perceived, a second time directly represented, and a third time exhibited in figured form in a picture, and so forth, indicates only *one* central concept" (§91, 191–92). Husserl depicts the object's mode of being as "prescribed,"[4] yet the constancy enabled by this prescription implies that within the object itself there is "'something'," "'self-same'," "determinable" (§131, 257), and "expressible":

> Logical meaning (*Bedeutung*) is an expression. The verbal sound can be referred to as expression only because the meaning which belongs to it expresses; it is in it that the expressing originally lies. "Expression" is a remarkable form, which permits of being adapted to every "meaning" (to the noematic "nucleus"), and raises it to the realm of the "Logos", of the *conceptual*, and therewith of the "*general.*" (§124, 273)

Thus the inherent position of the object, which is secured by the intentional framework, is not sufficient to ensure that we can grasp its logical meaning; rather, to do so, the object must carry within itself an expressible and positive force. The aim of Husserl's phenomenology was to uncover both the objective and the subjective conditions of knowledge. The illumination of these conditions throughout his work enabled the consolidation of the ideas of the subject and the object, which are proper to phenomenological investigation. Husserl explains: "The 'object' is referred to, is the goal aimed at, set in relation to the Ego only (and by the Ego itself)." Moreover, the attitude of the Ego to the object, which "bears the personal ray in itself is thereby an act of the Ego itself [that] 'lives' in such acts." However, he insists that "This life does not signify the being of any 'contents' of any kind in a stream of contents, but a variety of describable ways in which the pure Ego in certain intentional experiences, which have the general mode of the *cogito*, lives therein as the 'free essence' which it is" (§92, 195).

HUSSERL AND OTHER PHENOMENOLOGISTS

The involvement of the subject in the very positing of the phenomenological object, however, does not bring about its subjectivization, nor does the personal element pertaining to the phenomenological subject obstruct it from being involved in the elucidation of the conditions of knowledge. Quite the opposite, in the phenomenological investigation both the object and the subject are encompassed in the abstractedness which is precisely what enables approaching the desired "one" and "general" in phenomenology. Husserl's insistence on this abstractedness is apparent already in his early writings, where he asserts that even a practical discipline assumes a fundamental logical lawfulness that can be studied. With respect to the object, this refers to the validity of logical laws, while with respect to the subject, the search aims at the "*a priori* conditions of knowledge which can be discussed and investigated apart from all relation to the thinking subject and towards the idea of subjectivity in general."[5] Husserl responds to this challenge with his idea of "pure logic" that seeks to uncover the a priori logical laws that are necessary for all the uses of logic in all forms of knowledge.[6] The importance of "pure logic" lies precisely in its not being a normative discipline that articulates the correctness of the rules of logic.[7] Husserl explains: "If everything which has being is rightly recognized as having being, and as having such and such a being... then without doubt we may not reject the self-justifying claims of ideal being. No interpretive skill in the world can in fact eliminate ideal objects from our speech and our thought."[8] It follows from this that no matter whether the phenomenon under discussion is real or ideal, the phenomenologist will always seek its most general and ideal aspects.

This conspicuous abstractedness, especially when applied to the basic principles of Husserlian phenomenology, is central to my argument. As opposed to positive arguments, which one can accept or reject, an abstract infrastructure can serve as a framework for a wide range of approaches. Husserl's statement on the nature of phenomenological investigation—"there is nothing to limit us" in the first person—may thus be extended to the phenomenologists who followed him, who, while relying on the more general elements of his phenomenology, developed their own independent phenomenologies. This point is particularly relevant when we turn to Husserl's seminal idea of "givenness" (*Gegebenheit*). This term, which Heidegger called "the magic word" (*Zauberwort*) of phenomenology, entails not only Husserl's idea of reality as the realm where meaning is the product of reflection, but also the possibility of its continuous modification through repeated acts of reflection. This then is how I would characterize the status of Husserl's phenomenology for the phenomenologists who followed him—as something given—from which meaning can be derived and thus immediately and perpetually altered. This dynamic of modification and confirmation, which follows directly from Husserl's notion of mere givenness vis-à-vis self-givenness, and whose process I will delineate below, also characterizes the relation between his phenomenology and the phenomenologies that came in its wake.

My aim in taking Husserl's idea of givenness as a facilitating element—at once a firm ground and a secure point of departure—for the various transformations of post-Husserlian phenomenological discourse, is neither historical nor psychological, and deliberately avoids any reference to specific strands of phenomenology. Following Husserl, I see this discussion from "[t]he viewpoint of function," which "covers the whole phenomenological sphere pretty nearly, and in the last resort *all* phenomenological analyses enter its service" (*Ideas*, §86, 179). The importance of this functional viewpoint is that "[i]nstead of the single experiences being analyzed and compared, described and classified, all treatment of detail is governed by the 'teleological' view of its function in making 'synthetic unity' possible" (§86, 179). Husserl explains that this form of analysis

> seeks to inquire how this self-same factor, how objective unities of every kind... are "known" or "supposed," how the identity of these suppositions is constituted by conscious formations of very different type yet of essentially prescribed structure, and how these formations should be described on strict methodical lines. (§86, 179)

Husserl himself relates functional analysis to the reflexive-transcendental nature of phenomenology as a rigorous methodical framework. Accordingly, while my interpretation is the product of my own reflection on his ideas, it is supported by what I see as indispensable elements in his phenomenology that can clarify its relationship to the work of his followers. Obviously, my interpretation is subject to Husserl's insight that any mode of experience should aspire to be absolutely valid but ought to be regarded as "*a kind of secondary objectification* within the compass of the total objectification of the thing" (§44, 84).

From "Givenness" to "Self- Givenness"

The fundamental principle of Husserl's phenomenology is that "Natural Knowledge begins with experience (*Erfahrung*) and remains *within* experience."[9] This principle is succinctly expressed in the phrase he coined, which became the catchword of phenomenology: "back to the 'things themselves,'"[10] that is, to focusing on things that deliver themselves to one's observation or experience. According to Husserl, in any sense experience in which our consciousness is directed at an individual object, it "brings it to givenness" (*Ideas*, §3, 13). At the starting point of our relation to the world that surrounds us, the object (*Objekt*) has a formal ontological meaning that is everything that might be subjected to true or false predication.[11] One's addressing towards this object is signified as "an outer perception," which is simply part of our "primordial experience of physical things" (§3, 9–10). In *Logical Investigations*, Husserl clarifies that the ego as an empirical object "remains an individual, thing-like (*dinglicher*) object," and as such is given to its phenomenal properties in which it "has its own internal make-up (*inhaltlich Bestande*)."[12] Thus outer perception, which is unaware of the mutually constitutive processes that ties together the object and the subject, is what Husserl calls the "natural attitude" or "natural knowledge," which he describes as follows:

> I find continually present and standing over against me the one spatio-temporal fact-world to which I myself belong, as do all other men found in it and related in the same way to it. "This fact world", as the word already tells us, I find to *be out there*, and also *take it just as it gives itself to me as something that exists out there*. All doubting and rejecting of the data of the natural world leaves standing the *general thesis of the natural standpoint*. (§30, 55–56)

It is thus the immediate, datum-point givenness of things, when the "I, the real human being, am a real object just like others in the natural world" (§33, 62), that furnishes "the entrance gate of phenomenology" (§30, 55).

Yet, as Husserl explains, since human experience "compels our reason to pass beyond intuitively given things" towards "physical truth" (§47, 90), we cannot adhere to that datum-point where the meaning of the object and the subject is merely empirical. Indeed, he points out that already the word "phenomenon," his primary destination, "is ambiguous in virtue of the essential correlation between *appearance and that which appears*. φαινόμενον (phenomenon) in its proper sense means that which appears, and yet it is by preference used for the appearing itself, for the subjective."[13] Clearly, as Husserl's thinking matured, he realized that this ambiguity resulted from joining together the appearing object, whether real or ideal, and appearance, as that which appears to the subject. Thus the secure position of the object was the result of its being intended by the thinking and knowing subject. [14]

Having clarified these points, Husserl declares his aim: "*Instead now of remaining at this standpoint, we propose to alter it radically*" (§31, 56), and his confidence that "[e]mpirical or individual intuition can be transformed" (§3, 11). In this process "outer perception" is transformed into "inner perception" when "we mentally destroy the objectivity of things—as correlate of empirical consciousness" (§47, 91). And, with respect to the subject, this transformation means that "if we *cut* the ego-body from the empirical ego, and limit the purely mental ego to its phenomenological content, the latter reduces to a unity of consciousness."[15] This ego that has been cut is nothing peculiar, but floats above many experiences and is undiscernably part of them. One's body, which appears to inner perception like any other external object, is thus separated from the concept of the ego. The idea of the I that is acknowledged as establishing phenomenological investigation is then "a spiritual ego" that as such is identified with the unity of pure consciousness.[16] However, this spiritual ego should enable us to come to terms with our primordial experience (§1, 9–10).

Although the transformation of empirical observation into intuition is achieved by inner perception, it does not confine phenomenological inquiry to the inner realm but rather allows their interplay to continue. Moreover, it is through this interplay that the two dimensions of experience, the outer and the inner, are elucidated. Within these two the very of idea of givenness itself is illuminated through constant alteration and confirmation regarding what is given. I suggest that Husserl's idea of self-givenness transpires through this complex dynamic. Husserl's programmatic statement—"Our phenomenological sphere, the sphere of absolute clarity, of immanence in the true sense, reaches no farther than self-givenness reaches"[17]—thus defines both the outer and the inner boundaries of phenomenological investigation. One the one hand, the very designation of self-givenness as the desired outcome of reflection suggests that it exceeds mere givenness and that this potentiality implies further modifications. On the other hand, self-givenness is inherent to givenness, as only that which is given can achieve self-givenness. However, self-givenness does not simply supersede givenness, because, according to Husserl, between empirical observation and the intuition of essence there is "not a mere superficial analogy, but a radical community of nature" (§3, 14). This "radical community of nature" implies that empirical observation can never be entirely removed from phenomenological observation, which for Husserl is "the goal of the *science of the natural standpoint*" (§30, 56).

Husserl further explains that "under the heading 'givenness'... we *understand as an included factor the being apprehended*." However, since this relates to an experience that is "generally presented with certain *emptiness* of content and *vague* sense of *distance* which prevents its being employed in reaching conclusive results," a need arises for the shift of mere givenness to self-givenness, which denotes "*the way* in which experiences are given" in their intentional constitution, and not "for their own sake" (§67, 132). Self-givenness is also capable of eliminating the vagueness and emptiness that characterize the modes of presentation in empirical experience in which "a thing is necessarily given in mere '*modes of appearing*'" (§44, 82). In contrast, self-givenness implies that these experiences "are not vague but are presented with fullest clearness" and "an *absolute nearness*" (§67, 131). Thus by attaining self-givenness "the incoherent data would become coherent" and provide us with evidence for what we experience.[18] And although givenness also carries with it some form of evidence, it is blurred with vagueness and emptiness.[19] For Husserl, we should note, evidence is not a question of our convictions, our feelings, or what we consider obvious, but is open to observation and reflection, which is why inquiry always remains in action within the experience of evidence. [20]

It seems that just as some evidence exists already in mere givenness, thanks to which it can be elevated into self-givenness, so also in self-givenness there are still remnants of mere givenness. These remnants require continuous reflection and further investigation, and thus absolute self-givenness cannot be fully attained. [21]

Finally, self-givenness that appears in seeing (*Noein*), from which evidence is inseparable, is the basis of the methodical rigor of Husserlian phenomenology. Precisely because seeing is "immediate," yet "not merely the sensory seeing of experience, but *seeing in general as primordial dator consciousness of any kind whatsoever*," it can serve as "the ultimate source of justification for all rational statements. It has this right-conferring function only because and in so far as its object-giving is primordial" (§19, 36). This primordiality also implies the independence of the self-given, since it precedes any experiential element that expels the thing from itself or blurs its identity with itself. Genuine phenomenological science aims at exactly this primordial plane of appearance, where essence and the most general exist in their purity. Achieving self-givenness by reflection upon this plane is both the mechanism for achieving philosophical rigor and an indicator of it. At the end of this process, self-givenness on the side of the object uncovers its essence by approaching as close as possible to it, and on the side of the subject it is indicated by the reflection that achieves greater lucidity and abundance of phenomena. Obviously, the self-givenness of the subject and object is intertwined, and this obliges the phenomenological account to always report on both of them.

The following discussion will discern the two fundamental processes that are involved in the achieving of self-givenness. One deals with narrowing the scope of reality in the wide sense and focusing the phenomenological investigation on the relation between the object and the subject, both of which have undergone restraint and limitation. The second, which follows the first and assumes its achieving, aims at establishing deeper and wider knowledge regarding the essences that are implicit in mere givenness. Consequently, self-givenness is revealed as a realm of meaning in which the final deciphering of the objectivity of phenomenological study might be achieved.[22]

Achieving the Phenomenological Subject and Object: Narrowing and Cutting

In *The Idea of Phenomenology*, Husserl states that "the first and principal part of phenomenology as a whole" confines itself "to the task *of clarifying the essence of cognition and of being an object of cognition*,"[23] as well as "to exclude *givenness in that wider sense*" for achieving the self-given datum (*Ideas*, §67, 132). Within self-givenness, an internal perception might be achieved in which objects and subjects are not regarded as ontological beings with the fullness of their transcendency. Rather, these two are shrunken into the intentional sphere in which objects exist "for" the consciousness, while subjects are considered as intending their objects. Just as the transition from empirical observation to the intuition of essence forms one mental sequence, so too the transition from givenness to self-givenness realizes something that already inheres in the given datum. In Husserl's words: "the objective element

HUSSERL AND OTHER PHENOMENOLOGISTS

does not only meet one's gaze as 'itself' in general, and we are not only aware of it as 'given', but it confronts us as a self given *in its purity, wholly and entirely as it is in itself*" (§67, 131). It is clear that the objective aspect of givenness is an inseparable part of the transformation both from empirical to intuition and from givennness to self-givenness. Already in *Logical Investigations*, Husserl explains that the intention of the subject towards the object is "a *descriptive feature* of the experiences... whose sense it should be possible to fix and clarify by considering the experiences themselves."[24] Similarly, he later describes the internal perception involved in the intuition of essence as "the consciousness of something, of an 'object', a something towards which its glance is directed, a something 'self-given' within it" (§3, 13). Thus being an object intended by the subject is actually the object's givenness, within which the phenomenological investigation starts. However, the phenomenologist posits himself at the disposal of human experience and not before objects as such. Husserl maintains that

> everything out of the world of nature known through experience and prior to any thinking, bears in its totality... the character "present" out there, *a character that can function essentially as the ground for support for an explicit (predicative) existential judgment which is in agreement with the character it is grounded upon*. If we express that same judgment, we know quite well that in so doing we have simply put into the form of a statement and grasped as a predication *what already lay somehow in the original experience*. (§31, 56; my emphasis)

Thus the transition from the empirical to the essential does not occur ex nihilo and should in no way be considered an interpretation that adds something to it, but as meeting the modes of appearing in experience. Rather, this shift from mere givenness to self-givenness implies the inadequacy and imperfection of both objects and subjects. As Husserl puts it: "In principle a thing in the real world, a Being in its sense, can within the finite limits of appearance appear only '*inadequately*'" (§138, 289), and "it is an essential mark of what is given through appearances that no one of these gives the matter in question in an 'absolute' form" (§ 44, 82). Obviously, this state of affairs results from givenness essentially being of appearances, that is, of things that are "necessarily given in mere '*modes of appearing*'" (§ 44, 84).

So the need to narrow down the object arises from the inadequacy characteristic of it in the experience of the subject before whom the object stands. In other words, the one-sidedness of the appearing of objects implies the more general inadequacy of one's way of experiencing things and essences in general. Husserl establishes that "This holds for every essence related to the *thing-like*... it even holds good... for all *realities* generally, whereby indeed the vague expressions 'one-sidedness' and 'more-sidedness' receive determinate meanings, and different kinds of inadequacy are separated out one from another" (§3, 12). It follows that not only transcendent but also intentional objects under phenomenological investigation appear one-sided and incomplete, which is why "*no rational positing which rests on appearance that presents itself so inadequately* can be '*definitive*', 'invincible'" (§138, 289). This all-encompassing assertion rests on the assumption that the essences underlying all things can never fully reveal themselves in appearances.[25]

The experiencing subject, like the object experienced, is also inadequate or limited, since experience (*Erlebnis*) "is not, and never is, perceived in its completeness" (§44, 84). This means that the elements that comprise our conscious experience of something are incapable of joining together because "our experiencing function swarms with oppositions that cannot be evened out either for us or in themselves." Our experience not only controverts "the suggestion that the things it puts together should persist harmoniously to the end" but it also "lacks the fixed order-schemes of perspectives, apprehensions, and appearances," and is "wholly incapable of constituting self-preserving 'realities', unities that endure and 'exist in themselves whether perceived or not perceived'" (§49, 93-94). The narrowing down of both the subject and the object within the intentional framework thus responds to their specific mode of appearing. Husserl derives from this insight his method of cutting that aims at "a scientific elaboration" in which empirical givenness is transformed and thus enables consciousness to be established as a unifying force within the phenomenological investigation:

> If we *cut* out the ego-body from the empirical ego, and limit the purely mental ego to its phenomenological content, the later reduces to a unity of consciousness, to a real experiential complex, which we (i.e. each man for his own ego) find in part evidently present, and for the rest postulate on good grounds. The Phenomenologically reduced ego is therefore nothing peculiar, floating above many experiences: it is simply identical with their own interconnected unity.[26]

We see, then, that the elimination (*Ausschalten*) of all elements that related to the empirical dimensions of experience establishes the subject that is proper to the "pure phenomenological experience." Thus, too, the outer perception that "one's own ego as much" as "someone else's... and each ego as much as any physical thing, a house or a tree etc.," gives way to an inner perception in which "the appearing of things does not itself appear to us, [rather] we live through it." Consequently, "the appearing of the thing (the experience) is not the thing which appears," but we experience the appearing of things "as belonging in the phenomenal world." Things, then, do not simply appear but appear *before us*. The phenomenological subject is crucial since "we live through" the appearing of things and this experience is typified as "an animating interpretation of sensation" (§2, 82–84). This narrowing of the subject culminates in Husserl's view of subjective experience as personal, for "experiences in the purely phenomenological sense" "an adequate perception can only be 'inner' perception... [which] can only be trained upon experiences simultaneously given, and belonging to a single experience with itself."[27] In *Ideas* Husserl reformulates this point by saying that in our relation to the world "we can best carry on in the first person" (§27, 51).

However, there is no contradiction between the high level of generality characterizing the search for essences and the personal element of inner perception, for, although phenomenological investigation is carried out by individuals, the knowledge they produce is general and public. Husserl, already in his early criticism of psychologism, did not see the subject in logical judgments as an obstacle to achieving objectivity. Thus the involvement of the subject in observing an object does not necessarily bring about its subjectivization, as shown by the potential of inner perception to become an origin for universal truth by means of reflection:

> Living in the *cogito* we have not got the cogitatio consciously before us as intentional object; but it can at any time become this: to its essence belongs in principle the possibility of a *"reflexive" directing of the mental glance* towards itself. ... In other words, every cogitation can become the object of so-called "inner perception", and eventually the object of a *reflexive* valuation (§38, 71).

Finally, the process of narrowing and cutting that is bound up with achieving self-givenness, on the part of both the object and the subject, is the first step in the phenomenological investigation, and Husserl's phenomenology is a one-time and powerful exemplar to its performance. It transpires, then, that methodical rigor cannot be achieved without restraining and limiting the scope of one's gaze towards one's objects. Rather, phenomenological observation itself is impossible except within its own boundaries that are delineated by the demands and the spirit of self-givenness. However, this step does not stand by itself but requires the following step that carries out what is only apparently its opposite.

Achieving Meaning: Completion and Widening

The establishment of the phenomenological subject and object, which is bound up with the recognition of inadequacy in the wide sense and with an initiated cut within it, is critical for achieving self-givenness. Only then will phenomenology be founded as the "first philosophy" (*Erste Philosophie*) whose self-grounding and self-justifying might enable it to be the basis for any other science. [28]

However, self-givenness is not a target that stands for itself. Rather, the accessibility and closedness of self-givenness to the primordial layer of things is harnessed to the study of the essences that underlie all phenomena. Given, as we have seen, that experience (*Erlebnis*) "is not, and never is, perceived in its completeness," the search for underlying essences also necessarily involves a narrowing down. However, whereas our inadequacies in intuiting essences, compared to those in dealing with appearances, remain rather latent at the first stage of phenomenological investigation, at the second stage of investigation they come to the fore and assume their rightful place as the foundation of all things. Their centrality seems indispensable for the very objective of completing our knowledge of essences, for they remain concealed as long as other elements manifest themselves. Thus the focus on essence in the second stage of phenomenological investigation seems to respond to this insight and to enable the attainment of a genuine adequate self-givenness. Only then, I suggest, can the entire complex of structures and contents of the object of investigation open out before the phenomenologist. [29]

The second stage of phenomenological investigation thus centers on the transition from the empirical to the intuition of essence, which according to Husserl, "is itself not to be understood as empirical but as essential possibility." Moreover, "the object of such insight is then the corresponding *pure* essence or eidos, whether it be the highest category or one of its specializations, right down to the fully 'concrete'" (§3, 12). This shift extricates the individual's phenomenological observation from its apparently unavoidable particularity in favor of locating it in the common realm of reason. Although "*At first* 'essence' indicated that which is, the intimate self-being of an individual discloses to us '*what*' it is. But even more importantly, "*The essence (Eidos) is an object of a new type. Just as the datum of individual or empirical intuition is an individual project, so the datum of essential intuition is a pure essence*" (§3, 12–13). However, this widening does not restore the elements that were initially removed from givenness, nor does it add to our knowledge of objects; rather, it relates to the experience of subjects in relation to objects and thus confers value on the personal gaze of the phenomenologist upon the world of phenomena that appears before him. And, what is more, this shift generates new experiences, as Husserl puts it: "All actual experience refers beyond itself to possible experiences, which themselves again point to new possible experiences, and so *in infinitum*" (§47, 92). Consequently, the same contents might be given new interpretations by different phenomenologists. However, "interpretation itself can never be reduced to an influx of new sensations; it is an act-character, a mode of consciousness, of 'mindedness' (*Zumuteseins*)." [30] Husserl thus emphasizes the reflexive nature of phenomenology, for "*Every variety of 'reflexion' has the character of a modification of consciousness*" to the extent that "under the concept of reflexion must be included all modes of immanent apprehension of the essence and... all modes of immanent experience (*Erfahrung*)" (§78, 152–53). Indeed, reflection "itself is assuredly a general modification of a new type—this self-*directing* of the ego upon its experiences" (§78, 154).

HUSSERL AND OTHER PHENOMENOLOGISTS

The plurality of different experiences, which in Husserl's phenomenology mirrors the variety of the world of phenomena,[31] is offered here as an explanation of the variety of phenomenological approaches. The possibility of attaining knowledge about essences relies especially on the determinacy of "the undetermined marginal field," which, according to Husserl, encompasses "thing-experiences themselves" and exists in each actual experience. However, although this indeterminacy is essential, it still "leave[s] open possibilities of a filling out."[32] Just as these possibilities are "in no sense arbitrary," so also the modifications of our consciousness "belong to *every* experience as ideally possible changes, and... they can be repeated *in infinitum*" (§78, 154). In any event, since the indeterminacy is determined, and the possible variations of experience are essential, also empirical occurrences should be regarded in phenomenological investigations as manifesting an essence. It is not surprising, then, that Husserl pours into the process of intuiting essences an element of necessity by claiming that "In principle a thing can be given only in one of its aspects, and that not only means incompletely... but precisely that which presentation through perspectives prescribes." It is thus the plurality of perspectives that frees our individual gaze from our single, inadequate perspective and enables us to attain some degree of determinacy: "It [the object] may be 'the same', only given with other predicates, with another determining content; 'it' may display itself only in different aspects whereby the predicates left indeterminate have become more closely determined." Similarly, "*separated* acts, as for instance, two perceptions of a perception and memory" of the same thing do not dismantle it but "*close up together in an identical unity*, a unity in which the 'something', the determinable which lies concealed... is consciously grasped as self-identical." Moreover, not only does the plurality of perspectives or acts that are addressed to a single thing achieve a "harmonious" unity and determine "in common accord the same 'object'," but also this unity itself "is clearly not foreign to the essential being of the acts thus lined together" (§131, 273). Finally, the reflexion that was mentioned before as responsible for the modifications that take place in consciousness is also "the title for types of experience which belong essentially together" (§78, 152). That is to say, that the requirement of a plurality of perspectives that appears to be an answer to the structured inadequacy of appearance does not violate the essential lawfulness of both the phenomenological object and subject.

At first sight, the plurality of perspectives may seem to compensate for narrowing and cutting the elements of the given in the process of achieving self-givenness. However, the plurality of perspectives is not a quantitative factor in the process of achieving determinacy. On the contrary, only empirical observation can be quantitative and, as such, is necessarily one-sided and inadequate. The intuition of essence assumes, in contrast, that quality is always more than a single perspective or even a collection of individual perspectives. Paradoxically, as Husserl explains, such extrication is possible because "in principle a margin of determinable indeterminacy always remains over, however far we go along our empirical way." For, as he adds, "*to remain for ever incomplete... is an ineradicable essential of the correlation Thing and Thing-perception.*" It would seem that for Husserl every perception and very mode of intending objects "must require such incompleteness."[33] Since no single gaze or plurality of such is capable of eradicating the inadequacy that is structured in givenness as such, possibilities of a filling out remain always open. At the same time, this confirms Husserl's view that "the object of experience is progressively constituted" (*Ideas*, 11). This "stretch of givenness," which "stretch[es] out in an infinite number of directions *in systematic strictly ordered ways*," is again not arbitrary but "always dominated throughout by some unity of meaning" (§44, 83). I believe that the depth and novelty of Husserlian thinking at this point lies in its implicit understanding that despite the unbeatable particular elements that shape the experience of individuals before phenomena, there is always a transcendent element that exceeds the boundaries of actual experiences and guides us along the path to achieve meaning.

Conclusion

Husserl's early testimony that the difficulty he faced in his studies "stretches far beyond all peculiarities of special forms" and "forced" him "into discussions of a very general sort... towards a universal theory"[34] was an important guideline for untangling the relation between his phenomenology and the phenomenologies that followed. Accordingly, my discussion has focused on the general question of what elements in Husserlian phenomenology facilitated the variety and diversity that characterize post-Husserlian phenomenologies. Guided by this perspective, I endeavored to unveil and decipher the general constituting dynamic that enabled the post-Husserlian phenomenological discourse. Yet this in no way diminishes the value of particular studies of Husserl's influence on his followers. On the contrary, the contributors to this special issue were invited to respond to this challenge. Their work can thus be regarded as a test of my argument on the facilitating element in Husserl's thinking. The most important conclusion I myself draw from reading Husserl relates to the precedence of the metaphysical infrastructure of reality over the study of its specific elements. Even more so, the case of the phenomenological discourse makes conspicuously evident that philosophers cannot walk on this path by themselves, for genuine philosophizing always calls for ways of doing philosophy together with others.

Unavoidably, Husserl's struggle with "the difficulties of pure phenomenological analysis"[35]—which confronted him with "the close interdependence of... various epistemological concepts" and "leads back again and again to original analyses, where the new confirms the old, and the old confirms the new"[36]—also confronted the post-Husserlian phenomenologists. They could not help but return to his foundational idea of givenness against which to test their own observations. His phenomenology, however, seems to have been at once too wide and too narrow for them. Consequently, some of them ignored some of his ideas, while others developed ideas that were marginal or only briefly discussed by him, thus the entire phenomenological discourse was enriched and granted with new faces and diversified. This dynamic transformation, as Husserl himself wrote, occurs with any object subjected to phenomenological analysis. For the post-Husserlian phenomenologists, however, the object was first and foremost the phenomenology of Husserl himself.[37]

Furthermore, the dynamic of progress in a "zig-zag fashion," to which Husserl testified—in which "one can only proceed securely, if it repeatedly breaks with such systematic sequence, if it removes conceptual obscurities which threaten the course of investigation *before* the natural sequence of subject-matters can lead up to such concepts"[38]—was also the lot of his followers. Husserl states: "the realm of truth is objectively articulated into fields: researches must orient themselves to these objective unities."[39] This determination might serve as a framework for phenomenology's different paths while preserving their basic affinity to Husserlian phenomenology as an "objective" beginning that cannot be ignored. It would seem, then, that the variety that is structured in Husserl's most fundamental insights

HUSSERL AND OTHER PHENOMENOLOGISTS

on the phenomenon of givenness could not but leave its mark on his followers both in relying upon his phenomenology and no less in distancing themselves from it.

However, if my interpretation is tenable, then Husserl's phenomenology must also be subjected to the cutting and completion process that is the core of his idea of givenness. This means that not only did the post-Husserlian phenomenologists need the infrastructure of the founding father in order to achieve their own phenomenological view, but also that Husserl's own phenomenology is and must remain in need of further "cuts" and completions. One may therefore agree with Spiegelberg's evaluation that "phenomenology is at best unfinished business."[40] That is to say, that the certainty that motivates phenomenological philosophy is deliberately transcendent, for although philosophical observation is an expression of the innermost truth of the individual, transcending it is not only unavoidable but also desirable.

Notes

1. Herbert Spiegelberg, *The Phenomenological Movement*, 2 vols. (The Hague: Martinus Nijhoff, 1960), 1.xxvi, xxviii, xxvii, xxxvii. Spiegelberg presents a more critical view of the subjectivity of phenomenology in "How Subjective is Phenomenology?" in *Essays in Phenomenology*, ed. Maurice Natanson (The Hague: Martinus Nijhoff, 1969), 137–43.
2. Dorion Cairns, "An Approach to Phenomenology," in *Philosophical Essays in the Memory of Edmund Husserl*, ed. Marvin Farber (New York: Greenwood Press, 1968), 3, 4; all emphases follow the original, unless stated otherwise.
3. Husserl Edmund, *Ideas I, General Introduction to Pure Phenomenology* (1913), trans. W. R. Gibson (London: Routlegde, 2012), §132, 275; hereafter cited in the text. Originally published as *Ideen zu einer reinen Phänomenologie und phänomenologischen Philosphie*, vol. 1, Husserliana 3 (The Hague: Martinus Nijhoff, 1950).
4. Edmund Husserl, *The Idea of Phenomenology*, trans. William P. Alston and George Nakhnikian (The Hague: Martinus Nijhoff, 1964), 8.
5. Edmund Husserl, *Logical Investigations*, vol. 1, trans. *John* Niemeyer Findlay, ed. Dermot Moran (London: Routledge, 2001), Prolegomena §65, 150. The original title "Idee der Subjektivität überhaupt" was mistranslated as "Idea of Subjectivity in Science."
6. Husserl, *Logical Investigations*, vol. 1, §§67–69.
7. Husserl, *Logical Investigations*, vol. 1, §§12–14, 26–33; §20, 44–45.
8. Husserl, *Logical Investigations*, vol. 1, §8, 250.
9. Husserl, *Logical Investigations*, vol. 1, §1, 9.
10. Husserl, *Logical Investigations*, vol. 2, Introduction, §2, 168. In this work this determination meant focusing on logical lawfulness and most fundamental ideal essences of things. See Husserl, *Logical Investigations*, vol. 1, §66, 151–52.
11. The term *objekt* is distinguished from *Gegenstand*, see Dermot Moran and Joseph Cohen, *The Husserl Dictionary* (London: Bloomsbury, 2012), 228.
12. Husserl, *Logical Investigations*, vol. 2, §4, 85.
13. Husserl, *The Idea of Phenomenology*, 11.
14. Husserl, *Logical Investigations*, vol. 1, §7, 177. In a manuscript, probably from 1989, titled "Keine Wahrnehmung ohne wharnehmende Subjekt" (Ms. A VI 11 I , 186), Husserl notes: "The entire observation is valid for psychic acts in general in relation to the I." Cited in Eduard Marbach, *Das Problem des Ich in der Phänomenologie Husserls* (The Hague: Martinus Nijhoff, 1974), 6, n. 6.
15. Husserl, *Logical Investigations*, vol. 2, §4, 85–86; my emphasis.
16. Husserl, *Logical Investigations*, vol. 2, §8, 92–93.
17. Edmund Husserl, *The Idea of Phenomenology*, 8.
18. See Husserl, *The Idea of Phenomenology*, 12.

HUSSERL AND OTHER PHENOMENOLOGISTS

19. Elisabeth Ströker explains that for Husserl evidence "is the *experience of self-givenness* of a thing [*Sache*]. This implies that an epistemological difference obtains between the mere givenness of a thing and its self-givenness." Ströker Elisabeth, *Husserl's Transcendental Phenomenology* (Stanford, CA: Stanford University Press, 1933), 30.

20. Husserl, *The Idea of Phenomenology*, x. On Husserl's view of self-evidence regarding intuitive data as testifying to truth, see Herbert Spiegelberg, "Phenomenology of Direct Evidence," *Philosophy and Phenomenological Research* 2.4 (1942): 427–56. Elsewhere, Spiegelberg cites Husserl's words in the "Platform" of his *Jahurbuch für Philosophie and phänomenologische Forschung*, where he establishes that what unites different phenomenologists is "the conviction that only by a return to the primary sources of direct intuition and to insights into essential structures derived from them" may we be able to approach, clarify and eventually solve (at least in principle) philosophical and conceptual problems. Spiegelberg, *The Phenomenological Movement*, 1.5.

21. For Husserl self-givenness is not a requirement of phenomenological investigation only but of science in general, in his words: "Every science has its own object-domain as field of research, and... to all its correct assertions, there correspond as original sources of the reasoned justification that support them certain intuitions in which objects of the region appear as self-given and in part at least as *given in a primordial (originärer) sense*" (*Ideas*, §1, 9). In the background of this insight stand the principles of "descriptivity" and "lack of supposition," which were foundational for Husserlian thinking from its very beginning and were designed to save knowledge from various speculative and scientific theories and to consolidate phenomenology as a non-constructivistic theory.

22. Both processes are finally crystalized in Husserl's phenomenology as two stages of the phenomenological method: the first largely corresponds to "phenomenological reduction," while the second corresponds to "eidetic reduction." While the discussion of Husserl's method of reduction exceeds the scope of this introduction, I argue that both processes are already implicit in his idea of givenness, which he shared with the phenomenologists who followed him, unlike the method of reduction, which was one of the issues that led to the split of the phenomenological movement.

23. Husserl, *The Idea of Phenomenology*, 18. This approach is already implied in the subtitle of the second volume of *Logical Investigations*: "Investigation into Phenomenology and the Theory of Knowledge."

24. Husserl, *Logical Investigations*, vol. 1, §7, 177; my emphasis.

25. As Husserl put it: "It belongs to the type of development peculiar to certain categories of essential being that essences belonging to them *can* be given only 'one-sidedly', whilst in succession more 'sides', though never 'all sides', can be given" (*Ideas*, §3, 12).

26. Husserl, *Logical Investigations*, vol. 2, §4, 85–86; my emphasis.

27. Husserl, *Logical Investigations*, vol. 2, §5, 82–86. For more on outer and inner perception, see the appendix "Beilge über inner und äußer Wahrnehmung," which appears in the German original only, Edmund Husserl, *Logische Untersuchungen*, vol. 2, part 1 (Hamburg: Felix Meiner, 1992), 751–75.

28. "Erste Philosophie" is the title of Husserl's Freiburg Lecture courses (1923–1924), later published as *Husserliana* 7 and 8.

29. The realist phenomenologist Hedwig Conrad-Martius (1888–1966) describes this as follows: "In order to be a phenomenologist... one should somehow shift the standards from our eyes. How does this happen? I cannot tell. However, we suddenly *see thousands of things that we did not see before*. Husserl, our honored and good teacher taught us this way... a secular action. We philosophized passionately, almost day and night... we did nothing other than to bring everything, absolutely everything, under the magnifying glass of eidetic inquiry" (presented at the congress of "Distinguished Service Cross," March 1958), in "Nachlässe Archiev," Bayerischen Staatsbibliothek (BSM) (Conrad-Martius, DII, 2), cited in Alexandra Elisabeth Pfeifer, "Ontological Phenomenology: The Philosophical Project of Hedwig Conrad-Martius," *Axiomathes* 18 (2008): 448; my emphasis.

30. Husserl, *Logical Investigations*, vol. 2, §14, 103.

HUSSERL AND OTHER PHENOMENOLOGISTS

31. See also *Logical Investigations*, vol. 2, §92.
32. Husserl, *Logical Investigations*, vol. 2, §47, 92.
33. Husserl, *Logical Investigations*, vol. 2, §43, 83.
34. Husserl, *Logical Investigations*, vol. 1, 1.
35. Husserl, *Logical Investigations*, vol. 1, Introduction, §3, 170.
36. Husserl, *Logical Investigations*, vol. 1, §6, 175.
37. As is well known, Husserl later established both methodical dispositions as two successive operative methodological steps, "phenomenological reduction" and then "eidetic reduction." The discussion of these two reductions exceeds the scope of this article. However, I argue that the main insights upon which these methodological steps are based are implicit already in Husserl's idea of givenness.
38. Husserl, *Logical Investigations*, vol. 1, §6, 175.
39. Husserl, *Logical Investigations*, vol. 1, §2, 12.
40. Spiegelberg, "How Subjective is Phenomenology?" in Natanson, *Essays in Phenomenology*, 143.

Husserl and Levinas: The Ethical Structure of a Philosophical Debt

Hagi Kenaan

Department of Philosophy, Tel Aviv University, Israel

ABSTRACT
The article examines Levinas's evolving relationship with Husserl. It shows how the critical dialogue with Husserl and, specifically, the transfiguration of Husserl's key notion of "intentionality," grounds the maturation of Levinas's ethical thinking. It does so by unpacking the manner in which the Levinasian critique of Husserl is tied to a concept of "debt" through which Levinas understands his long-lasting relationship with the founder of phenomenology.

For Emmanuel Levinas, the encounter with Husserl during the year he spent in Freiburg in 1928–29, had a long lasting impact, one that he consistently and explicitly acknowledged throughout his philosophical career. "To meet a man is to be kept awake by an enigma," Levinas writes. "Upon meeting Husserl, the enigma was always that of his work. Despite the relative simplicity of his welcome and the warmth found in his home, it was always phenomenology one met in Husserl… so, for me, the debt to the man is inseparable from the debt to his work."[1] With Husserl, in Freiburg, the young Levinas was initiated into phenomenology and thus "discovered," as he later recounts, "the concrete meaning of the very possibility of 'working in philosophy.'"[2] Husserl's philosophy provided a nurturing ground for Levinas's maturation as a thinker. And, indeed, the dissertation he wrote on Husserl's theory of intuition, together with a series of additional studies that he published on Husserl's phenomenology, typically mark, as in Jean-Paul Sartre's known declaration, the introduction of phenomenology to France.[3]

And, yet, when Levinas speaks of his debt to Husserl's work, he is not only referring to the influence it exerted on the early stages of his development. What he is evoking, rather, is the continual relevance Husserl's thought carries for his mature philosophy, an ethical philosophy that, over the years, explicitly distanced itself from Husserlian phenomenology. This becomes clear in Levinas's writings of the 1960s–1970s in which the philosophical debt to Husserl becomes a recurring theme that is typically interwoven with a range of critiques against Husserl and phenomenology. How exactly, then, should this acknowledged debt to Husserl's work be understood? How does Levinas understand the specificity of this debt in light of his wholesale critique of Husserl? Is there, for example, a sense in which Husserl's

Intentionality

The most common context in which Levinas expresses his debt to Husserl is in discussing the impact the Husserlian notion of intentionality had on his work. In prefacing *Totality and Infinity*, for example, he writes that "the presentation and the development of the notions employed owe everything to the phenomenological method. Intentional analysis is the search for the concrete." Or, in a later text, "Doubtless it is Husserl who is at the origin of my writing. It is to him that I owe the concept of intentionality animating consciousness."[4] Indeed, Husserlian intentionality is a theme Levinas has articulated over and over again, presenting it as the core concept of phenomenology or, as he puts it, "phenomenology is intentionality."[5]

Elucidating Husserl's philosophy in an early text, Levinas explains the term "intentionality" as follows:

> The characteristic that necessarily belongs to the whole sphere of consciousness... is to be always "consciousness of something." Every perception is perception of the "perceived"; every desire is desire of the "desired," etc. Husserl calls this fundamental property of consciousness intentionality.[6]

Intentionality refers to the structure of "about-ness" constitutive of consciousness: the fact that consciousness is always directed at something (an object, a state of affairs), that it is always a bearer of content. At the same time, as Levinas himself often emphasizes, Husserl's concept of intentionality denotes not only some property or faculty but refers to a deep and essential dimension of consciousness—a structure that turns consciousness into what it is. Intentionality is consciousness's fundamental form of being. What makes the Husserlian position revolutionary, according to the early Levinas, is the understanding that consciousness itself is a *relation* and that, as such, it cannot be understood only in itself, independently of the world toward which it is always open:

> It must be clearly understood that intentionality is not a bond... between consciousness on one side and the real object on the other. Husserl's great originality is to see that the "relation to the object" is not something inserted between consciousness and the object: it is consciousness itself. It is the relation to the object that is the primitive phenomenon—and not a subject and an object that would supposedly move toward one another.[7]

Consciousness is not an independent, closed, and self-contained domain confronting the world; it is not a private field of subjective events or the inside of some black box containing only copies, representations, or reflections of the real things outside. Instead, the intentional structure should be understood as an opening: consciousness is the very opening of a world. Consequently, what is revealed to us in the field of experience is not a *re*-presentation of the things and events belonging to the world, but the world itself.

In his early writing, Levinas expresses his admiration for Husserl's innovation, and particularly for the open structure of a consciousness that always transcends itself, invariably affected by dimensions of sense that precede any specific content. With Levinas's development as an independent thinker and, specifically, with his preoccupation with an ethics grounded in an experience of alterity, his way of embracing the phenomenological notion of intentionality becomes inseparable from an explicit critical turn toward Husserl: while consistently emphasizing the importance of Husserl's notion for his own project, Levinas nevertheless repeatedly criticizes Husserl for having ultimately missed the radical potential of his own discovery. In the preface to *Totality and Infinity*—in the passage we've already quoted—Levinas articulates his ambivalence in the following way:

> The presentation and the development of the notions employed owe everything to the phenomenological method. Intentional analysis is the search for the concrete. Notions held under the direct gaze of the thought that defines them are nevertheless, unbeknown to this naïve thought, revealed to be implanted in horizons unsuspected by this thought; these horizons endow them with a meaning—such is the essential teaching of Husserl. What does it matter if in the Husserlian phenomenology taken literally these unsuspected horizons are in their turn interpreted as thoughts aiming at objects! What counts is the idea of the overflowing of objectifying thought by a forgotten experience from which it lives.[8]

While the specific edge of these comments might be somewhat subtle, it should not be difficult to notice that Levinas's ambivalence is tied to what he understands as an overly narrow determination of "the essential teaching of Husserl." Whereas for him the essence of Husserl's intentionality lies in the openness of consciousness to horizons of meaning that are "unbeknown" and "unsuspected" by objective thought, he suggests that this essential dimension nevertheless gets covered up in Husserlian phenomenology in which "these unsuspected horizons are in their turn interpreted as thoughts aiming at objects." That is, despite the richness and heterogeneity of experience which intentional analysis originally uncovers, Husserl, according to Levinas, ultimately solidifies the intentional as intrinsically object-directed.

Levinas's insistence on the need to overcome the constrains of "objecthood" is, in itself, not unique in the post-Husserlian phenomenological tradition (e.g. Heidegger, Schutz, Sartre, Merleau-Ponty) whose significant developments all follow, in different ways, from a search for new areas and dimensions of non-objectified experience. What makes Levinas so unique, in this context, is that his critique of Husserlian intentionality is anchored in an ethical agenda.

Ethics and Critique

Levinas's ethics grows out of a critique targeting a predominant philosophical tradition that, in his view, consecrates the ego as its starting point and that, as such, remains closed to a radical alterity whose recognition is, for him, necessary for addressing the ethical. According to Levinas, this philosophical and conceptual closure characteristic of Western thought reproduces a central tendency in our daily life: the tendency to ignore the alterity of the other person, which, in itself, echoes an ethical demand. Hence for him, as he writes in *Totality and Infinity*, "as long as the ethical question "what do I owe the other person?" is asked within the horizons of egological thinking, it cannot resonate the unbridgeable distance separating self and Other, a distance that needs to be acknowledged in order to open the ethical question in a radical way. Consequently, ethical thinking must, according to him, precede ontology and take its place as a "First Philosophy." By pointing to the primacy of ethics, Levinas seeks to undermine the tradition's accepted understanding that ontology comprises the most basic domain of philosophical questions. And for him, when the primary goal of thought is to obtain knowledge about the essence and being of a thing, the ethical question is ineluctably forced into second place. Furthermore, as First Philosophy,

HUSSERL AND OTHER PHENOMENOLOGISTS

Levinas understands the ethical as developing from a distinctive intentionality, "a critical intention… beyond theory and ontology." That is, whereas "Philosophy is egology," ethics, for Levinas, is primarily a form of critique, one that challenges and ultimately transforms philosophy's egological ethos. In particular, ethical critique (or ethics *as* critique) aims at opening philosophical thought to the otherness of the other person, a troubling alterity that cannot be interpreted within the conceptual order of what Levinas terms "the same" (*le Meme*): "Critique does not reduce the Other to the same… but calls into question the exercise of the same." Moreover, since the Other's otherness could never become apparent to us from within ourselves, the possibility of its revelation depends on a rupture occurring in the closed structure of the ego, a disturbance that no longer allows the ego to assume itself as obvious and self-evident: "we name this calling into question of my spontaneity by the presence of the Other—ethics."[9]

For Levinas, as is already clear, this kind of ethical vision cannot develop within the object-based paradigm of intentionality offered by Husserl. In the Husserlian paradigm of an "intentionality where thought remains an *adequation* with the object," no room can be made for the encounter with the unique presence—the alterity—of the other person, which, according to Levinas, grounds the possibility of the ethical. The primary experience of the other person which, for him, is so crucial, cannot register within the domain of objective thought since it is "not an ideal essence or a relation open to intellectual intuition. Instead, it is pre-eminently the presence of exteriority… an original relation with exterior being." As such, the presence of transcendence requires an "intentionality of a wholly different type":

> "If, as this book [*Totality and Infinity*] will show, ethical relations are to lead transcendence to its term, this is because the essential of ethics is in its *transcendent intention*, and because not every transcendent intention has the noesis-noema structure. Already *of itself* ethics is an 'optics.'"[10]

Levinas on Cartesian Meditations

Levinas's critique of intentionality is most typically directed at the predominance of the object in Husserl, and yet, as suggested, what underlies this critique are more specific concerns about the manner in which the Husserlian paradigm ineluctably levels the unique human presence of the Other. What triggers Levinas's critique, in other words, is not only a general objection to what he understands as Husserl's uniform (or, ultimately schematic) use of intentional analysis, but, more specifically, the implication such an analysis carries for Husserl's engagement with the question of the other person. "Intersubjectivity" was the topic of the Husserl seminar Levinas audited in 1928–29, but the more concrete backdrop of his critique is the lesson he gleans from Husserl's famous treatment of the other person in a text with which Levinas was intimately familiar: *Cartesian Meditations*.

In *Cartesian Meditations*, a text that influenced the young Levinas who was also its French translator,[11] Husserl poses the question of the Other's phenomenality in new, unprecedented terms. The need to deal with the question of the Other's appearance emerges in the context of Husserl's attempt to answer "what may seem to be a grave objection. The objection concerns nothing less than the claim of transcendental phenomenology to be itself transcendental *philosophy*,"[12] that is, a philosophy that discloses the primary conditions that precede the actual structures of consciousness and make human experience possible.

Husserl understands his method as a new possibility of uncovering a transcendental layer in the ego's experience of the world, even while recognizing that his call for philosophy's immersion in the ego's field of experience gives rise to a problem of method: "When I, the meditating I, reduce myself to my absolute transcendental ego by phenomenological epoché do I not become *solus ipse*; and do I not remain that, as long as I carry on a consistent self-explication under the name phenomenology?"[13] What troubles Husserl, then, is the validity of the intentional analysis that he himself had proposed. Could his phenomenology be trapped, despite its pretension of dealing with the "things themselves," within the limits of subjective consciousness? Husserl therefore seeks to show why his phenomenology does not ultimately collapse into subjectivism or solipsism. And, in this context, the idea of grounding the existence of what is in principle exterior to consciousness in the Other's form of givenness is critical for his entire phenomenological project. However, while Husserl's discussion is initially motivated by these methodological concerns, it eventually leads him to an analysis of the concrete modalities of the Other's givenness to consciousness. For Levinas, this analysis is ultimately more interesting than the discussion's conclusive demonstration. "This reduction," he writes in "From Consciousness to Wakefulness,"

> is not only directed against the solipsism of the "primordial sphere" and the relativism of truth that results from it, in order to ensure the objectivity of knowledge in the form of an agreement between multiple subjectivities. The constitution or the explication of the meaning of an I other than me… tears the ego away from its hypostasis… from the center of the world.[14]

Reading Husserl in ways that resonate his own ethical concerns, Levinas points to dimensions of the intersubjective reduction that go beyond the master's explicit aims. What Husserl asks to do, rather, is to dispel the threat of solipsism by showing that, even at "zero level," the ego's intentional experience never consists only of a substratum of private experiences but is always part of an intersubjective world. He wishes to show that the very core of consciousness, consciousness at the level of its immanent contents, already consists of what necessarily transcends it. For this purpose, he asks us to

> obtain for ourselves insight into the explicit and implicit intentionality wherein the alter ego becomes evinced and verified in the realm of our transcendental ego; we must discover in what intentionalities, syntheses, motivations, the sense "other ego" becomes fashioned in me and, under the title, harmonious experience of someone else, becomes verified as existing and even as itself there in its own manner.[15]

Husserl sets to explore the unique intentionalities constitutive of the daily experience by which other human beings appear to us, that is, the "harmonious experience of someone else." Here, however, his analysis interestingly turns to focus on those dimensions of the alter ego's presence that cannot be understood in terms of consciousness's paradigmatic relationship with objects of knowledge. For Levinas this is not a coincidence but a fulfillment of the essential promise of intentional analysis: "It is this relation to the other *I*, that constitutes the non-gnoseological event necessary… to the egological Reduction itself."[16]

Husserl's analysis thus shows that, despite the apparent similarities between the appearance of the Other and that of the object in the field of consciousness, the presence of a human other is unique in that it necessarily creates a gap, a distance that consciousness cannot bridge:

> Since another subjectivity… arises with the sense and status of a subjectivity that is other in its own essence, it might at first seem to be a mystery how community… becomes established. The other organism, as appearing in my primordial sphere, is first of all a body in my primordial Nature. … [But] How can I speak at all of *the same* body, as appearing within my primordial sphere in the mode There and within his and to him in the mode Here? These two primordial

spheres, mine which is for me as ego the original sphere, and his which is for me an appresented sphere—are they not *separated* by an abyss I cannot actually cross, since crossing it would mean, after all, that I acquire an original... experience of someone else? If we stick to our de facto experience... we find that actually the *sensuously seen body* is experienced forthwith as *the body of someone else* and not merely as an indication of someone else. Is not this fact an enigma?[17]

The presence of the Other is always pervaded by a dimension of inaccessibility, an absence, that accentuates, for the perceiving consciousness, its own limits, thus challenging its ego-centric structure. In other words, the encounter with another subjectivity is irreducible to what consciousness can process *as* content and, as such, poses an enigma for consciousness, a disconcerting, albeit "non-gnoseological" experience, that intentional analysis must learn to recognize. For Levinas, this "moment" in Husserl's reduction is a crucial one:

> In the identity of presence to self, in the silent tautology of the pre-reflexive, a difference between the same and the same takes shape—a dephasing, a difference at the heart of interiority. This difference is irreducible to adversity which remains open to reconciliation... the other splits the same of consciousness which thus lived; the other that calls it deeper than itself. *Waches Ich*—myself awake.

Furthermore,

> The explication of the meaning that an *I* other than me has *for me*... describes the way in which the Other Person tears me away from my hypostasis, from the here at the heart of being or the center of the world in which, privileged, and in this sense primordial, I place myself... the ultimate meaning of my "mineness" is revealed in this tearing away.[18]

Husserl's language in the *Meditations* is clearly far from being as dramatic as Levinas's, but, given the difference in their philosophical style, is Levinas right in reading the Husserlian analysis as implying that the experience of the other destabilizes the egocentric structure and orientation of consciousness? Is he simply reading into Husserl more than Husserl himself intended or, should we, perhaps, understand his reading as an uncovering of "the overflowing of objectifying thought by a forgotten experience," of the "unbeknown" or "unsuspected horizons" that "in Husserlian phenomenology... are in their turn interpreted as thoughts aiming at objects"?[19]

What is clear is that in the intersubjective reduction, the Other, *qua* Other, is revealed in ways that are intended to challenge any positive description and thus render the phenomenal surface that meets the eye as essentially insufficient. The concrete modalities of presence that Husserl associates with the other person lack the form of a "something" and appear, rather, more as a "some-non-thing" woven into the movements of the other person's body, gait, speech, acts, or face expressions. As such, to encounter another person necessarily means seeing more than what you see, and what concerns Husserl in the "Fifth Meditation" is indeed the decoding of those mechanisms of "actualization" and "presentification" that enable consciousness to see more than it seemingly sees. Husserl focuses on specific structures of intentionality, on unique kinds of syntheses that open up for consciousness the possibility of experiencing the Other's subjectivity, even if this subjectivity will never fully become an object of consciousness.

In this respect, Husserl can indeed be said to pave the way for Levinas's metaphysical understanding of the relationship with the Other. First, Husserl articulates the experience of encountering the Other as grounded in an intentionality that should be studied *sui generis*. This intentionality is essentially different and, therefore, irreducible to the object's frame of appearance, but, at the same time, it cannot be understood only in contrast to the object.

HUSSERL AND OTHER PHENOMENOLOGISTS

The Other has a singular kind of presence, which, according to Husserl, requires not only special handling but also an alternative philosophical sensibility, expressed in the ability to accept the philosophical contact with what cannot be grasped, with what invariably appears as the uncontainable or, as Levinas would have it: the transcendent.

As suggested, however, Levinas's reading of Husserl's intersubjective reduction is twofold. While he finds in Husserl the potential articulation of a radical event of otherness that would serve as the key for grounding his own ethical project, he concomitantly criticizes Husserl for attenuating, or for simply not recognizing, the radical implications of his analysis, thus falling back into the self-contained sphere of egological immanence. To be more specific, when presenting what he understands as the essence of Husserl's subjective reduction, Levinas speaks of its achievement in terms that completely comply with his own philosophy. He puts this as follows:

> Husserl's theory of the intersubjective reduction describes the astonishing or traumatizing (*trauma* not *thauma*) possibility of a sobering up in which the *I*, facing the Other, is freed from itself, and awakens from dogmatic slumber. The Reduction, repeating as it were the disturbance of the Same by the Other who is not absorbed into the Same… describes the awakening, beyond knowledge, to an insomnia or watchfulness of which knowledge is but one modality. It is a fission of the subject, not shielded by the atomic consistency of the unity of transcendental apperception; an awakening coming from the other… that ceaselessly puts the priority of the same into question… it is the very event of transcendence as life.[20]

And, yet, while presenting Husserl as the source of his own ethical thinking, Levinas immediately qualifies his reading, by emphasizing how, in the last resort, Husserl's intersubjective reduction remains subservient to the self-sufficiency of the egological sphere with its traditional *telos* of scientific knowledge:

> But, all this is no longer Husserl. To him, the reduction remained the last passage from a less perfect to a more perfect knowledge. The reduction which the philosopher miraculously decided to perform was motivated solely by contradictions arising in naïve knowledge. The psychism of the soul or the intellectuality of the mind remains knowledge—the crisis of the European spirit is a crisis of Western science.[21]

What is it exactly in Husserl's intersubjective reduction that disappoints Levinas? What are the grounds for his claim that, despite its radical potential, "Husserl's philosophy attests to a sort of closure at the heart of the opening into the given, a drowsiness within spontaneous truth"?[22]

Some of the answers to these questions already lurk at the background of this discussion. Levinas's more general "complaint" against Husserl has to do, as suggested, with the manner in which Husserl's privileging of objective thought bars him from responding to the heterogeneity of concrete experience that he, himself, discovers. "In the phenomenological analysis of that concreteness of mind, there appears in Husserl—in conformity with a venerable Western tradition—a privilege of the theoretical, a privilege of representation, of knowing; and, hence, of the ontological meaning of being." [23] As a corollary of this, there is something primary in the manner in which Husserl construes the transcendence of the Other that, in principle, invalidates its radicalism. That is to say, his treatment of the Other's transcendence cannot, in principle, develop in any radical way because the framework within which it takes shape is, to begin with, egological, and its horizons of meaning are predetermined by the idea of representation whose other side is consciousness' containability. While this dimension of Husserl's thought is completely conspicuous throughout the

HUSSERL AND OTHER PHENOMENOLOGISTS

"Fifth Meditation," it can most clearly be seen in his conclusion celebrating the reduction's achievement in overcoming the charge of solipsism:

> What I demonstrate to myself harmoniously as "someone else"... is *eo ipso* the existing Other *for me* in the transcendental attitude: the alter ego demonstrated precisely within the experiencing intentionality of my ego. Within the bounds of positivity we say and find it obvious that, in my own experience, I experience not only myself but others. ... "In" myself I experience and know the Other; in me he becomes constituted—appresentatively mirrored, not constituted as the original. Hence it can very well be said, in a broadened sense, that the ego acquires... every transcendency.[24]

In a similar manner, we can look at the closing, somewhat dramatic, lines of *Cartesian Meditations* and try to imagine the kind of philosophical discomfort that they might have aroused in Levinas who, in 1930, was working on their translation.

> The Delphic motto "Know thyself!" has gained a new signification. Positive science is a science lost in the world. I must lose the world by epoche, in order to regain it by a universal self-examination. "*Noli foras ire*," says Augustine, "*in te redi, in interior homine habitat veritas.*" [Do not wish to go out; go back into yourself. Truth dwells in the inner man]. [25]

Leaving open the question of whether, as a matter of principle, the Husserlian paradigm can or cannot make room for radical alterity,[26] let us look now at two more specific, interrelated, aspects of Husserl's reduction that elicit Levinas's critical response: (1) Husserl's understanding of the constitution of the other person in terms of an essentially "harmonious experience;" and (2) the relational standing of Husserl's alter-ego vis-à-vis the perceiving subject.

Harmonious synthesis: The idea that the constitution of the meaningful is essentially harmonious is a recurrent theme in Husserl's conception of meaning, serving as a common presupposition. That is, for him, the phenomenological task of describing the processes of constitutive intentionalities and syntheses of meaning typically presupposes that the genesis and formation of meaning in the field of experience is a harmonious process. Meanings emerge, appear, and establish themselves when the constant multiplicity and change that are part of the stream of consciousness gather and coalesce around more or less clear and stable structures. These noematic structures, always dynamic and open to change, are essentially structures of harmony, consistency, and compatibility, of successful melding and coherence. In the Husserlian life-world, the appearance of things is described as a taking on of form, a perpetual movement of coalescence into conscious solidity.[27] And as a corollary of this, the encounter with the other person is understood in these same terms.

But this is precisely what is rejected by Levinas, who identifies in the encounter with the Other an experience "moving" in the opposite direction. To put this in Husserlian terms, what takes place in the encounter with the Other is a strong unravelling, a fracturing of the noematic structure. Whereas Husserl goes on thinking of the Other in the general terms of constitution and synthesis, Levinas points to a dimension of an uncontrolled, unorganized, non-synthetic upsurge. The encounter with the Other is essentially disharmonious; not an uncovering of what lies within the horizons of consciousness, but a revelation of what forces itself upon consciousness, doing so without "asking for permission," without taking consciousness into consideration, that is, in a manner that resists any kind of conformity with given forms of thought. "Husserl's theory of the intersubjective reduction describes the astonishing or traumatizing (*trauma* not *thauma*) possibility of a sobering up in which the *I*, facing the Other, is freed from itself, and awakens from dogmatic slumber." And yet, in describing this traumatizing affect Husserl, according to Levinas, fails to do justice to it:

24

trauma takes the form of *thauma*, no trace is left of a "fission of the subject" and the strong affect of disharmony is sublated into an understanding of the stream of experience guided solely by an ideal of harmony. Another way to put this is to say, with Levinas, that Husserl's description of experience lacks a dimension of intensity and that this lack has to do with the utterly intellectual form of his thinking. To put more specific, Husserl may be said to be impervious to the concreteness of the experience of alterity since his intentional analysis is predetermined by a conceptualization of alterity that unloads alterity of its affective impact.

Alter-ego and analogy: Indeed, in the "Fifth Meditation," alterity is that form of presence associated with an alter-ego, another-I, an I who is not I or, in other words, a consciousness that, while being symmetrical and analogous to the I's consciousness is also exterior to it. In this context, the phenomenon driving Husserl's investigation is not the alterity of the other consciousness as much as the external location—the exteriority—of one consciousness vis-à-vis the other. And in this respect, the problem that concerns Husserl is one pertaining to the multiplicity of consciousnesses and the conditions enabling such multiplicity, so that these identically structured consciousnesses only differ in their location in space. As such, the alterity of another ego cannot bear any immediate resonance because it is construed, to begin with, as a logical derivation from the objective fact of its differing, relational, position vis-à-vis the *I*. This means, in Levinas' view, that even when explicitly dealing with transcendence, Husserl cannot ever make actual room for the Other's *alterity* because his concern with the alter-ego remains grounded in identity and analogy.

Levinas's Debt

Given Levinas's critique of Husserl, let's return now to the question of debt with which this discussion started. The term "debt" (Levinas uses *la dette*) is, in itself, an interesting one, especially as it appears within the horizons of an intellectual relationship. Unlike the ordinary, practical, use of the term that typically refers to something that is owed or due and that, as such, needs to be returned or paid back to a giver, in an intellectual context, debts are not returned—they are acknowledged. That is, the conventional manner in which one pays back an intellectual debt is by mentioning it in public: "I owe him" or "this is my debt to her" are speech acts that, when appearing in writing, typically suffice for settling an intellectual debt, although one doesn't really give back anything, in any material sense. But, what exactly is one saying when one acknowledges a philosophical debt? In making such acknowledgments, we are typically saying something to the effect that we are not alone in our thinking, that we are not the ultimate source of our thoughts, and, more specifically, that another person has played a significant role—that he or she are present—in the thinking or writing we call our own. In other words, we are making a point about the relational character of the *cogito*, about our being *in* a relationship that precedes the solidification of an autonomous "I think." This non-symmetrical relationship that we present, in public, as an owing of a debt to someone, is not a factual relationship, but belongs, rather, to the sphere of the ethical. Indeed, it is in terms of a relation of debt that the fundamental question of ethics is often posed: what do I owe to the other person? That is, what kind of debt is imposed on—how is an owing part of—my relation to others? Being in debt, in this ethical sense, presupposes a particular kind of intentionality that, unlike a factual debt, has no object-correlate. It cannot be reduced to the form of owing some-thing, even if, it does happen to show itself in specific situations of owing to the other person a "this" or a "that."

HUSSERL AND OTHER PHENOMENOLOGISTS

An ethical debt, in other words, is the debt one is in when living a life whose infrastructure is the relation to others *qua* others. This debt can, at times, take on different—more or less satisfying—forms of being responsive to and responsible for the welfare of the other person. But, its inner form consists in relating to the other person in a manner that allows the exteriority, or transcendence, of that person to become part of our relation to them. In this sense, an ethical debt is what we "pay back" by remaining in debt; what we ethically owe the other person is not to relieve ourselves of that debt.

I think that this is what Levinas is alluding to when he writes that "to meet a man is to be kept awake by an enigma." That is, what we fundamentally owe the other person is to be kept awake by the enigma of his or her exteriority, an enigma that we can never solve, but that we can address, and fail to address, in a variety of ways. This enigma is also central, as we've seen, to Levinas' writing on Husserl. "Upon meeting Hussserl," he writes "the enigma was always that of his work," implying that, in being kept awake by that enigma, Levinas lived his debt to the Master, a debt, that he thematized again and again, while accepting the impossibility of such a thematization. Hence, in describing his debt—which is concomitantly his relation with the enigma of exteriority—Levinas recurrently points to that which was offered to him in the teachings of Husserl. To recall, let's return to a passage from which we've already quoted:

> Doubtless it is Husserl who is at the origin of my writings. It is to him that I owe the concept of intentionality animating consciousness, and especially the idea of the *horizons of meaning* which grow blurred when thought is absorbed in *what it thinks*… *Horizons of meaning,* which "intentional" analysis rediscovers when it focuses on the *thought* that "has forgotten," in reflection, and revives those horizons of the *entity* and of *being*. Above all, I owe to Husserl… the principles of such analyses, the examples and models that have taught me how to get at those horizons and how to look for them. For me, that is the essential contribution of phenomenology.[28]

For Levinas, Husserl's work offered a new understanding of the unfolding of meaning whose gist is that in facing the meaningful, one always sees more than one sees and always thinks beyond the thoughts one entertains. What Levinas thus found in Husserl's teaching and, particularly in his conception of intentionality, was an understanding that the meaningful is structured as an enigma, one that keeps the philosopher awake, as he or she returns to its continual unpacking. Moreover, Levinas tells us that, embodied in Husserl's "examples and models," he found a form of openness (of a wakefulness) with which he could access the enigmatic structure of the unfolding of meaning. This openness was, for him, a necessary key to unlocking "forgotten" horizons of meaning that uphold the determined intelligibility of phenomena. In utilizing the key he found in Husserl's teaching, Levinas was able to develop his own philosophical vision aiming at the radical alterity of the other person. But, Husserl who provided the key to such a vision, stayed behind, remaining exterior to that vision. What Husserl gave Levinas was something that he himself never had. This unique kind of giving is a theme Levinas intermittently touches on in *Totality and Infinity* when referring to what he understands as a genuine teaching relationship.

> Teaching does not simply transmit an abstract and general content already common to me and the Other. It does not merely assume an after all subsidiary function of being midwife to a mind already pregnant with its fruit. Speech first founds community by giving, by presenting the phenomenon as given; and it gives by thematizing. The given is the work of a sentence. In the sentence the apparition loses its phenomenality in being fixed as a theme. (98–99)

HUSSERL AND OTHER PHENOMENOLOGISTS

For Levinas, the relationship of teaching is based on a giving, one that is different from the Socratic model. The measure of this giving may, at first sight, wrongly appear to be that which a teacher thematizes: i.e. a given representation of things. But, a giving can never be reduced to what is given. The Saying cannot be reduced to the Said.[29] "The first teaching of the teacher is his very presence as teacher from which representation comes" (100). And, analogously, the core of being a student lies in how, in the midst of attending to the Said, one is "capable of a relation with the exterior" (180), capable of being kept awake by the enigma of a giving that comes from the exteriority of another person.

It is in this sense, I take it, that Levinas understood his debt to Husserl's teaching and especially to the Husserlian concept of intentionality that he so radically transformed precisely because, in recognizing the concrete truth of this concept, he was fully indebted to it. "Teaching is a way for truth to be produced such that it is not my work, such that I could not derive it from my own interiority. In affirming such a production of truth we modify the original meaning of truth and the noesis-noema structure, taken as the meaning of intentionality" (295).

Notes

1. Emmanuel Levinas, "The Ruin of Representation," in *Discovering Existence with Husserl*, trans. Richard A. Cohen and Michael B. Smith (Evanston, IL: Northwestern University Press, 1998), 111.
2. Emmanuel Levinas, *Ethics and Infinity: Conversations with Philippe Nemo*, trans. Richard A. Cohen (Pittsburg, PA: Duquesne University Press, 1985), 28.
3. Jean-Paul Sartre, *Situations IV* (Paris: Gallimard, 1964), 190.
4. Emmanuel Levinas, "Non-Intentional Consciousness," in *Entre Nous*, trans. Michael B. Smith and Barbara Harshav (New York: Columbia University Press, 2000), 123.
5. Levinas, "The Ruin of Representation," 112.
6. Emmanuel Levinas, "On Ideas," in *Discovering Existence with Husserl*, 13.
7. Levinas, "On *Ideas*," 13.
8. Emmanuel Levinas, *Totality and Infinity: An Essay on Exteriority*, trans. Alphonso Lingis (Pittsburg, PA: Duquesne University Press, 1991), 29.
9. Levinas, Totality and Infinity, 43–44.
10. Levinas, *Totality and Infinity*, 27, 66, 29.
11. Edmund Husserl, *Méditations cartésiennes*, trans. G. Peiffer and Emmanuel Levinas (Paris: Armand Colin, 1931).
12. Edmund Husserl, *Cartesian Meditations: An Introduction to Phenomenology*, trans. Dorion Cairns (The Hague: Martinus Nijhoff, 1960), 89.
13. Husserl, Cartesian Meditations, 89.
14. Emmanuel Levinas, "From Consciousness to Wakefulness," in *Discovering Existence with Husserl*, 164.
15. Levinas, "From Consciousness to Wakefulness," 90.
16. Levinas, "Philosophy and Awakening," in *Entre Nous*, 86.
17. Husserl, Cartesian Meditations, 123.
18. Levinas, "Philosophy and Awakening," 85–86.
19. In this context, it is interesting to notice that, while Levinas is preoccupied with the ethical implications of Husserl's theory of intersubjectivity, he does not show any particular interest in Husserl's ethical writings, with which he is likely to have been familiar. On Husserl's ethics, see Edmund Husserl, *Vorlesungen über Ethik und Wertlehre 1908-1914*, in *HUA*, vol. 28, ed. Ullrich Melle (Dordrecht: Kluwer Academic Publishers, 1988); Ullrich Melle, "From Reason to Love," in *Phenomenological Approaches to Moral Philosophy: A Handbook*, ed. J. Drummond and L. Embree (Dordrecht: Kluwer Academic Publishers, 2002); Joacim Siles i

HUSSERL AND OTHER PHENOMENOLOGISTS

Borras, *The Ethics of Husserl's Phenomenology* (London: Continuum, 2010); see Sophie Loidolt, "A Phenomenological Ethics of the Absolute Ought: Investigating Husserl's Unpublished Ethical Writings" in *Ethics and Phenomenology*, ed. Mark Sanders and J. Jeremy Wisnewski (Lanham, MD: Rowman & Littlefield, 2012).

20. Levinas,"Philosophy and Awakening," 87.
21. Levinas, "Philosophy and Awakening," 87–88
22. Levinas, "Philosophy and Awakening," 87–88
23. Levinas,"Philosophy and Awakening," 87–88
24. Levinas, "The Ruin of Representation," 148–49.
25. Levinas, "The Ruin of Representation," 148–49.
26. Since Husserl could not offer a rejoinder on this point, it remains open whether Levinas's interpretation of Husserl's understanding of the "experience of the stranger" succeeds in doing justice to his position. Furthermore, Levinas also tends to disregard a question that Husserl would certainly pose to him, as Derrida later did, concerning the very possibility of making room, in philosophical terms, for radical transcendence. Is not the Levinasian manner of introducing radical transcendence into philosophical discourse a contradiction in terms? Is not the very attempt to conceptualize transcendence already a betrayal of the uncontainable essence of the transcendent?
27. On Husserl's discussion of the "inverse movement" that ultimately leads to the "explosion" of the noematic structure, see Hagi Kenaan, "Subject to Error: Rethinking Husserl's Phenomenology of Misperception," *International Journal of Philosophical Studies* 7 (1999): 55–67.
28. Levinas, "Non-Intentional Consciousness," 123.
29. On Levinas's conception of the Said and the Saying, see Hagi Kenaan, "The Plot of the Saying," in *Etudes Phenomenologiques: Levinas et la phénoménolgie* 22.43–44 (Brussels: Ousia, 2006), and *The Ethics of Visuality: Levinas and the Contemporary Gaze* (London: I.B. Tauris, 2013), pt. 2 "Talk."

Husserl, Heidegger, and Sartre: Presence and the Performative Contradiction

James Mensch

Faculty of Humanities, Charles University, Prague 5, Czech Republic

ABSTRACT

In this essay I explore the divide that separates Heidegger and Sartre from Husserl. At issue is what Derrida calls the "metaphysics of presence." From Heidegger onward this has been characterized as an interpretation of both being and knowing in terms of presence. To exist is to be now, and to know is to make present the evidence for something's existence. Husserl's account of constitution assumes this interpretation. By contrast, Heidegger and Sartre see constitution in terms of our pragmatic engagements with the world, engagements that they trace to the essential nothingness at our core. Who is correct: Husserl or those who give his phenomenology a negative basis? At issue is the nature of transcendence. Do we transcend ourselves toward the world by constituting both our own and the world's presence or do we do so by virtue of an inner nothingness that allows us to assume various identities as a consequence of our pragmatic engagements? Husserl claims that to argue against presence is to argue against evidence. It is to enter into a performative contradiction, one where you undercut the evidence you present for your position. His theory of constitution can, in fact, be seen as an attempt to avoid this contradiction. Implicit here is a claim that Heidegger and Sartre, in their appeal to nothingness, must fall into this contradiction. The contradiction thus becomes a way of deciding between their positions. I do so by exploring their accounts of constitution and the rationality they see implicit in it.

If there is one thing that Husserl's successors, from Heidegger to Derrida, agree on, it is that "[f]rom Parmenides to Husserl, the privilege of the present has never been put into question."[1] This privilege, Heidegger asserts, is that of "determining the meaning of being as *parousia* or *ousia*, which signifies presence in an ontological-temporal sense. An entity in its being is taken as presence [*Anwesenheit*]; it is understood in relation to a distinct temporal mode, that of the present [*Gegenwart*].[2] For Derrida, "the privilege granted to the present... is the ether of metaphysics." It marks our conception of consciousness. In its self-awareness, consciousness is self-present. Thus "[t]he privilege granted to consciousness... signifies the privilege granted to the present."[3] What happens when we contest this privilege, when, in Derrida's words, we turn from "a philosophy of presence" to "a meditation on non-presence"?[4] From the perspective of Husserl's successors, we reform and renew philosophy. In their view, the interpretation of being as presence fails to grasp the special nature of the subject or its relation to its world. From a Husserlian perspective, to contest presence is to contest evidence. It is to enter into a performative contradiction, where in arguing for your position, you undercut the evidence you present for it. In what follows, I am going to examine this Husserlian response. In doing so, I shall trace what Derrida calls the "metaphysics of presence" inherent in Husserl's position.[5]

Presence and the Performative Contradiction

The simplest example of a performative contradiction is the assertion "I am dead." As is obvious, the assertion contradicts the presuppositions for making it. At least from the time of the *Logical Investigations* (1900s), Husserl's work can be characterized as motivated by the goal of avoiding this type of contradiction. In epistemology, it occurs in theories that "imply that the logical or noetic conditions for the possibility of any theory are false."[6] Husserl argues that if such theories are self-referring, then in contradicting their own presuppositions, they are "self-destroying." They have destroyed their own noetic and logical possibility. On the other hand, if they are not self-referring, they are epistemologically meaningless. They do not have the meaning given by the notions of noetic and logical possibility. This is because a non-self-referring thesis about "the laws on which the rational possibility of any thesis and the proof of any thesis depend" is outside the horizon of sense given by these laws. As such, it has no meaning as defined by them. The thesis is of a different order or type than that which it speaks about. If it were the same type, then some self-reference to its epistemological possibility would implicitly occur. Lacking this, we have no way of ascertaining our position regarding it.

To make this concrete, we can imagine a debate between a Marxist, a Freudian, and a biological determinist. Each will appeal to the hidden motives for a person's action. The Marxist will assert that a person's views are determined by his position in the class system, the Freudian will assert their determination by the unconscious, and the biological determinist will point to the chemical actions of the brain as being the decisive factor. How will we decide among them? All will see our actual views as traces of what cannot appear to us. The difficulty can be put in terms of the knowing relationship. Each asserts a relationship—be it that of the class struggle, or that of the unconscious to the conscious mind, or that of the brain to the mind—that is beyond the knowing relationship, i.e., beyond what we can know as based on the contents of our consciousness. Such contents, in fact, are asserted to be determined by this relationship. It governs what the person counts as the evidence for what he claims to know.

To resolve their debate, the participants would have to justify their claims, that is, to show that they "know" what they are talking about by giving some evidence for the relation that they are claiming to be determinative. This, however, would involve exempting this evidence from the arguments they make that undercut evidence as such. The same holds for the logic of their argumentation. It also cannot be relativized. The biological determinist must, for example, exempt his reasoning from the assertion that "even logic alters with the development of the brain."[7] But in implicitly exempting the justification of their theories from the skeptical consequences these theories entail, they are both denying and implicitly presupposing the independence and priority of the knowing (noetic) relationship.[8]

For Husserl, this points to the necessary priority of the knowing or epistemological standpoint. Whenever some other relation is taken as prior to this, we fall into a self-undermining skepticism. This holds not just for the attempt to understand knowing in terms of economic, psycho-analytical, or biological factors; it also obtains for the relationships of history, language, culture, and so on when we take them as external to the knowing relationship and as determinative of its content. The point follows, since to justify the claim that some particular relationship is the determining one, one has to argue for its truth—to attempt to justify it as an item of knowledge. But to do so is to presuppose the independence and priority of the knowing relationship—the very thing that one is attempting to deny. Given this, Husserl concludes that "epistemology must not be understood as a discipline that follows metaphysics or even coincides with it, but rather as one which precedes metaphysics just as it precedes psychology and all other disciplines."[9] As prior, it determines their claims to knowledge. Because it does so, it cannot take its standards from them, but must supply these standards itself.

These standards, Husserl believes, are provided by intuitive evidence—the evidence of either straightforward, sensuous perception or that provided by intellectual, "categorial" insight—the intuition that allows us to grasp states of affairs. His reason for this is that the standards for intuitive evidence are not externally provided. They are inherent in the perceptual process itself. Intuitive evidence can be more or less clear, more or less distinct, detailed and so forth. It can either match or fail to match what we claim we are seeing. Given that claims to knowledge find their justification in the evidence presented for them, we have to say that the standards of intuitive evidence are the inherent ones that the epistemological relation provides.

Constitution and Presence

In the *Logical Investigations*, the working out of this view occurs in the context of the relation of intention to fulfillment. To intend to see something is, for Husserl, to try to make sense of what we perceptually experience. The goal is a "unity of meaning." The process of intending such a meaning is apparent when we regard a visual illusion—for example, that of an arrow that seems to be pointing inward and then outward from the page. As we regard it, the two senses of the arrow appear alternately. This is not by chance since visual illusions are constructed to provide data that support different interpretations. Such illusions, in fact, show that "perception is interpretation." As Husserl explains this: "It belongs to perception that something appears within it, but *interpretation* makes up what we term appearance—be it correct or not, anticipatory or overdrawn. The *house* appears to me through no other way but that I interpret in a certain fashion actually experienced contents of sensation. I hear a *barrel organ*—the sensed tones I interpret as *barrel organ tones*. ... They are termed 'appearances' or, better, appearing contents precisely for the reason that they are contents of perceptive interpretation."[10] Husserl's point is that to intend to see something is, concretely, to form an interpretative intention. It is to attempt to interpret what one sees in terms of a unitary sense. As experience shows, not every intention is fulfilled. Our interpretative intentions are constantly adjusted in terms of the perceptual evidence. For example, what looked like a rabbit hiding under a bush can turn out, on closer inspection, to be merely a play of light and shadow. As Husserl makes clear, this process of adjustment between intention and perceptual fulfillment is one where neither side dominates the other. Even though every sense of the object is a sense intended by consciousness, consciousness in its intending the object cannot, in its act of interpretation, inform the object with every possible sense.[11] Only those senses that are fulfilled or embodied by the intuitive presence of the object pertain to it as such.[12] In other words, consciousness's interpretive, intending sense informs the object's intuitive presence only to the point that the object's intuitive presence fulfills or embodies this interpretive sense. Implicit in this account is *the equation of evidence with presence*. The claims of our intentions to see something find their evidence in a confirming intuitive presence.

The relation of intention to fulfillment that the *Logical Investigations* describes is actually an early version of Husserl's theory of constitution. Here, the role of interpretation in grasping a unity of sense is understood as "synthesis."[13] "Synthesis" signifies "placing together" (Gk. *sun tithemi*, 'to put together'). Its goal, as with interpretation, is the grasp of a unity of meaning. Thus, as we walk into a room, we are confronted with a myriad of shifting perceptions. How do we interpret these as perceptions of the various objects within it? According to Husserl, we do so by recognizing distinct patterns of perceptions—those that present the perspectively arranged views of distinct objects. Placing a set of these views together, we grasp a pattern. As we do so, we interpret it as having a distinct referent and assert that the members of the pattern are views *of* this referent. Suppose, for example, I turn a box in my hands. As I do so, first one side and then another appears. These different appearances are linked perspectively in a series. Grasping the pattern in the series, I proceed through it to grasp the box. As is obvious, the box is not any one of the views I have of it. It is the one thing that the many views have in common. As a one in many, it is, in fact, a unity of sense. It is, in other words, the goal of my attempt to make sense of what I perceive. As such, it is present as the object of my interpretative intention. On the one hand, this object is immanent within my perceptual experience. Its presence is established through my connecting my different perceptions, that is, my act of synthesis or placing them together. On the other hand, it also transcends them. This transcendence is ontological: The box is ontologically distinct from the perceptions presenting it. An individual perception cannot present itself perspectivally. We cannot shift it about to see its backside.[14] Only the box can show itself in a perspectival series. Only it has the qualities that would allow us to designate it as a spatial-temporal object.

Two points follow from this analysis. The first is that intentionality, the quality of a single view's being a view *of* an object, is the result of the constitutive process. It involves the generation of the presence of the referent through the synthesis. The second is that the transcendence of this referent is also the result of the constitutive process. The synthesis generates that which transcends it. Thus the transcendence of consciousness for Husserl, its quality of going beyond itself, is a function of its own activity.

Sartre sees this as a betrayal of Husserl's fundamental insight. He writes: Husserl "defines consciousness precisely as a transcendence. .... This is his essential discovery. But from the moment that he makes of the *noema* an *unreal*, a correlate *of* the *noesis*, a noema whose *esse* is *percipi*, he is totally unfaithful to his principle."[15] Sartre's contention is that Husserl is engaged in a kind of Berkeleyan idealism, one that asserts that the *being* of the noema (or object of consciousness) is its *being perceived*. For Sartre, this makes the noema something "unreal." It has its being, not in itself, but only as a correlate of a noesis or synthetic act of consciousness. Two things argue against this view. The first is the ontological transcendence of the object. As a one-in-many, it is neither the individual views through which it is posited nor the individual synthetic act that engages in such positing. The second is the fact that our attempts to posit an object can fail. Suppose, for example, that on approaching a bush on a bright sunny day, we seem to see a rabbit hiding under it. As we move to get a better look, its features appear to become more clearly defined. One part of what we see seems to be its head, another its body, still another its paws. Based upon what we see, we anticipate that further features will be revealed as we approach: this pattern of light and shadow will be seen as the rabbit's ears, another will be seen as its eyes, and so forth. If the interpretations that guide our acts of synthesis are correct, then our experiences should form a part of an emerging pattern that exhibits these features, that is, that perceptually manifests the object we assume we are seeing. If, however, we are mistaken, at some point our experiences will fail to fulfill our expectations. What we took to be a rabbit will dissolve into a collection of flickering shadows and light. Our attempts to place our perceptions together into a pattern presenting the rabbit will fail. The possibility of failure points again to the role of perceptual presence in confirming our claims. Husserl's linking intentionality to constitution is based on this role. It presents an account of knowing that privileges intuition. Here, the justifying content of our claims to know are internal to the constitutive process by which we grasp the object. As such, it is an account designed to avoid the performative contradiction inherent in skeptical theories.

Rationality and Constitution

A further element in Husserl's attempt to avoid this contradiction occurs in his equation of constituted presence with rationality. Influenced by the Darwinism current at the time, many of his contemporaries believed that "even logic alters with the development of the brain."[16] Nietzsche, perhaps, is the most direct exponent of this view. He writes that "we have senses for only a selection of perceptions—those with which we have to concern ourselves in order to preserve ourselves." This means that "the measure of that of which we are in any way conscious is totally dependent upon the coarse utility of its becoming conscious." We are conscious of things if this helps preserve us. The same holds for our knowledge. To cite Nietzsche again: "The meaning of 'knowledge'... is to be regarded in a strict and narrow anthropocentric and biological sense. ... The utility of preservation—not some abstract-theoretical need not to be deceived—stands as the motive behind the development of the organs of knowledge—they develop in such a way that their observation suffices for our preservation."[17] The performative contradiction inherent in such remarks is obvious. If, in fact, our rationality were determined by the peculiar line of our evolutionary development—by the exigencies of preservation that it incorporates—then how could we know this? To assume that our "organs of knowledge" were capable of this would be to assume that they had developed so that they could objectively grasp the evolutionary process that produced them. But nothing in evolutionary theory, understood as the working of purely mechanical causes, points to this. Other species make what, from our perspective, are category mistakes. Why should we assume that we are unique in avoiding such mistakes? But if we cannot, how can we assure ourselves of the objective validity of the evidence and argument of evolutionary biology?

HUSSERL AND OTHER PHENOMENOLOGISTS

Husserl's alternative to this impasse is to claim that appearing is inherently rational. By this he means that the laws of formal and material logic structure appearing. They do so because such laws express the laws of constitution. Given this, we can assert with Husserl that "'truly existing object' and 'object capable of being rationally posited' are equivalent correlates."[18] In fact, we have Husserl's claim that "an all-sided... solution of the problems of constitution"—the problems involving the positing of objects—"would obviously be equivalent to a complete phenomenology of reason in all its formal and material formations."[19] One way to understand this claim is to note that a completely senseless, irrational world would be one where we could not posit objects on the basis of our experiences. Our perceptions would not fit together to form repeating patterns. As a result, no synthesis of perceptions and no assigning referents to the resulting patterns would be possible. By way of contrast, a rational world is one where we can posit objects from our perceptions. Similar objects are posited from similar patterns and, as a result, we have the possibility of forming logical classes such as all A's, all B's, et cetera. To assert, in this context, a logical contradiction—to say that at the same time and place an object has and has not some property—would be to assert that an appearing pattern allowed simultaneously two different interpretations. It would be to reduce the appearing world to a series of visual illusions, thereby frustrating the intention of the synthetic act to grasp a unity of meaning. This, however, is not the world we experience. The fact that we can apply logic to it and infer consequences that actually obtain points to Husserl's assertion that "the *ordo et connexio rerum* must direct itself according to the *ordo et connexio idearum*."[20] There is no "blind ordering" that makes this necessary. Behind it is the fact that constitution aims at a unity of meaning and that such unity embraces not just objects but also their relations. The fact that what is irrational—that is, contradictory—cannot appear simply points back to the formal necessities of constitution.

The Husserlian response to the performative contradiction implicit in Nietzsche's extension of Darwinianism involves not just taking the concept of an "'object' as a title for the essential connections of consciousness"—namely, those "rational connections" through which the object "receives its rational positing."[21] It is also based on the fact that logical relations are not causal ones. To assert "All A's are B's; all B's are C's; therefore all A's are C's" is not to claim a material-causal relation between the terms. Similarly, the fact that P implies Q does not signify that P causes Q. Given this, we cannot equate logic with the material causal processes of our brains as we do when we assert that logic evolves along with the brain. Logic, as opposed to biology, considers formal rather than material necessities. Logic's relation to the constitutive processes by which we posit objects involves, correspondingly, non-material objects. Now, the individual views that we connect into patterns are not spatial-temporal, material objects; neither are the patterns that are formed from them. At issue in our attempt to make sense of what we perceive is not physical matter, but rather our perceptual content along with the "unities of sense" that we attempt to draw from this. To all these, logic, rather than causality, pertains; and because it does so we can reason about what appears without falling into a performative contradiction. Such a contradiction can only appear when the grounds of reason are outside of appearing and yet determinative of it. It is at this point that we violate the priority of the epistemological standpoint. Husserl's account of constitution, which makes rationality internal to our grasp of objects, is designed to avoid this. To see what happens when we abandon this "metaphysics of presence," we have to consider the alternatives presented by Heidegger and Sartre.

HUSSERL AND OTHER PHENOMENOLOGISTS

Selfhood and Nothingness

In a letter dated Meßkirch, 22 October 1927, Heidegger writes to Husserl:

> Which kind of being [*Seinsart*] is the being in which the 'world' constitutes itself? This is the central problem of *Being and Time*, i.e., a fundamental ontology of Dasein. At issue is showing that human Dasein's kind of being is totally distinct from all other beings and that it is precisely this [kind] that contains in itself the possibility of transcendental constitution.[22]

In emphasizing the distinctness of Dasein's kind of being in *Sein und Zeit*, Heidegger asserts that it is not a "what," but rather a "who" (45). The entities that count as a "what" have definite properties, and we can, accordingly, describe "what" they are. The "who," however, escapes such characterization. While the entities with given properties can be characterized as present—that is, as "present to hand" or, if they are useful, "ready to hand"—Heidegger takes Dasein as having a distinct kind of being, one characterized "by the nothingness [*Nichtigkeit*] of the being of its basis [*Grundseins*]." This means that it "is itself essentially null [*nichtig*]" (285).

These characterizations rest on a non-Husserlian, pragmatic account of constitution. According to Heidegger, we constitute the senses of the objects of our world through our practical engagements. Such engagements constitute—"disclose" or make present—things as means for our various projects. Thus, if my goal is to cross a lake in a sailboat, I disclose or make present the wind as "wind to fill my sails." If my project is to build a bookcase, I disclose the senses of hammer, nails, and wood as means for my purpose. Now, what makes such projects possible is my "projective being." For example, in deciding to cross the lake, I grasp this as a possibility I am capable of and project myself forward as actualizing it. Engaging in this activity, I not only disclose my being as the person who is crossing the lake in a sailboat, I also exhibit both the boat and the wind as means for my purposes. This grasping of crossing the lake as a possibility is part of my understanding of how I make my way in the world. *Understanding something as something* (e.g., wind as wind to fill my sails), *and projecting myself forward* as the person who will accomplish something (e.g., cross the lake in a sailboat), mutually imply each other. I understand things as means for my purposes because I can conceive of such purposes, that is, project myself forward as accomplishing them. The reverse also holds. I project myself forward because I can grasp things as means for my projects. Heidegger thus writes: "As understanding, Dasein projects its Being upon possibilities"—possibilities it can accomplish. This "Being-towards-possibilities, which understands, is itself a potentiality-for-Being [of Dasein], and it is so because of the way these possibilities, as disclosed, exert their counter-thrust [*Ruckschlag*] upon Dasein" (148). Their counter-thrust is their role in defining Dasein's being as having realized one of its possibilities.

This definition gives Dasein its characteristics—but such characteristics are distinct from those that a thing exhibits. They are the result of Dasein's own action, that is, the projects it engages in. Unlike a thing, Dasein faces the choice of what it will do and, hence, become. For Heidegger, this signifies that "Dasein, when understood ontologically, is care" (57). "Care" is a care for our own being since Dasein, for Heidegger, is the entity for whom its own being is an issue (12). It has to decide what it will be. In other words, its being is a matter of its choices as it makes its way in the world. Such choices involve its projects, the things it wants to accomplish. These, however, constantly change. Having accomplished one project, Dasein turns to another. Now, if we ask what Dasein is "in itself," apart from such

35

projects, we can only get a *negative* answer. Inherently, Dasein is simply its projecting itself, its being ahead of itself as it considers which possibilities of itself it should actualize. This means that, even before it chooses, "Dasein is already ahead of itself in its being. Dasein is always [in considering these possibilities of itself] 'beyond itself' ['*über sich hinaus*']" (192). This insight into Dasein's being is the same as that which Sartre expresses in *Being and Nothingness* when he writes that Man is a being "who is what he is not, and who is not what he is" (112). Separated from myself in my being *ahead* of myself, I am *not* what I *presently* am. Given this, I can only "be" what I am not, that is, be as projected toward those goals or possibilities which I actualize through my projects.

This being ahead of myself is, according to Heidegger, part of the structure of my being as care. In his words, "The being of Dasein signifies, being ahead of yourself in already being in the world as being there with the entities that one encounters within the world. This being fills in the meaning of the term *care*" (*Sein und Zeit*, 192). This complicated terminology should not conceal from us the basic phenomenon that Heidegger is pointing to. In engaging in a project, I am in anticipation, ahead of myself; I am there at the goal. Guided by the latter, my being is stretched out in time, I am *also* there with the entities I encounter. Thus, guided by the goal of building a bookcase, I hammer the nails into the wood. My being-in-the-world is that of directing myself according to my projected future as the person who *has* built the bookcase.

If, in projecting myself, I can only *not* be what I presently am, then as projection, I am defined by this *not*. With this, we return to our citations about the nothingness at the core of Dasein's being. Extended, they read: "Not only is the projection, as one that has been thrown, determined by the nothingness [*Nichtigkeit*] of the being of its basis [*Grundseins*], but also, as projection, [Dasein] is itself essentially null [*nichtig*]... the nothingness meant here belongs to Dasein's being-free for its existential possibilities" (285). The point follows since Dasein has to choose what it will be—which of its "existential possibilities" it will actualize through its projects. To insist that it has some given properties—that it is some thing—is to assert that there are essential limits, rooted in its nature, to such "existential possibilities." Such limits, however, are only accidental. They are given by Dasein's personal history and that of its generation. Thus, by virtue of my own past, I have the materials needed for the bookcase. Their presence makes its construction possible. By virtue of the "past of my generation," my place in history, there are such things as books and bookcases and, hence, the possibility of forming the intention of constructing a bookcase. But for a being that is incapable of projecting—and, hence, of projects—such possibilities do not exist.

The nothingness that Heidegger is referring to thus has a multiple sense. It signifies that Dasein is no-thing and cannot be characterized as such. Unlike a thing, it is neither present to hand nor ready to hand. It further signifies the "not" of its projective being—the fact that, as ahead of itself, it cannot be identified by what it presently is. Finally, and most radically, it indicates the self-alterity that characterizes its being. Dasein is, at its basis, other than all the possibilities of selfhood that it can realize through its projects. In the "null basis" of its being as care, it is also distinct from all the particular beings it can disclose. Its inner alterity is such that it places it beyond everything worldly that it can imagine or know. It is, in its inner nothingness, non-representable and, hence, *anonymous*. The freedom of this anonymous human existence has, as we should expect, no inherent limits. "Freedom," Heidegger writes, "is the abyss [*Ab-grund*] of Dasein."[23] The nothingness that grounds freedom makes it an abyss since it signifies that it has no ground that would place essential limits on it.

HUSSERL AND OTHER PHENOMENOLOGISTS

Sartre, while following Heidegger in his account of pragmatic disclosure, derives the inner nothingness of the self directly from his account of the intentionality of consciousness. He argues that to say that consciousness is consciousness *of* something is not to say that it *is* that thing. Intentionality, insofar as it implies transcendence, is an "openness to," rather than an identity. As Sartre expresses this in *Being and Nothingness*: "*presence to* always implies duality. ... If being is present to itself, it is because it is *not* wholly itself. Presence is an immediate deterioration of coincidence, for it supposes separation" (124; second italics added). Given that consciousness, to be consciousness, must be self-aware, such separation must also characterize it. This self-separation is the nothingness at its core. In Sartre's words: "The being of consciousness *qua* consciousness is to exist *at a distance from itself* as presence to itself, and this empty distance which being carries in its being is Nothingness. Thus, in order for a *self* to exist, it is necessary that the unity of this being include its own nothingness as the nihilation of identity" (125). Such nothingness makes the self a "For-itself" rather than a thing (an "In-itself") with its given properties. Thus, Sartre writes, "The For-itself is the being which determines itself to exist inasmuch as it cannot coincide with itself" (125–26). Its determination is through its projects and its projective being is based on the nothingness, which prevents it from ever coinciding with itself. As with Heidegger, the self's freedom results from this inner nothingness. Sartre puts this in terms of the detachment or withdrawal from being that freedom implies. In his words, "For man to put a particular existent out of circuit is to put himself out of circuit in relation to the existent. In this case, he is not subject to it; he is out of reach; it cannot act on him, for he has retired *beyond a nothingness*. Descartes, following the Stoics, has given a name to this possibility, which human reality has, to secrete a nothingness which isolates it—it is *freedom*" (60).

We "secrete" this nothingness every time we reflect upon ourselves, every time we "step back" from ourselves and grasp our relation to some existent. The fact that intentionality is not identity means that the reflecting consciousness is not the consciousness reflected upon. For Sartre, this non-identity is the possibility of our withdrawal, of our detaching or *freeing* ourselves from the self that we reflexively grasp. As such, it is also a withdrawal from the conditions determining this self. It is, according to Sartre, a freeing ourselves from them. As Sartre makes clear, this detachment is a possibility grounded in our very being as a For-itself, that is, as a mode of being that, because of its inherent nothingness, exists as a continuous decomposition of the identity of the In-itself. Affected as an In-itself, the decomposition frees us from this. For Sartre, then, "human reality can detach itself from the world—in questioning, in systematic doubt, in skeptical doubt, in the epoché, etc.—only if, by nature, it has the possibility of self-detachment" (60). The possibility of this detachment is the same as that of our freedom, which is the same as that of our self-presence or consciousness. At its basis is the nothingness that is the nihilation of our identity. Given this, it follows that "what we call freedom is impossible to distinguish from the *being* of 'human reality'... there is no difference between the being of man and his *being-free*" (126). Both point to the nothingness that makes our human being distinct from all other beings.

The Contingency of Reason

The above accounts yield a very different view of reason than that presented by Husserl. For Husserl, reason reflects the relation of evidence to positing that informs constitution. As we pursue the implications of our intuitively established assertions, the reasonable is what can be borne out by the evidence of perception, be this our sensuous perception or our founded "categorial" (intellectual) perception. For Heidegger, however, what appears is relative to our choices. It is a function of the projects that we choose to engage in and, hence, ultimately, of our freedom. Water, for example, appears as a liquid to drink or as something to douse a fire with or something to wash with depending on our purpose. Here, the appeal to intuitive evidence does not have an objective, confirming force. In fact, since what we choose to disclose often conceals what we have not chosen to make present, such evidence can often function as a form of concealment. Thus, a world in which economic decisions take precedence, one ruled by strict standards of utility, may evince the rationality of the marketplace. But such rationality will conceal other forms of behavior, other standards for rational choices. The difficulty here is the limiting of disclosure to pragmatic engagements, engagements that necessarily depend on our choices. The fact that the freedom underlying these choices has no ground—is an abyss—signifies both the openness of our freedom and the lack of inherent limits to our pragmatic disclosures.

It may seem that we can escape this concealment by turning to the historical record. Can we not look back and see the results of the decisions of past generations, thereby gauging our own? Not according to Heidegger. In fact, "[i]n no other science are the 'universal validity' of standards and the demands for 'universality'... less possible as criteria for truth than in genuine history [*eigentlichen Historie*]" (*Sein und Zeit*, 395). The reason for this is that there is no "factual" nature of mankind. Dasein's "factuality [*Tatsächlichkeit*] constitutes itself in its resolute projection of itself upon a chosen potentiality for being [*gewähltes Seinskönnen*]" (394). We are, factually, what we choose to be. This, however, depends on the future we envisage for ourselves. The same holds for what we learn from history. In Heidegger's words, "even historical disclosure temporalizes itself in terms of the future. The '*selection*' of what should be a possible object for history *has already been made* in the factual existential *choice* of Dasein's historicity. History first arises and uniquely *exists* in this choice" (395). The point is that our interests in history are determined by our present concerns. In an era that strives for gender equality, for example, the selection of possible objects for historical study will include those individuals who strove for such equality. Histories will appear of the "women's movement." In Heidegger's terms, the "remains, monuments and records" of this movement will have a "*world-historical* character." This, however, depends upon their "interpretation," which is, itself, determined by "the historicity of the historian's existence" (394). In other words, it depends upon the historian's epoch, on its common interests and projects.

In Sartre's terms, the rationality of an age is that of the "hodological space" it inhabits. This space is structured by the practical necessities of the projects it engages in. Such necessities exhibit a determinate order, one that links actions to consequences. Just as an overall project involves a number of subsidiary projects each of which may, in turn, require further projects for its realization, so too we find a corresponding hierarchy of means in achieving our goals. Thus, if I live in a suburb, to get to the store, I must drive. To drive, I require a car, but to use it, I must take my keys. I must also be careful to fill the car's tank with gasoline so that it won't run out. This, however, requires cash and a stop at the gas station. If I am out of cash, I must first stop at a cash machine and use my bank card. This use, however, first requires that I have applied for one. As is obvious, were I so minded, I could continue this description until I sketched out the instrumental complexes by which I make my way in my world. The order of these complexes is, in fact, "the practical organization of existents into a *world*." Within it, "each instrument refers to other instruments, to those which are its *keys* and to those for which it is the *key*" (424). The "paths" connecting these determine the "hodological space" (from the Greek *hodos* for 'path') that characterizes this world.

The rationality of this space is given by this order of instrumental complexes. A rational person makes use of it to accomplish his purposes. A rational person, for example, would not attempt to drive a car without its key or get money from a cash machine without a bank card. Such rationality, however, is contingent. It depends on our epoch and on the instrumental complexes that we happen to inherit. The hodological spaces, say, of Paris and a remote Andean village are as much features of our contingency as the facts of our birth, race or physical condition. Both Paris and the village exhibit a rationality, a set of paths connecting their respective sets of instruments. That this rationality is contingent, that it takes its origin from contingently given circumstances, does not lessen its necessity for those who live within it. It does, however, localize it. In so doing, it points to the fact that the world only exhibits the pragmatic rationality that men and women put into it. Since this depends on their choices, this rationality need not continue. It can, as was the case in the French Revolution, collapse and be replaced with a new set of practical necessities and corresponding rationality. This contingency comes from the freedom of the selves who construct a given world. Ultimately, for Sartre, it arises from their inability to coincide with themselves, to be determined or fixed as a thing is. As such, this contingency is a consequence of the nothingness that, for both Sartre and Heidegger, is at the core of our selfhood.

The Performative Contradiction

The performative contradiction inherent in this account of reason appears when we apply its conclusions to the account that presents them. If reason is, per se, contingent, then so is the argumentation that the account uses to justify itself. This contingency can be expressed in terms of Heidegger's equivalence of understanding and projection. If the two are the same, then we never initially grasp anything as it is in itself apart from the uses to which we can put it. Such uses presuppose a general understanding of how to make our way in the world, a grasp, in Sartre's terms, of the "hodological space" that we find ourselves in. Given this, all interpretation of things involves presuppositions. In Heidegger's words, "An interpretation is never a presuppositionless apprehending of something presented to us" (*Sein und Zeit*, 150). It articulates a tacit understanding—a way of being in and using the world—that is given in advance. If this understanding is contingent, then so is the interpretation that is based on it.

As Heidegger's remarks on history make clear, this contingency affects our "historical interpretation" of the world. Such interpretation can never be without presuppositions. It is always circular and, thus, can never "be as independent of the standpoint of the observer as our [scientific] knowledge of nature is supposed to be." The point follows since understanding expresses the possibilities that we project forward in our engagement with the world. Such possibilities, however, are rooted in both our personal histories as situated, finite beings and in the transpersonal history that defines our common historical situation. Both change over time. The possibilities of our childhood are distinct from those that we now possess as adults. Similarly, the possibilities available to the ancient Greeks were distinct from our own. In each case they express different pragmatic engagements with the world. The contingency of the engagements is, thus, the contingency of the historical interpretation of the world.[24]

The application of this to Heidegger's own endeavor comes when he considers the implications of this conclusion. He asks: if all interpretation presupposes a pre-given understanding, "how is it to bring any scientific results to maturity without moving in a circle?" The circle consists of the results of interpretation presupposing the understanding that interpretation makes explicit. Heidegger's response to this is not to deny such circularity but, rather, to affirm the circular nature of human understanding. To see the circle as vicious, he claims, is to misunderstand the act of understanding—its basis in projection (152). The interpretations that follow from Dasein's understanding express his projecting himself forward in terms of the possibilities he has to use things. In Heidegger's words, "the fore-structure of understanding and the as-structure of interpretation show an existential-ontological connection with the phenomenon of projection." This points back "to a primordial state of Dasein's Being" (151). Given this, we have to affirm that "[t]he 'circle' in understanding belongs to the structure of meaning, and the latter phenomenon is rooted in the existential constitution of Dasein, that is, in the understanding that interprets. An entity for which, as Being-in-the-world, its Being is itself an issue, has, ontologically, a circular structure" (153).

If this, however, is the case, then what about Heidegger's own attempt to understand being? Does not his attempt to derive the sense of being by interpreting Dasein also involve circularity? In his words, "Does it not then become altogether patent in the end that this problem of fundamental ontology, which we have broached, is one which moves in a 'circle'?" The reply is the same as that given earlier: human understanding is, as such, circular. In Heidegger's words, "We have indeed already shown, in analyzing the structure of understanding in general, that what gets censured inappropriately as a 'circle' belongs to the essence and to the distinctive character of understanding as such." What is presupposed is not "some proposition from which we deduce further propositions." It is, rather, something that has "the character of an understanding projection" (314). As such, it is rooted in the nature of Dasein's understanding. Thus, "[w]e can never 'avoid' a 'circular' proof in the existential analytic" (363). We cannot, because "Dasein is already ahead of itself. As being, it has in every case already projected itself upon definite possibilities of its existence; and in such existential projections it has, in a pre-ontological manner, also projected something like existence and Being." Thus the inquiry into the question of Being, as a research carried out by Dasein, "is itself a kind of Being that disclosive Dasein possesses." Given this, "can such research be denied this projecting which is essential to Dasein?" For Heidegger, it cannot. The objection of moving in a circle thus "fails to recognize that entities can be experienced 'factually' only when Being is already understood, even if it has not been conceptualized." In other words, it "misunderstands understanding" because it fails to grasp Dasein's "circular being" (363).

Given this response, we have to say that ontological research is in the same position as historical research. It bears within itself an implicit, if unacknowledged performative contradiction. The fact that "all entities can be experienced 'factually' only when Being is already understood," when applied to the factual experience of Dasein, undercuts the conclusions that Heidegger draws. The contingency of this tacit, not yet conceptualized understanding, affects these conclusions. To put this in terms of the priority of the epistemological standpoint, it can be said that Heidegger violates this priority when he makes the knowing relation dependent and, hence, contingent on a historically determined pragmatic engagement with the world. Reason, in Heidegger's view, does not set this engagement. It is rather set by it.

The situation does not essentially change when Heidegger in the 1930s sees each historical age as determined by a given standard for what counts as real and a corresponding method for disclosing reality—our present standard being that of power, be it material, economic, or

HUSSERL AND OTHER PHENOMENOLOGISTS

any other variety, and the method of disclosure being that of the corresponding technology that allows us to access such power. For Heidegger, each such standard is an appearing of Being. Insisting on this standard, we interpret Being in terms of the beings that we disclose by following this standard. The very distinction of Being from such beings is, however, forgotten in our insistence.[25] The same distinction, however, places the determining factor outside of the knowing that it promotes. Again we have the determination of reason by something external to it.

Transcendence and Presence

A Heideggerian might well respond to the above by asserting that the existential analytic involves nothing less than the transformation of philosophy. Our inability to avoid the circle indicates an inability to remain within the boundaries that traditionally distinguished philosophical argumentation—namely, those set by premises and conclusions linked by syllogistic reasoning. What remains is a kind of *Denken*, a thinking that, aware of its own interpretative presuppositions, embraces its circular structure, investigating its presuppositions ever more deeply. A follower of Sartre might add that Husserl avoids the performative contradiction by misunderstanding the nature of the subject. In taking being as presence, he undermines the non-presence that is essential to transcendence. More particularly, by ignoring the nothingness at the core of the self, Husserl reduces Dasein to an "In-itself," a mere thing. To answer this objection is to show how Husserl can account for transcendence in terms of constitution. How can constitution, with its focus on presence, incorporate the self-separation that Heidegger and Sartre see as essential for our selfhood?

The answer to this question has, in general terms, already been given. Since what is constituted is ontologically distinct from the elements that enter the constitutive synthesis, transcendence is inherent in constitution. Thus, the appearing object is not its appearances. It transcends these as their common referent, that is, as the one thing that the many appearances are appearances "of." Transcendence, here, is a function of presence. The synthetic entity (the one-in-many) that is present through the synthesized elements transcends their presence. For Husserl, the same schema applies to the separation of the self from itself. To see this, we have to turn to the lowest level of constitution—that of our sense of time.

This constitution begins with presence—the presence of the "primordial impression." The presence of an impression is its immediate appearing. There is no constitution at work here; rather, the impression is the "source-point" for constitution. In Husserl's words, "The 'source-point' with which the 'production' of the enduring object begins is a primal impression."[26] This means, he adds in an appendix, "Consciousness is nothing without impression." It does not generate impressions: the impressions are "the 'new,' that which has come into being as alien to consciousness, that which has been received, as opposed to what has been produced through consciousness's own spontaneity" (100–106; translation modified). What consciousness does with such impressions is attempt to hold fast to them. The necessity here is that, without this activity, our consciousness would not extend beyond the present moment. We would never be able to gather together the perceptions required to make a spatial-temporal object present. We would also never be able to grasp a melody, which we do by attending to the relations of the tones. The fact that we can do this means that, as the new tones sound, within a certain margin of diminishing clarity, the previous tones continue to be present. These already sounded tones are not present the way the sounding ones are;

41

HUSSERL AND OTHER PHENOMENOLOGISTS

if they were, we would hear a clanging discord. As Husserl observes, the tones undergo continuous modification; they "die away"; they get fainter and fainter. There is here a certain analogy with an object receding and contracting as it spatially departs from us. In a similar manner, as Husserl writes: "In receding into the past, the temporal object contracts and in the process also becomes obscure" (26–28). Ultimately, it disappears altogether. The same holds for the tones that we attempt to retain. What we experience are a series of fadings that become fainter and fainter. Now, for Husserl, a "retention" is this experience. A retention is a consciousness of the dying away, the sinking down of what we impressionally experience (31–33). This experience is one of continuous modification of what we retain, that is, of its dying or fading away.

This kind of experience does not itself give us a sense of departure into pastness. We need to learn to interpret this fading presence as temporal departure. With this, the retentional fadings come to "carry primary interpretations that, in their flowing connectedness, constitute the temporal unity of the immanent content in its receding into the past." Thus, just as we interpret a spatial object's getting smaller and contracting together as its spatial departure, so too we interpret a primary content's fading as its temporal departure from the now that we occupy. Attached to each retention there is, then, "a primal interpretation" (92). The series of such interpretations gives us the ongoing interpretation of the fading (but still retained) content as sinking into the past—as departing further and further from our now. Crucial to this account is the assertion that we actually perceive the pastness of the past in our "primary memory" of such fading.[27] Such perception is synthetic. It is the result of a constitutive process with its elements to be synthesized and the corresponding interpretation that assigns them a referent. The individual elements are the fadings, which Husserl calls the "adumbrations" or "shadings off" of what we posit through them, namely, the given temporal position. The interpretation takes these fadings as depicting its departure into the past.[28]

This perception of the past involves the same ontological transcendence that perception in general exhibits. The departing temporal moment transcends the elements from which it is constituted. It is a one-in-many that has different ontological status from its multiple adumbrations. Temporally, the transcendence is that of the past in its departure from the now that the self inhabits. Given this, in constituting the departing moments of time, "I exist," Husserl writes, "in the streaming creation of transcendence, of self-transcendence, of [self-transcendent] being as self-pastness."[29] The "mode of being" in which I exist is, he adds, that "of a multiple, continuous transcendence of my primal-modal being as now."[30] All this affects my self-perception. Because synthesis takes time—the time to gather and interpret the content-filled moments that are being synthesized—my synthetic self-perception apprehends me not as I am, but as I was. The living, functioning ego is now. As such, it has moved on in the time it took me to engage in such synthesis. Thus, what I apprehend "is always myself, not as the primordium that I am, but rather the primordium that I was."[31]

With this, we have Husserl's version of the "immediate deterioration of coincidence" that Sartre speaks about. This deterioration is not the result of some inner nothingness. The self-separation that it brings about is an effect of the constitutive process. We can stand back from ourselves because the self that we judge is *not* the living self that acts in the now—the self that can say "I act now and only now, and I 'continuously' act."[32] It is, rather, the self that *has* acted, the self whose past action we can praise or condemn. We also have Husserl's version of the anonymity of Dasein. This anonymity does not signify its nothingness. It rather points to the distinction between the constituting and the constituted. Given that

42

HUSSERL AND OTHER PHENOMENOLOGISTS

I cannot apprehend myself in my functioning nowness, the self that I presently am must remain anonymous. As Husserl puts this, the self "that is the counterpart (*gegenüber*) to everything is anonymous. It is not its own counterpart as the house is my counterpart. And yet I can turn my attention to myself. But then this counterpart in which the ego comes forward along with everything that was its counterpart is again split. The ego which comes forward as a counterpart and its counterpart [e.g., the house it was perceiving] are both counterparts to me. Forthwith, I—the subject of this new counterpart—am anonymous."[33] This anonymity springs from the constitutive process. Given that the constituted is distinct from the constituting, the self that is at the origin of all constitution is distinct from all that appears in the constituted world. As such, it cannot be represented in its terms. Like Dasein, it is ontologically distinct from the things it makes present. This distinction, however, is one of presence. The constituting self has, at its core, the presence of sheer nowness.

To complete this account of Husserl's "metaphysics of presence," one further comparison must be made. For Heidegger and Sartre, our freedom is a result of our self-alterity. At its basis is the nothingness at our core. For Husserl, as well, our freedom can be traced to the alterity that allows us to transcend ourselves. This alterity, however, is a result of the constitutive process. As such, it *includes the rationality* that, for Husserl, is essential to this process. Thus, by virtue of this alterity, we can distance ourselves from ourselves. We can address ourselves in a moment of conscience and say, "You should not have done that. It was wrong to take that line of conduct." This freedom, however, does not undermine the rationality that is inherent in the constitutive process. We are free insofar as we can step back from constituted presence, but such freedom does not include the possibility of our overturning the rules through which such presence is generated. Reason, for Husserl, is not primarily pragmatic. It does not, in the first instance, refer to the order of a "hodological space" that can be overturned by changing our choices. For Husserl, although we can choose not to constitute or bring to presence a particular object or state of affairs, we cannot choose to alter the rules through which such presence comes about. To take an example, the *categorial objects* that are made present through constitutive processes of categorial intuition *cannot be made objects of sensuous perception*. To attempt to do so, Husserl writes, is like trying to paint elliptical functions or play them on the fiddle. Not even "divine omnipotence can manage this."[34] The same holds for trying to make a three-dimensional object present without recourse to the perspectival views through which it appears. Freedom for Husserl is, thus, not absolute. Rather than being the abyss—the *Ab-grund*—of Dasein, it is limited by the constitutive process that generates the self-separation that makes it possible.

For Husserl, this signifies that we are free to step back from the world. We are also free to suspend our positing of its objects as we do when we perform the phenomenological epoché. But we are bound if we wish to posit a stable presence. The point is that freedom is not outside of rationality, but rather part of presence. As rational, it accords with the priority of the epistemological standpoint. Such a view, of course, does not mean that destructive actions are not open to us. There is nothing in Husserl's account of rationality that would, for example, prevent Heidegger from making his infamous *Rektoratsrede* of 1933. There is also nothing that would prevent Husserl from writing his last work, the *Krisis*, a few years later. The distinction concerns the responsibility for these actions. The appeal to presence is, for Husserl, the appeal to evidence. Responsibility is responsibility to evidence in making one's claims. It is, in fact, a holding of one's freedom to account. For Husserl, as for Kant, this self-limitation of freedom is essential to morality.

HUSSERL AND OTHER PHENOMENOLOGISTS

Acknowledgements

This article was supported by the Ministry of Education, Youth and Sports of Czech Republic, Institutional Support for Long-term Development of Research Organizations, Charles University, Faculty of Humanities. It is an output of the program PRVOUK P18 Phenomenology and Semiotics.

Notes

1. Jacques Derrida, "Ousia and Grammé: Note on a Note from *Being and Time*," in *Margins of Philosophy*, trans. Alan Bass (New York: Harvester Wheatsheaf, 1982), 34.
2. Martin Heidegger, *Sein und Zeit* (Tübingen: Max Niemeyer, 1967), 25. I generally follow the translation of *Being and Time*, trans. John Macquarrie and Edward Robinson (New York: Harper & Row, 1962). Since this work gives the page numbers of *Sein und Zeit*, I cite the original pagination, which is hereafter cited in the text.
3. Jacques Derrida, "Différance," in *Margins of Philosophy*, 16.
4. Jacques Derrida, "Speech and Phenomena," in *Speech and Phenomena and Other Essays on Husserl's Theory of Signs*, trans. David Allison (Evanston, IL: Northwestern University Press, 1973), 63.
5. Derrida, "Speech and Phenomena," 63. Derrida identifies presence and evidence in the following words: "this privilege of the present-now defines the very element of philosophical thought, it is *evidence* itself, conscious thought itself" (62). Thus to contest presence is to move beyond philosophical thought.
6. Edmund Husserl, *Logische Untersuchungen*, ed. Ursula Panzer, in *Edmund Husserl, Gesammelte Schriften* (Hamburg: Felix Meiner Verlag, 1992), 2.120. All translations from the German edition of *Logische Untersuchungen* (*Logical Investigations*) are my own.
7. Husserl, *Logische Untersuchungen*, 2.151–52, fn.
8. The difficulty here is the same as that presented by Frederic Fitch with regard to the claim of universal scepticism. As he notes, the sceptical view according to which "nothing is absolutely true" is actually a "theory about all theories." It thus casts doubt upon itself. Its theoretical thesis is that no proposition can be asserted as true for certain. Allowing for self-reference with respect to this assertion, it becomes inconsistent. On the one hand, it casts doubt on its own validity. On the other hand, if it is really valid, then it wrongly casts doubt on its own validity in casting doubt on the validity of *all* statements. In Fitch's words, "if it is valid, it is self-referentially inconsistent and hence not valid at all." We can also say that, as a universal statement, it is invalid since it must except itself from its own claims to universality. See Frederic B. Fitch, "Self-Reference in Philosophy," in *Contemporary Readings in Logical Theory*, ed. Irving M. Copi and James A. Gould (New York: Macmillan, 1967), 156–57.
9. Husserl, *Logische Untersuchungen*, 2.226.
10. Husserl, *Logische Untersuchungen*, 4.762.
11. See Husserl, *Logische Untersuchungen*, 4.605–6, 717.
12. Husserl, *Logische Untersuchungen*, 4.623.
13. Husserl's preferred term is "constitution," though he does use "synthesis." Both terms are taken as equivalent to Kant's concept. In Husserl's words: "What is called constitution, this is what Kant obviously had in mind under the rubric, 'connection as an operation of the understanding,' synthesis" (Ms. B IV 12, 2–3, 1920). I wish to thank Professor Rudolf Bernet for permission to cite from Husserl's unpublished manuscripts.
14. Edmund Husserl, *Ideen zu einer reinen Phänomenologie und phänomenologischen Philosophie, Erstes Buch*, ed. R. Schuhmann (The Hague: Martinus Nijhoff, 1976), 88. All translations from the German edition are my own.
15. Jean-Paul Sartre, *Being and Nothingness*, trans. Hazel Barnes (New York: Washington Square Press, 1966), 23; hereafter cited in the text.
16. Husserl, *Logical Investigations*, 2.120.
17. Friedrich Nietzsche, *The Will to Power*, trans. Walter Kaufmann and R. J. Hollingdale (New York: Vintage, 1968), §493, 272; §473, 263; §480, 266–67.

HUSSERL AND OTHER PHENOMENOLOGISTS

18. Husserl, *Ideen zu einer reinen Phänomenologie*, 349.

19. Husserl, *Ideen zu einer reinen Phänomenologie*, 380.

20. Husserl, *Ideen zu einer reinen Phänomenologie*, 118.

21. Husserl, *Ideen zu einer reinen Phänomenologie*, 356.

22. This letter appears in the textual critical notes to Husserl's *Phänomenologische Psychologie*, ed. W. Biemel (The Hague: Martinus Nijhoff, 1962), 601.

23. Martin Heidegger, "Vom Wesen des Grundes," in *Wegmarken* (Frankfurt am Main: Vittorio Klostermann, 1967), 69.

24. Does this mean that historical knowledge is less rigorous than that of the exact sciences of nature? According to Heidegger, for a science to make this claim is a sign that it misunderstands its own understanding, i.e., the historical presuppositions that the understanding involves. As I cited him, "interpretation is never a presuppositionless apprehending of something presented to us." The difference is that "the ontological presuppositions of historical knowledge transcend in principle the idea of rigor held in the most exact sciences." They do so insofar as the "existential foundations relevant for it" are broader (*Sein und Zeit*, 153). Those of mathematics, for example, "lie within a narrower range" than history. Now, for Heidegger, historical research can never be completed. The interpretations that it advances are not independent of the standpoint of the researcher, and this standpoint changes with the advance of history. By implication, the same holds for science.

25. See Martin Heidegger, "Vom Wesen der Wahrheit," in *Wegmarken* (Frankfurt am Main: Vittorio Klostermann, 1967), 91–94.

26. Edmund Husserl, *Zur Phänomenologie des inneren Zeitbewusstseins*, ed. Rudolf Boehm (The Hague: Martinus Nijhoff, 1966), 29; English translation, *The Phenomenology of the Consciousness of Internal Time (1893–1917)*, trans. John Barnett Brough, vol. 4 of Edmund Husserl, *Collected Works*, ed. Rudolf Bernet (Dordrecht: Kluwer Academic Publishers, 1991), 30. Unless otherwise indicated, I follow Brough's translation; hereafter page numbers refer to the original and to the English translation, respectively, and are cited in the text.

27. As Husserl puts this: "But if we call perception the *act in which all 'origin'* lies, the act that *constitutes originally*, then *primary memory is perception*. For only in primary memory do we *see* what is past, only in it does the past become constituted—and constituted presentatively, not re-presentatively. The just past, the before in opposition to the now, can be directly seen only in primary memory; it is its essence to bring this new and original past to primary, direct intuition, just as it is the essence of the perception of the now to bring the now directly to intuition" (*Zur Phänomenologie des inneren Zeitbewusstseins*, 41–43).

28. As Husserl writes, the sense of such departure "springs from the interpretation of the temporal representatives of the temporal positions" [*Zeitstellenrepräsentanten*], such representatives being the fadings. "This interpretation too is continuously maintained in the flow of modification" in that we continuously interpret the process of fading as departure into pastness (*Zur Phänomenologie des inneren Zeitbewusstseins*, 66–69, translation modified). Thus, in taking the tone "as identical in the flow of the modification of the past," "the interpretation that belongs essentially to this modification... lets the continuous process of being pushed back into the past appear." We experience the tone that has sounded as both "held fast in its matter" and as receding into the past (66–67, 69, translation modified). Calling such modifications "adumbrations," he writes in an appendix, "The elapsed now... presents itself in the new actually present now in a certain *adumbration*; and each such adumbration represents [*vertritt*], so to speak, what has been in the actual now" (275–76, 285–86, translation modified). Thus the "elapsed duration" of the tone is "represented [*repräsentiert*] by means of a continuity of fading modifications." Such modifications are "the flow of adumbrations in which the identical tone 'presents' itself [*sich 'darstellt'*]" (277–87).

29. "Ich bin im strömenden Schaffen von Transzendenz, von Selbsttranszendenz, von Sein als Selbstvergangenheit und Selbstzukunft." Ms. C7, 21a, 9 July 1932, in *Späte Texte über*

HUSSERL AND OTHER PHENOMENOLOGISTS

Zeitkonstitution (1929–1934), Die C-Manuskripte, ed. Dieter Lohmar (Dordrecht: Springer Verlag, 2006), 130.

30. Husserl, "Ich bin—ich bin im Währen, der ich bin, und bin als das immer schon in dieser Seinsart einer vielfältigen kontinuierlichen Transzendenz meines urmodalen Seins als Jetzt." Ms. C7, 21a, 9 July 1932, in *Späte Texte*, 130.

31. Husserl, Ms. C7, 21a-b, 9 July 1932, in *Späte Texte*, 130.

32. Husserl, Ms. BIII 9, 15a, Oct.-Dec. 1931. As he also describes my being as functioning nowness, my act flows away, "but I, the identity of my act, am 'now' and only 'now' and, in my being as an accomplisher [*Vollzieher*], am still now the accomplisher." Here, "I, the presently actual ego, am the now-ego" [*jetziges Ich*]." Ms. C10, 16b, Sept. 1931, in *Späte Texte*, 200.

33. Husserl, Ms. C2, 2b-3a, Aug. 1931, in *Späte Texte*, 2.

34. Husserl, *Ideen zu einer reinen Phänomenologie*, 129.

Intentionality, Consciousness, and the Ego: The Influence of Husserl's *Logical Investigations* on Sartre's Early Work

Lior Levy

Department of Philosophy, University of Haifa, Haifa, Israel

ABSTRACT

Jean-Paul Sartre's early phenomenological texts reveal the complexity of his relationship to Edmund Husserl. Deeply indebted to phenomenology's method as well as its substance, Sartre nonetheless confronted Husserl's transcendental turn from *Ideas* onward. Although numerous studies have focused on Sartre's points of contention with Husserl, drawing attention to his departure from Husserlian phenomenology, scholars have rarely examined the way in which Sartre engaged and responded to the early Husserl, particularly to his discussions of intentionality, consciousness, and self in *Logical Investigations*. This essay focuses on Sartre's critical response to *Logical Investigations*, arguing that Husserl's understanding of these three notions shapes and informs Sartre's own approach to them in *The Transcendence of the Ego* (1936–37), "Intentionality: A Fundamental Idea of Husserl's Phenomenology" (1939), and *Being and Nothingness* (1943). By carefully reading Sartre side by side with Husserl, this essay articulates the ways in which Sartre allowed himself to think along with, and not against, Husserl.

Introduction

Jean-Paul Sartre refers to the influence Edmund Husserl's phenomenology exerted on the development of his thinking on numerous occasions. In his philosophical texts, he often comments on Husserl's position regarding diverse topics such as emotions, time-consciousness, imagination, and one's relations to others. At times, Sartre builds on Husserl's accounts to support his own philosophical arguments; on other occasions, he articulates his own position in direct opposition to him. In his diaries and in numerous interviews and conversations now in print, Sartre reflects on his relationship to Husserl's work and recounts his first encounters with it.

Despite the wealth of these sources, few studies examine the concrete ways in which Husserl influences Sartre's work.[1] Recently, Beata Stawarska provided a much-needed account of Sartre's introduction to Husserl's phenomenology and a detailed and illuminating analysis of his relationship with it. Stawarska studies Sartre's early existential texts, where he enters into a conversation with Husserl's philosophical positions. Through an examination of Sartre's notion of intentionality, his applications of the phenomenological method, his critique of the transcendental ego, his philosophical investigation of human imagination, and his approach to human emotions, she outlines Sartre's ambivalence toward Husserlian phenomenology, suggesting that he is faithful to "the perceived spirit of phenomenology, but not to its word."[2] Indeed, though Sartre himself admits the effect Husserl's phenomenology had on him, saying on one occasion that "Husserl had gripped me... I was 'Husserlian' and long to remain so,"[3] he continuously tries to disentangle himself from Husserl's grasp. To mention only two well-known examples, in *The Transcendence of the Ego* Sartre criticizes Husserl's conception of the transcendental ego as incompatible with his (Husserl's) definition of consciousness, and thus his own interpretation of the ego as an object is held against Husserl's position. In *Being and Nothingness* he criticizes Husserl's account phenomenological experience of the other as incapable of escaping solipsism, despite the "undeniable advantages" of his theory. There, Sartre again opposes his own existential understanding of the self-other relationship to Husserl's epistemological view.[4]

Stawarska suggests that Sartre's paradoxical stance toward Husserl extends beyond methodological and doctrinal disagreements and is rooted in a crucial disagreement over fundamental philosophical commitments. As she puts it, the tension "touches on the problem, what are we, philosophers, to do?"[5] It is clear that the two differ on philosophy's ultimate task: Whereas Husserl thinks of phenomenology as "making possible a strictly scientific philosophy,"[6] Sartre conceives of it as "a philosophical foundation for an ethics and a politics."[7] For Husserl phenomenology is first and foremost a detached science, concerned with epistemic issues like clarity, evidence and truth: "Here we have a field of *attainable* discoveries, fundamentally involved in the possibility of a *scientific* philosophy. Such discoveries have indeed nothing dazzling about them: they lack any obviously useful relation to practice or the fulfillment of higher emotional needs" (1.172). According to Sartre, phenomenology's task is to investigate questions of existence, not of knowledge. Accordingly, *Being and Nothingness* is "An Essay on Phenomenological Ontology" in which Sartre does not apply the epoché. In exploring this crucial difference in their philosophical orientation, Stawarska limits her discussion to Sartre's response to Husserl's *Ideen* (1913). Consequently, she centers on the ways in which he labors to modify Husserlian phenomenology and redeem it from its transcendental overtones.[8] As she puts it:

> Sartre employs the phenomenological method adopted from Husserl to suspend the validity of the claims and concepts posited by Husserl; his loyalty is in the approach and not in the doctrine, and his goal is to purify the phenomenological field established by Husserl by clearing it of any mental furniture adopted from the philosophical tradition. ... The promise of phenomenology is revolutionary, the fruit overly saturated with the usual juices of academic thinking; Sartre's goal is then to liberate Husserl from himself.[9]

However, alongside philosophical passages and personal statements that lend support to this reading, Sartre provides grounds for construing a different account of his relationship to Husserl's work. While reflecting on his relationship to Heidegger's philosophy, he admits his attraction to Husserl's scientific spirit and attempts to think through traditional philosophical problems:

> [T]he essential thing was certainly the revulsion I felt against assimilating that barbarous and so unscientific philosophy, after Husserl's brilliant, *scholarly* synthesis. With Heidegger, it seemed as though philosophy has relapsed into infancy. I no longer recognized the traditional

problems in it—consciousness, knowledge, truth and error, perception, the body, realism and idealism, etc.[10]

Here, the exposition of traditional problems—touching directly on questions of knowledge and self-knowledge—are singled out to explain Husserl's strong appeal. Sartre also clearly indicates his admiration for the "academic" tone of Husserl's philosophy, as well as for his clarity and precision.

Although this and other autobiographical remarks cannot be the sole foundation for a reappraisal of Sartre's relationship to Husserl's work, and although they do not alter the fact that he manifests at times his discomfort with Husserl's philosophical positions, they may nevertheless enable us to envision a different narrative of Sartre's relationship to Husserl. In this alternative narrative Sartre is not "a parasitic reader of Husserl, who is leaching the available intellectual resources to the very bone and acknowledging the master's authority by repeatedly testing the validity of his claims."[11] Instead, he acknowledges the master's authority by allowing himself to think along with, and not against him.

In what follows, I will present an alternative, positive account of Husserl's influence on Sartre's philosophical development, by exploring their deep philosophical affinities. To this end, I will focus on the role Husserl's *Logical Investigations* (1900/1901; 1913/1921) played in shaping Sartre's approach to basic philosophical problems such as the nature of intentionality, consciousness, and the self. I will concentrate on two texts: *The Transcendence of the Ego* (published in 1936–37), and "Intentionality: A Fundamental Notion in Husserl's Phenomenology" (published in 1939, but written around the same time as the earlier work).

My alternative narrative is meant to supplement rather than supplant Stawarska's account of Sartre's relationship to Husserl's thought. She is right, of course, to point to Sartre's criticisms of Husserl's transcendental phenomenology in *Ideas* and *Cartesian Meditations*, criticisms that appear in the very same texts in which I locate the positive influence of Husserl's *Logical Investigations*. The point is that in as much as Sartre criticizes the late Husserl, he does it out of a position of allegiance to the early one. In this respect, I agree with her claim that "Sartre's goal is... to liberate Husserl from himself."[12] I want to emphasize that in liberating Husserl from himself, Sartre deems the liberated Husserl, the one who can return to his earlier self, as a crucial point of reference for his own philosophical project.

Intentionality: Theoretical and Methodological Considerations

Husserl refers to *Logical Investigations* as his "breakthrough-work" that inaugurates his phenomenological project (1.43), by abandoning his earlier attempt to provide a "psychological foundation" for logic and mathematics.[13] In the *Philosophy of Arithmetic* (1891), where such a foundation was to be laid, Husserl argued that the act of grasping the meaning of logical or arithmetical truths is tantamount to having a psychological state. This was a form of psychologism whereby the clarification of concepts consisted in determining their psychological origin.[14] Yet, as Husserl describes it in the "Foreword" to the first edition of *Logical Investigations*, this position left "doubts of principle, as to how to reconcile the objectivity of mathematics, and of all science in general, with a psychological foundation for logic."[15] In other words, as long as the meanings that are grasped (e.g., logical or numerical concepts) are identified with psychological states, they remain subjective and lose their claim to objectivity. Nonetheless, if objectivity is to be maintained, Husserl argues, we are faced with the question of "[H]ow... to understand the fact that the intrinsic being of objectivity becomes 'presented,' 'apprehended' in knowledge, and so ends up by becoming subjective? What does it mean to say that the object has 'being-in-itself,' and is 'given' in knowledge?" (2.169). In other words, the question we face is what renders knowledge possible. How can we aim at something that possesses independent being without reducing it to a mental process?

Husserl's principle of intentionality provides an answer to this question. With it, he is able to distinguish between the thought processes or acts by which consciousness *intends* something and the objects that these processes or acts are about, which are *intended* by them. To develop a proper understanding of how it is possible to think of objectivity, Husserl insists that we need to rid ourselves of the Cartesian framework, according to which the mind is a substance that can only come into contact with its own ideas or mental contents. Instead, he continues, "we must go back to the 'things themselves'" (2.168).

The need to return to "the things themselves" is not a call to develop a metaphysics that deals with the being of the things in question. Rather, Husserl is concerned, first and foremost, with "*basic questions of epistemology*" (2.169). In other words, he is interested in studying the ways in which the things themselves are given to consciousness from a first-person perspective. His emphasis on the centrality of experience sheds light on his claim that a "theory of knowledge, properly described, is no theory" (2.178). Theoretical presuppositions about the nature of the mind determine what is available in experience. A Cartesian theory of mind, for example, limits the "things" that subjects can encounter and know to ideas or mental representations alone. If we want to establish a genuine theory of knowledge, we need to abandon theoretical considerations and return to seeing, thinking, judging, and knowing, and see what these very experiences yield, what is given in them, and what they refer to.

When we turn to experience, we are bound to discover that it is never purely subjective. Multiple experiences, actual and possible, are directed to objects and not to subjective contents contained in this or that mind. Objects as such can be seen differently by different subjects, or by the same subject at different moments in time. It is precisely the sameness and objectivity of "the things themselves" that render possible the multiplicity of experiences of them: "[T]he essence of meaning is... in its 'content', the single, self-identical intentional unity set over against the dispersed multiplicity of actual and possible experiences of speakers and thinkers" (2.228). Put differently, particular acts yield different points of views on one and the same thing. These acts, which are perspectival and singular, do not exhaust the object, which they are about. Objectivity, then, is irreducible to a particular point of view, yet it can only be given from a subjective point of view.[16]

Husserl's return to first-person experience and the givenness of things themselves in experience, is precisely what drew Sartre to his work. According to Sartre's own account, he was attracted to Husserlian phenomenology because of its ways of engaging with concrete experience: "That's why, when Aron said to me, 'Why, we can reason about this glass of beer ...'", says Sartre, "that knocked me out. I thought to myself: 'Now here at long last is a philosophy.'"[17] In "Intentionality: A Fundamental Idea of Husserl's Phenomenology," Sartre expresses his enthusiasm at Husserl's turn to the concrete, offering his reflections on the relationship between our experience of the world and the world itself. Sartre's account of intentionality in this essay is often understood as importing an ontological twist into Husserl's ontologically neutral principle.[18] If one focuses on Husserl's *Ideas*, where the epoché is exercised and the notion of *noema* (the object as intended qua intended) is introduced, it could indeed seem as though Sartre were imposing foreign ontological weight onto the notion of intentionality.

HUSSERL AND OTHER PHENOMENOLOGISTS

Yet, if our point of reference is Husserl's notion of intentionality in *Logical Investigations*, and if we keep in mind both the methodological considerations that motivate it and its conclusions, then we see that Sartre's reading is in fact attentive to Husserl's own view. For, as mentioned above, according to Husserl himself act-transcendent objects are necessary for the possibility of knowledge.

As is clear from Sartre's account in "Intentionality," the rejection of the Cartesian model of consciousness as a container for mental objects is a crucial step toward the construction of a viable philosophy. Sartre is disturbed by the prospects offered by traditional philosophy for thinkers wishing to understand the objectivity of the world: "The simplest and plainest among us vainly looked for something solid, something not just mental, but could encounter everywhere only a soft and very genteel mist: themselves." He bluntly calls this position, which makes the subject both the starting and end point of philosophizing, "illusion." Yet what is illusory about traditional philosophy is not simply its reduction of all knowledge to the subject, for, as Sartre says, illusion is "common to both realism and idealism."[19] Even realists, who think that the objects that we know are *not* mental entities, are caught in this illusion when they think that knowing entities is a psychological or mental state.[20] Thus illusion threatens realists and idealists alike, since it is rooted in a particular theory of mind and not in a certain ontological vision of the world. This theory of mind is none other than the Cartesian or representational theory that Husserl wants to dispel and that Sartre, in a more expressive manner, describes as a conception of consciousness as a "spidery mind," a "dark stomach," or "immanence."

Sartre thus identifies with the liberating force of Husserlian intentionality. First, as we saw, Husserl refuses to inherit a theory of knowledge that imposes certain structures or features on thinking. According to the Cartesian model, which in Sartre's account in "Intentionality," becomes a variant of "digestive philosophy," the mind can only know its mental contents, its own representations of the world. Husserl's insistence that experience itself shapes our theory liberates us from metaphysical presuppositions about consciousness. Consequently, as Sartre points out, "consciousness is purified." With this, we learn that in knowing, seeing, or thinking about X, consciousness does not know, see, or think about itself: "Husserl persistently affirmed that one cannot dissolve things in consciousness. You see this tree, to be sure. But you see it just where it is: at the side of the road, in the midst of the dust, alone and writhing in the heat, eight miles from the Mediterranean coast" (4–5).

With Husserl's introduction of the principle of intentionality in his *Logical Investigations*, we no longer know only mental states or "see" what appears before our mind's eye. We see and know things themselves. Again, Sartre builds here on what was already made explicit in *Logical Investigations*: "all thought and knowledge have as their aim *objects* or *states of affairs*, which they putatively 'hit' in the sense that the 'being-in-itself' of these objects and states is supposedly shown forth, and made an identifiable item, in a multitude of actual or possible meanings, or acts of thought" (1.169). And later in the Fifth Investigation he reiterates: "*the intentional object of a presentation is the same as its actual object, and on occasion as its external object, and… it is absurd to distinguish between them*" (2.595, original emphasis). On the basis of these and other remarks, Sartre insists that Husserl's notion of intentionality brings back to philosophy "something solid, something not just mental" (4). Intentionality, according to Sartre, forces us to take the world into our philosophical considerations. The particular worldly object on which Sartre focuses his philosophical attention is the ego. Despite the fact that his account of the objectivity of the ego draws

51

heavily on Husserl's own position in *Logical Investigations*, scant attention has been given to the similarity between their approaches to this issue. Before I turn to it, however, I examine how Husserl's understanding of the nature and structure of consciousness informs both Sartre's account of consciousness and his rejection of the notion of a transcendental ego.

Consciousness and the Ego

Sartre's early essay "Intentionality: A Fundamental Idea of Husserl's Phenomenology" ends with the claim that Husserl's call to return to "the things themselves" has freed us from being held captive by a belief in the interiority of mind or soul, which prevented us from exploring the world at large. With Husserl, Sartre says, "We are... delivered from the 'internal life': in vain would we seek the caresses and fondling of our intimate selves, like Amiel, or like a child who kisses his own shoulder—for everything is finally outside: everything, even ourselves. Outside, in the world, among others" (5). In *The Transcendence of the Ego*, published before this essay, but written around the same time, Sartre elaborates on the latter point. The aim of the book, he declares in its very first page, is "to show ... that the ego is neither formally nor materially *in* consciousness: it is outside, *in the world*. It is a being of the world, like the ego of another."[21] The book itself develops as a response to the question "is the *I* that we encounter in our consciousness made possible by the synthetic unity of our representations, or is it the *I* which in fact unites the representations to each other?"[22] As the question makes clear, Sartre admits that the *I*, ego, or self is part of our experience, but he asks whether it is a condition for, or an outcome of, conscious experience. His answer is that consciousness makes the *I* possible and not the other way around.

Sartre argues in *The Transcendence of the Ego* that the ego or *I* is neither a formal condition for the unity of consciousness nor a constituent part of consciousness (existing materially in it). This is a radical position. Intuitively, we think of different conscious states, the different perceptions, thoughts, and desires that we experience, as emanating from our*selves*. In this respect the ego, self, or *I* seems to be the source of consciousness (understood most generally as the totality of experiences), and conscious activity seems to be an aspect of the ego. This is a rather commonsensical position, which assumes that a unified and unchanging self underlies the infinite changes that one undergoes through life. This self makes the young girl identical to the mature woman. Indeed, it grounds her very identity, despite the fact that the two may have very little—psychologically and physically—in common. This self can be understood either materially as a definite set of character traits, personality, motivations and drives, or formally, as a transcendental structure that supports conscious acts, gathering their multiplicity into one conscious stream. By addressing both philosophical variants of the intuitive notion that an ego, self, or *I* governs conscious life and is the source and end of actions, emotions, and thoughts, Sartre attempts to refute the idea that consciousness *belongs* to one's self and the ego is prior to consciousness.

Sartre articulates his own position vis-à-vis Kant's theory of the transcendental ego and Husserl's adaptation of this theory in *Ideas*. According to Kant, the 'I' is a formal subject-term that unifies all synthetic-conscious acts. In the *Critique of Pure Reason* the transcendental subject is not a substantial self but a function or an ability to synthesize experience, and hence a condition for the possibility of experience.[23] Kant distinguishes the transcendental ego from the empirical ego, the latter being the person's physical body and personality, the former being a formal principle.[24] Furthermore, Kant seems at times

HUSSERL AND OTHER PHENOMENOLOGISTS

to identify the transcendental self with the noumenal self, which is never given in experience.[25] Responding to Kant, Husserl rejects the notion of a transcendental ego in *Logical Investigations*, to which we shall soon return. However, later in *Ideas*, he postulates an ego as the source of intentional activity, and thus as the subject of consciousness. In the later work, Husserl says that the pure ego "belongs essentially to every cogito."[26] While Kant distinguishes between a transcendental and an empirical subject, Husserl does not think that two different selves exist, nor does he take the transcendental ego to be an abstraction from the empirical ego. Rather, he thinks of the transcendental self and the empirical self as two aspects of the same concrete ego.[27] Perhaps this is the reason why Sartre finds Husserl's position so problematic: Husserl "personifies" the conscious field, so that in any given act there is not only an activity (seeing, hearing, tasting) and an object (birds, rock concerts, ice cream) but also an ego—a "me" who watches, reads or hears.

Sartre rejects this view and argues instead that experience is at first selfless, consisting of conscious events that simply occur, not to "me" or to my "self" but to a pre-personal conscious field. The ego is not prior temporally or transcendentally to consciousness. It is transcendent, external to consciousness, an object *for* consciousness like any other object in the world: chairs, dogs, and other people. To prove this point, he examines a series of moments devoid of an ego, such as being absorbed in reading, or running after or away from something. The choice of examples seems to beg the question. In order to prove that consciousness is egoless, Sartre turns to experiences that do not involve an ego. However, the examples of conscious activities that are not mediated by an ego are meant to show that the ego is not necessary for consciousness. For if the ego were necessary, it would have had to appear as an actual component of every experience. It is therefore sufficient to show that there are experiences devoid of an *I*, in order to demonstrate the actual independence of consciousness from an ego.

With the elimination of the transcendental ego, however, one needs to find a different explanation for the unity and individuality of consciousness. According to Sartre, a conscious center of gravity is possible without recourse to an ego, and the cause of conscious unity and individuality does not lie outside consciousness (or behind it, using the language of Kant or of Husserl in *Ideas*). Sartre attributes the unity and individuality of consciousness to two of its fundamental features—intentionality and temporality.

Consciousness, says Sartre, does not require "any such unifying and individualizing *I*. Indeed, consciousness is defined by intentionality."[28] Returning to Husserl's claim in *Logical Investigations* that consciousness is always consciousness *of* something—"the fact that all thought and knowledge have as their aim *objects* or *states of affairs*" (1.169)—Sartre finds that the unity of consciousness is grounded in the objects which consciousness intends. At this point, he explicitly builds on Husserl's understanding of the intentional relationship between acts and objects. Recall that, according to Husserl, objects are not immanent to consciousness. He clearly indicates that regardless of the question of the existence or non-existence of the intended objects, these objects are external and can never be understood as psychic contents.[29] As we saw in the previous section, he insists that the intentional object is irreducible to the intending act. Thus he says, for example, that in any perceptual act "the object is not actually given, it is not given wholly and entirely as that which it itself is" (2.712). The object is given to perception in profiles, or, as he puts it in *Ideas*, it is revealed "through mere adumbrations."[30] Particular acts give different, restricted views of one and the same object. The object is not exhausted by the acts (by the perceptual acts of seeing

HUSSERL AND OTHER PHENOMENOLOGISTS

it at T1, T2, and so forth). On the contrary, the acts become what they are—that is, *acts of perceiving X*—by virtue of their being directed to one and the same object. This is what Husserl means when he says that the unity of the acts is not caused by any further act, but by "the thing itself, as a perceived unity" (2.789).

Sartre develops this line of reasoning when he says that intentionality, through its relation to objects, unifies consciousness.[31] Since the objects of experience are the same, consciousness is able to notice the repetition of acts by which it intends them. To use Sartre's example, the unity of acts of addition "by which I have added, do add, and shall add two and two to make four," is the transcendent object "two and two make four."[32] Furthermore, the identity of objects contributes to the experience of temporal continuity. It enables consciousness to consider a current act as a variation or continuation of former ones. For example, "seeing the apple tree" at t^1 is considered the same kind of act as "seeing the apple tree" at t^n, precisely because it is a seeing of one and the same thing—the apple tree.

However, Sartre continues to note that something else is needed "if the continual flux of consciousness is to be capable of positing transcendent objects outside the flux."[33] The experience of objects as different or the same requires an awareness of their sameness or difference. In other words, to realize that something is "self-identical" or "the same" means to see it as the same *as it was*. One needs to remember past experiences and integrate them into present acts in order for conscious experience to emerge as a unified whole. Without the ability to retain prior perceptions and relate them to present ones, consciousness would not have been able to realize that the object perceived now *is the same* as the object perceived yesterday. So a minimal capacity for retention is required for consciousness to be unified.

In addition, consciousness must be able to retain not only the object phase (be conscious that what it perceives now is the same as what it perceived yesterday) but also the act phase (retain the past act by which *it* intended the object, so that it can judge now that *it* grasps the same object). Consciousness needs to be able to grasp *itself* as the same consciousness both now and yesterday. Unless it grasps itself as the same consciousness, it cannot issue judgments about the objects present to it. Consequently, the unity of objects that seemed at first to grant consciousness its unity depends, in fact, on a second kind of unity: the unity of consciousness as a self-aware whole.

The idea of a self-temporalizing consciousness is introduced in *Logical Investigations* with Husserl's short discussion of the "presentative form of *time* which is immanent in the stream of consciousness." About this form of time, immanent in consciousness, he says that "in each actual phase of the stream of consciousness the *whole* time-horizon of the stream is presented, and it thereby possesses a form overreaching all its contents, which remains the same continuously, though its content steadily alters" (2.545). In other words, each act appears in light of a horizon of that-which-has-just-appeared as well as of that-which-will-appear. And since through the integration into this pattern one stream of consciousness is created, we find that this structure of temporalization constitutes a unity within diversity. Despite the fact that the acts continuously change ("its content steadily alters"), consciousness remains the same ("possesses a form overreaching all its contents").

It is clear that Sartre's position regarding the individuality and unity of consciousness and the gratuitousness of all transcendental support is influenced by Husserl's own approach to consciousness in *Logical Investigations*. Sartre himself admits that his thinking on the matter is in complete unison with Husserl's. In answering the question whether "one [need] double it [consciousness] with a transcendental *I*" in the negative, he mentions that Husserl too has given this reply: "After having determined that the *me* is a synthetic and transcendent production of consciousness, he reverted... to the classic position of a transcendental *I*." Yet Sartre continues to ask in a somewhat disappointed voice: "Was this notion necessary"?[34] Sartre's presentation of the development in Husserl's thought on the question of the ego reveals his desire to bring Husserl back to his former line of thinking. He takes his own work as a revival of Husserl's original response to the crucial question of the necessity of the transcendental 'I', a question to which he responded in the negative, given his understanding of the ability of consciousness to unify and individualize itself. Yet despite the fact that he later retracts his position, Husserl does not omit his account of the egoless nature of consciousness from the subsequent editions of *Logical Investigations*. However, in a footnote he adds that "the opposition to the doctrine of a 'pure' ego, already expressed in this paragraph, is one that the author no longer approves of, as is plain from his *Ideas* cited above" (2.542, n. 1). And after having said in Section 8, in response to Paul Natorp's discussion of the pure ego, "I must frankly confess, however, that I am quite unable to find this ego, this primitive, necessary center or relations," he adds, in a note, "I have since managed to find it, i.e. have learnt not to be led astray from a pure grasp of the given through corrupt forms of ego metaphysics" (2.549). Whereas in the body of the work he maintains that consciousness is a unified whole, an identical "interconnected unity" (2.541), he nevertheless qualifies this claim later in the notes, arguing that the stream of consciousness depends on the existence of a pure ego.

In one of these footnotes (in section 6), Husserl explains what led him to modify his earlier position. The empirical ego, which he identified in the first edition of *Logical Investigations* with the stream of consciousness, is a transcendent thing that "falls" or is suspended with the phenomenological reduction. Yet the reduction does not eliminate the evidence of the *I am*. Even after the psychological or empirical ego has been bracketed, all conscious acts are experienced as emerging from a conscious center. And it is by virtue of emanating from this center and referring back to it that they are part of one conscious stream, a stream that is *mine*. As he puts it in *Ideas*, "[e]very 'cogito', every act in a specially marked sense, is characterized as an act of the Ego, 'proceeding from the ego', 'actually living' in it."[35] With this, consciousness becomes egological; it possesses an ego as a center of gravity of any possible intentional act. Itself not appearing as an object of these acts, the transcendental ego is nonetheless living each of these acts. In Husserl's own words:

> In every actual *cogito* it [i.e. the pure ego] lives out its life in a special sense, but all experiences also with the mental background belong to it and it to them, and all of them, as belonging to *one* single stream of experience, that, namely, which is mine, *must* permit of being transformed into actual *cogitations* or of being inwardly absorbed into such; in the words of Kant, "The '*I think*' must be able to accompany all my presentations."[36]

Kant's claim about the "I think," which Husserl uses to lend support to his own notion of a transcendental ego, is also Sartre's starting point for the rejection of any transcendental ground for consciousness in *The Transcendence of the Ego*. Sartre agrees that the "I think" must *be able* to accompany all my presentations, if they are indeed to be *mine*. He nonetheless thinks that it is wrong to pass from claims about its possible ability to claims about its actual presence. The "I think" is necessary for the personification of consciousness. However, according to Sartre, consciousness is not first and foremost personified. We have seen that in *The Transcendence of the Ego* Sartre adopts Husserl's notion of consciousness and sees it as the foundation for all experience. Following the early Husserl, he maintains that as long as we live in our acts we do not encounter an *I*. We are directed to the objects intended by these acts. It is not *I* who is thinking, but simply a pre-personal, anonymous consciousness intending objects through various acts. Sartre says, "[w]hen I run after a streetcar, when I look at the time, when I am absorbed in contemplating a portrait, there is no *I*."[37] With this, he reiterates Husserl's point in *Logical Investigations*: "if we simply 'live' in the act... become absorbed, e.g., in the perceptual 'taking in' of some event happening before us, in some play of fancy, in reading a story, in carrying out a mathematic proof etc., the ego... becomes quite elusive" (2.561).

Husserl's emphasis on the manner in which we live in the act is crucial for Sartre, who wishes to capture the immediacy and intimacy of our relation to the world in his philosophical thinking. If we take *Logical Investigations* as a starting point for Sartre's discussion of the relationship between consciousness and the ego, we can come to understand his dismissal of Husserl's later discovery, reported in the famous footnote to section 8. The ego is to consciousness as the footnote is to the text: both are added retrospectively and with their addition what was originally present is radically changed. Husserl, reflecting on his earlier work, was able to find an "ego" where he originally saw none. According to Sartre, this is not accidental, since the ego is indeed revealed only in hindsight. Moreover, after living in reflection long enough, living in the "shadow" of the ego, so to speak, consciousness becomes tainted by its presence, for it acquires a semblance of a personified conscious field. Contra the late Husserl, who argues that "the ego belongs to each coming and going mental process" and that in each act "the ego lives out its life in a special sense,"[38] Sartre insists that while living in our acts we are in the presence of things, absorbed in them to such a degree that precludes the existence of an ego on that level. The attentiveness to objects enables us to live in what Alfred Schutz termed "the vivid present."[39] This is a spacious present in which consciousness dwells, or which it, in fact, is.[40]

Both Husserl and Sartre connect the appearance of the ego with a withdrawal from the absorption in the world and with a fundamental change in the temporal structure of consciousness. The appearance of the ego is an outcome of the re-direction of the conscious gaze. When we reflect on our immediate experience, says Husserl, "[t]he original act is no longer simply there, we no longer live in it, but we *attend to it and pass judgment on it*." Reflection brings a specific past moment to the forefront and halts the flow of the vivid present. Both Sartre and Husserl identify reflection with a radical change in consciousness. According to Husserl, with reflection "an essential descriptive change has occurred" (2.562), and according to Sartre, "the consciousness which says *I think* is precisely not the consciousness which thinks."[41]

Conclusion: Consciousness and Freedom

There are, no doubt, further affinities between Husserl and Sartre, beyond those I have examined regarding intentionality, consciousness, and the self. Some are explicit, such as their approach to the question of imagination and image, and their interpretation of self-awareness; some are implicit and require careful exegesis of their work, such as their understanding of the self-other relationship. The scope of this essay does not allow me to examine all these issues. I hope to have shown, however, that Husserl's early work shapes and informs Sartre's own philosophical agenda in the most concrete ways. I read these texts chronologically in order to highlight the ways in which specific themes from

HUSSERL AND OTHER PHENOMENOLOGISTS

Husserl's *Logical Investigations* can be traced through Sartre's *Transcendence of the Ego* and "Intentionality." In this respect, my reading uncovers Husserl's "footprints" in Sartre's work. Yet now I would like, by way of a conclusion, to reverse the order of the reading. Beginning with Sartre's notion of consciousness in *Being and Nothingness* and his emphasis on the relationship between consciousness and freedom, I wish to trace him back to Husserl's *Logical Investigations* and thus to highlight a vein in Husserl's own thinking that is not fully explicit. This is not meant to impose Sartrean concepts on Husserl's work, but rather to articulate and explicate certain strains in it that, I think, form the horizon upon which Sartre's own understanding of philosophy's genuine concerns is shaped and articulated.

As we saw, Sartre's reading of Husserl in "Intentionality" and in *The Transcendence of the Ego* emphasizes that Husserlian phenomenology culminates in the purification of the conscious field. Consciousness is cleared not only of mental residue but also of the ego. The elimination of selfhood in both its transcendental and material form, argues Sartre, allows us to see that consciousness has direct contact with the world. Indeed, according to Sartre's reading Husserlian phenomenology understands consciousness as nothing other than a relation to the world.

This line of thinking is further developed in *Being and Nothingness* (1943). In this later work Sartre turns to the question of the being of consciousness and no longer offers a purely descriptive science of consciousness. Yet even that work begins with a reference to Husserl's principle of intentionality.[42] Consciousness's relation of 'aboutness', its directedness to objects, reveals, according to Sartre, that consciousness itself is not an object; it is not a thing, or it is *nothing*, in the sense that there is nothing substantial in it. For in order for it to be conscious of something, consciousness must be conscious of itself (self-conscious, that is) as other than that thing. The intelligibility of experience hinges on consciousness's ability "to withdraw itself from the full world of which it is consciousness and to leave the level of being in order frankly to approach that of non-being."[43] By virtue of its ability to withdraw from the plenum of being, consciousness is identified with nihilation and, consequently, with freedom. Consciousness is *nothing*; that is, it is not a thing, but rather a negating movement that creates distance between itself and the world, allowing for a world to appear in the first place. For Sartre, consciousness is free since it is a not a thing. Rather, it is a non-being or a relation to things, which makes every "this" or "that" appear. Consciousness's nothingness, its freedom, is the "original condition of the questioning attitude and more generally of all philosophical and scientific inquiry."[44] Thus questioning and reflecting are only possible because consciousness is free. The possibility of assuming a perspective on things, which is necessary for understanding both itself and the world, is grounded in consciousness's lack of self-identity. Our ability to question both grounds and reveals our transcendence and our freedom: we question because we are not identical to the world, to others, or to ourselves. We question too because we are always able to make our relationship to things explicit, to reflect on this relationship, and to know that "it is thus and not otherwise."[45]

This very idea of the interconnectedness of freedom, reflection, and knowledge seems to underlie Husserl's project in *Logical Investigations*. In the introduction to the first volume, Husserl elaborates on the fundamental role of reflection in the phenomenological project:

> The source of all such difficulties (whether we aim at pure essence of experiences or treat experiences from an empirical, psychological standpoint) lies in the unnatural direction of intuition and thought which phenomenological analysis requires. Instead of becoming lost in the performance of acts built intricately on one another... we must rather practice 'reflection',

57

HUSSERL AND OTHER PHENOMENOLOGISTS

i.e. make these acts themselves, and their immanent meaning-content, our objects. … Here we have a direction of thought running counter to deeply ingrained habits which have been steadily strengthened since the dawn of mental development. (1.170)

Without going into the details of Husserl's notion of reflection, which is not monolithic, I want to suggest that for Husserl, just as for Sartre, reflection, and, indeed, the possibility of philosophical knowledge more generally, is intimately linked with freedom. Husserl presents the phenomenological project in this passage as dependent on the possibility of reflection. Ordinary thinking, and perhaps even some forms of scientific thinking, are habitual and hence feel natural, but they distort our understanding of experience. Only by uprooting thought from its attachment to habits of thinking can we gain a clear grasp of our experience. Reflection reorients thought. By repositioning thought, distancing it from all that is familiar and natural, one is able to open up to new possibilities for understanding. Here, Husserl connects reflection with freedom, for he tells us that the former allows consciousness to resist even "deeply ingrained habits." In other words, consciousness is not merely conditioned; rather, it can always reflect on the conditions in which it finds itself, distance itself from them, and question its own situation.

Husserl's *Logical Investigations* provided Sartre with a set of problems that he explored as his own philosophical project—from the structure of consciousness and its relationship to the world, to the peculiar being of the self. In this project we also find, albeit in an implicit and restrained way, at least in the early stage, a sentiment that Sartre later makes explicit, namely, that through its relentless efforts to understand itself and the world, consciousness expresses its own freedom. Freedom, manifested most clearly in reflection and questioning, makes possible philosophical thinking itself and opens the door to understanding the human condition.

Notes

1. Most studies examine specific points of conflict or disagreement between Sartre and Husserl. For instance, their different understanding of the nature of selfhood, otherness, memory, and imagination. Dealing with these disagreements, scholars either try to rehabilitate Husserl's position and defend it from Sartre's criticism, or develop Sartre's critique. Examples of the former approach are Beata Stawarska, "Memory and Subjectivity: Sartre in Dialogue with Husserl," *Sartre Studies International* 8 (2002): 94–111; Beata Stawarska, "Defining Imagination: Sartre between Husserl and Janet," *Phenomenology and Cognitive Sciences* 4 (2005): 133–53. The latter approach is taken by Alfred Schuetz in "Sartre's Theory of the Alter-Ego," *Philosophy and Phenomenological Research* 9 (1948): 181–99; and Dan Zahavi, "Intersubjectivity in Sartre's *Being and Nothingness*," *Alter* 10 (2002): 265–81.
2. Beata Stawarska, "Sartre and Husserl's *Ideen*: Phenomenology and Imagination," in *Jean-Paul Sartre: Key Concepts*, ed. Steven Churchill and Jack Reynolds (Durham, NC: Acuman, 2013), 12.
3. Jean-Paul Sartre, *War Diaries*, trans. Quintin Hoare (New York: Pantheon, 1985), 183.
4. Jean-Paul Sartre, *Being and Nothingness*, trans. Hazel Barnes (New York: Washington Square Press, 1956), 317.
5. Stawarska, "Sartre and Husserl's *Ideen*," 13.
6. Edmund Husserl, *Logical Investigations*, vol. 1, trans. John Niemeyer Findlay, ed. Dermot Moran (London: Routledge, 2001), 4; hereafter cited in the text.
7. Jean-Paul Sartre, *The Transcendence of the Ego*, trans. Forrest Williams and Robert Kirkpatrick (New York: Hill & Wang, 1960), 106.

HUSSERL AND OTHER PHENOMENOLOGISTS

8. Forrest Williams and Robert Kirkpatrick express a similar position in their introduction to *The Transcendence of the Ego*. They focus on "what is under attack by referring to the philosophy of Husserl... to suggest how this disagreement with Husserl seems to have facilitated the transition from phenomenology to the existentialist doctrines of *L'Etre et le Neant*." Sartre, *The Transcendence of the Ego*, 12.

9. Stawarska, "Sartre and Husserl's *Ideen*," 17–18.

10. Sartre, *War Diaries*, 183.

11. Stawarska, "Sartre and Husserl's *Ideen*," 17.

12. Stawarska, "Sartre and Husserl's *Ideen*," 18.

13. For a comprehensive account of the itinerary of Husserl's thought, see Jitendra Mohanty, "The Development of Husserl's Thought," in *The Cambridge Companion to Husserl*, ed. Barry Smith and David Woodruff Smith (Cambridge: Cambridge University Press, 1995), 45–77.

14. In the *Philosophy of Arithmetic* Husserl claims that his aim is "at a psychological characterization of the phenomena on which the abstraction of that concept rests." Edmund Husserl, *Philosophy of Arithmetic*, trans. Dallas Willard (Dordrecht: Kluwer, 2003), 22.

15. Edmund Husserl, *Logical Investigations*, vol. 2, trans. John Niemeyer Findlay (London: Routledge, 1970), 2; hereafter cited in the text.

16. For a detailed account of the distinction between real and ideal and Husserl's rejection of the mentalistic framework, see Lillian Alweiss, "Between Internalism and Externalism: Husserl's Account of Intentionality," *Inquiry* 52 (2009): 53–78.

17. Jean-Paul Sartre, *Sartre by Himself*, trans. Richard Seaver (New York: Urizen Books, 1978), 26.

18. Stawarska, for instance, refers to "Sartre's decidedly realist reading of intentionality," in "Sartre and Husserl's *Ideen*," 21. According to her, Sartre picks up undercurrents in Husserl's *Ideas*, which he then weaves into "the cloth of his own ontology" (Ibid.) As I hope to show, though Sartre certainly radicalizes Husserl's understanding of intentionality, he is articulating a line of thinking that appears in an explicit manner in *Logical Investigations*, according to which the objects of consciousness are irreducible to the acts by which consciousness intends these very objects.

19. Jean-Paul Sartre, "Intentionality: A Fundamental Idea of Husserl's Phenomenology," trans. Joseph Fell, *Journal of the British Society for Phenomenology* 1 (1970): 4; hereafter cited in the text.

20. This is exactly what realists think, according to Sartre: "Is not the table the actual content of my perception? Is not my perception the present state of my consciousness?" ("Intentionality," 4).

21. Sartre, *The Transcendence of the Ego*, 31.

22. Sartre, *The Transcendence of the Ego*, 34.

23. Sartre offers an interesting reading of Kant. According to Sartre's revisionary account, from the fact that the "I think" must be able to accompany all our representations, it does not follow that it does in fact always accompany them. Kant is asking a question of possibility says Sartre, not a question of fact.

24. Immanuel Kant, *Critique of Pure Reason*, ed. and trans. Paul Guyer and Allen Wood (Cambridge: Cambridge University Press, 1999), A 106–7, 232.

25. See Kant, *Critique of Pure Reason*, A 492/B 520, where "the transcendental subject" is equated with "the self proper, as it exists in itself." As a noumenal object, the transcendental self is not subject to any of the categories and cannot be said to be in space or time. At the same time, it cannot be said to be a self in any sense. Insofar as it is a condition for all experience, not just mine or yours, the transcendental ego has no particularities.

26. Edmund Husserl, *Ideas Pertaining to a Pure Phenomenology and to a Phenomenological Philosophy—First Book: General Introduction to a Pure Phenomenology*, trans. Fred Kersten (The Hague: Nijhoff, 1982), 261.

27. Husserl returns to this point in his *Encyclopedia Britannica* essay on phenomenology, where he says: "Transcendental subjectivity... is none other than again 'I myself'... not, however, as found in the natural attitude of every-day or of positive science; i.e., apperceived as components of the objectively present world before us, both rather as subjects of conscious life, *in* which this world and all that is present – for 'us' – constitutes itself through certain apperceptions."

HUSSERL AND OTHER PHENOMENOLOGISTS

"'Phenomenology' Edmund Husserl's Article for the *Encyclopaedia Britannica* (1927): New Complete Translation by Richard E. Palmer," *Journal of the British Society for Phenomenology* 2 (1971): 85. For an interpretation of the transcendental self as the ordinary self under a change of aspect, see David Carr, "Kant, Husserl, and the Nonempirical Ego," *The Journal of Philosophy* 74 (1977): 682–90. For the alternative reading, see Herbert Spiegelberg, "Husserl's Phenomenology and Existentialism," *The Journal of Philosophy* 57 (1960): 62–74.

28. Sartre, *The Transcendence of the Ego*, 38.

29. Commenting on Franz Brentano's notion of intentionality, where "every psychical phenomenon is an object of inner consciousness," Husserl says that Brentano's "grave misgivings... keep us from assenting to this" (*Logical Investigations*, 2.557). He also explicitly argues that "[H]owever we may decide the question of the existence or non-existence of phenomenal external things, we cannot doubt that the reality of each such perceived thing cannot be understood as the reality of a perceived complex of sensations in a perceiving consciousness" (2.862).

30. Husserl, *Ideas*, 91.

31. "By intentionality consciousness transcends itself. It unifies itself by escaping from itself." Sartre, *The Transcendence of the Ego*, 38.

32. Sartre, *The Transcendence of the Ego*, 38. This example is also interesting since it shows that Sartre accepts ideal entities as examples of external entities, just as Husserl does. When Sartre says that number is a "transcendent object," he obviously does not mean that it exists in the world.

33. Sartre, *The Transcendence of the Ego*, 38–39.

34. Sartre, *The Transcendence of the Ego*, 37.

35. Husserl, *Ideas*, 232.

36. Husserl, *Ideas*, 172–73.

37. Sartre, *The Transcendence of the Ego*, 49.

38. Husserl, *Ideas*, 132.

39. Alfred Schutz, "Sheler's Theory of Intersubjectivity and the General Thesis of the Alter Ego," *Philosophy and Phenomenological Research* 2 (1942): 342.

40. This is what Husserl calls a "phenomenological stream of consciousness" (*Logical Investigations*, 2.541).

41. Sartre, *The Transcendence of the Ego*, 45.

42. "All consciousness, as Husserl has shown, is consciousness *of* something." Sartre, *Being and Nothingness*, 11.

43. Sartre, *Being and Nothingness*, 560.

44. Sartre, *Being and Nothingness*, 44.

45. Sartre, *Being and Nothingness*, 36.

From Husserl to Merleau-Ponty: On the Metamorphosis of a Philosophical Example

Meirav Almog

Kibbutzim College of Education, Technology and the Arts, Tel-Aviv, Israel

ABSTRACT
This essay outlines the transformation of the ostensibly mundane example of two hands touching each other in Husserl's *Ideas II* into the pivotal concept in Merleau-Ponty's ontology of flesh and notion of embodied subjectivity. By focusing on the contexts in which the example appears in the works of Husserl and of Merleau-Ponty, it seeks to explicate Merleau-Ponty's fascination with Husserl's example, its role in the development of his own thought and in the conceptual shift in his late works on the body. I explore the various stages in the metamorphosis of Husserl's example of touching hands, originally used merely to differentiate the sense of touch from that of sight, into Merleau-Ponty's radical concept of flesh that overturns "our idea of the thing and the world, and... results in an ontological rehabilitation of the sensible."

Every reflection is after the model of the reflection of the hand touching by the hand touched.

— Maurice Merleau-Ponty, *The Visible and the Invisible*

Husserl's Philosophical Example

While the influence of Edmund Husserl on Maurice Merleau-Ponty's work has been thoroughly researched, there is an ongoing debate as to the extent of his influence and the extent to which Merleau-Ponty may be said to have transcended Husserl's thought.[1] Merleau-Ponty has mainly been credited in this context with shedding light on and developing lesser-known aspects of Husserl's thought, which he discovered in Husserl's manuscripts, published posthumously as *Ideas II* and *The Crisis of European Sciences and Transcendental Phenomenology*.[2] Merleau-Ponty's reading of Husserl's transcendental reduction (*Epoché*) in *Ideas II*—the phenomenological suspension, or bracketing, of any judgment regarding the existence of the world—is commonly taken as a key moment in the dramatic shift in his late thought from an inquiry mainly focused on perception and the human body to his unfinished ontology of flesh as the carnal "essence" of the world.[3] Interestingly, when he indirectly comments on Husserl's effect on this shift, he refers to a simple, mundane example of hands touching each other. For Merleau-Ponty this example of reflexive touch turns out to be no mere example but a revolutionary event that "results in an ontological rehabilitation of the sensible."[4] To understand how a simple philosophical example can have such a dramatic effect, we must turn to Husserl's original description of the touching hands:

> Touching my left hand, I have touch-appearances, that is to say, I do not just sense, but I perceive and have appearances of a soft, smooth hand, with such a form. ... But when I touch the left hand I also find in it, too, series of touch-sensations, which are 'localized' in it. ... If I do include them, then it is not that the physical thing is now richer, but instead *it becomes Body, it senses*. ... The hand that is touching, which for its part again appears as a thing, likewise has its touch-sensations at the place on its corporeal surface where it touches (or is touched by the other). (original emphasis)[5]

Husserl introduces this example in section 36 of *Ideas II* as part of a more general exploration of the "The Constitution of Psychic Reality through the Body" and, more specifically, of the "Constitution of the Body as bearer of localized sensations" (152). His starting point in this section is the discovery that the body is part of every experience of spatio-temporal objects. In order to explore this corporeal ability, Husserl turns to the unique case in which the body itself is the spatio-temporal object of bodily experience. In order to present this experience as closely as possible to that of any other spatio-temporal object, he focuses first on the body parts available to both touch and sight at once, and disregards, momentarily, the parts that can be grasped by touch but not by unaided sight, such as one's back—"I can look at them and feel them, just like other things, and in this respect the appearances have entirely the same nexus as do other appearances of things." "But, now," Husserl continues, "there is a distinction between the *visual* and the *tactual* regarding, e.g. a hand" (152, original emphasis). The point of this example is initially to discern these abilities, which he further develops in the following section on "Differences between the visual and tactual realms" (155–59).

Through the reflexive touch, unlike the sense of sight, the body tactilely senses one hand as an object and, at the same time, senses the hand that touches that "object" from within. What interests Husserl here is the unique ability of the body to feel touch-sensations on or in the body while it touches. Yet this unique sensation is not confined to tactile reflexivity. As Husserl writes: "My hand is lying on the table. I experience the table as something solid, cold, and smooth. Moving my hand over the table, I get an experience of its thingly determinations. At the same time, I can at any moment pay attention to my hand and find on it touch-sensations" (153). That is, sensations of movement (moving my hand on the table), of weight (lifting a thing from the table), and so forth—are all localized in the body while experiencing an object.

What differentiates *reflexive* touch from any other tactile experience is that it serves as the constitution of the lived-body [*Leib*]. Thus the example of the hands manifests the body's constitution in a twofold manner: as an object, "it is a physical thing, *matter*," with properties such as color, smoothness, hardness, warmth, yet, at the same time, the body functions as a subject: it is also what "I find on it, and *sense* 'on' it and 'in' it: warmth on the back of the hand, coldness in the feet, sensations of touch in the fingertips." And when I include both sensations (that of the "object" and that of the "subject"), the body, Husserl emphasizes, does not become a richer object, but rather "*it becomes Body, it senses*" (153, original emphasis).

For Merleau-Ponty, as mentioned, this example is a definitive event. Responding emphatically to it, he writes: "It is imperative that we recognize that this description also overturns our idea of the thing and the world, and that it results in an ontological rehabilitation of the sensible" (S, 167). Yet what does Merleau-Ponty mean by such a rehabilitation? Why precisely does the sensible need to be rehabilitated? What do "ontological" and "sensible" mean here? And, of course, how can an ordinary example of two hands touching each other "overturn our idea of the thing and the world"? Moreover, although Merleau-Ponty first came across Husserl's example back in 1939 during his visit to the Husserlian archive in Louvain,[6] it resurfaces almost twenty years later and becomes extremely significant to him. What then motivated his renewed interest in this example, and why did he endow it with such ontological importance?[7]

In what follows I attempt to answer these questions by looking at the close relationship between the organic development of Merleau-Ponty's thought and Husserlian thought. I suggest that Merleau-Ponty's interpretation of Husserl's example underlies the dramatic shift in his phenomenological ontology, which also affects his complex approach to Husserlian thought.

Merleau-Ponty's Embodied Self

The question that grounds Merleau-Ponty's phenomenological project from its very beginning concerns the relations between subjectivity and objectivity, mind and body, consciousness and world. Dissatisfied with traditional ideas of the self, especially the behaviorist and the Cartesian conceptions and their accompanying epistemologies, he sees Western thought's forgetfulness of carnality as projecting the self as a sublimated being whose subjective correlative is a look that comes from *nowhere* and, hence, dominates and encompasses everything. As Françoise Dastur explains:

> Merleau-Ponty set himself the task of finding an intermediate position between intellectualism and empiricism, that is, between an insular subject and a pure nature. The world and consciousness, the outside and the inside, are not distinct beings that the full force of philosophical thought must contrive to reunite; rather, they are interdependent, and it is precisely this interdependence that becomes legible in the phenomenon of incarnation.[8]

Thus Merleau-Ponty places as the starting point of any philosophical inquiry the incarnated, "impure" consciousness of embodied human beings, whose essence is no longer "I think," but, borrowing from Husserl, the "I can."[9] In his *Phenomenology of Perception* he uses Husserl's distinction between the inanimate physical body (*Körper*) and the living, animated body (*Leib*),[10] taking the latter as the point from which any philosophical thought should begin. He does so, firstly, because for him the lived body renders the interdependence between consciousness and world most legible,[11] since "nature and consciousness can only truly communicate *in us* and through *our incarnate being*" (emphasis added).[12] And secondly, because, as he also learns from Husserl, the lived body is a structure of meaning that enables the world to appear as meaningful. Yet, unlike Husserl, who remains captive to a conception of intentionality that is governed by consciousness, Merleau-Ponty, as Taylor Carman argues, "bases his entire phenomenological project on an account of bodily intentionality and the challenge it poses to any adequate concept of mind."[13] Incarnation, for him, in its most fundamental form is the point of reference for all human existence: it is "our sensibility to the world, our synchronized relations to it... the thesis underlying all our experiences."[14] The lived body is, at the same time, my particular reference point around which the world is oriented, and what determines my point of view on the world in the deepest sense.[15] It determines, for instance, my directional orientation in the world: what is "up," "down," "left," or "right," and so forth. It is thus the (transcendental) anchor from which the self receives its place in the world with regard to time, meaning, language, space, and primal connection to physical objects.

Hence we see that Merleau-Ponty conceives the embodied subject in terms that are neither exclusively mechanistic nor entirely intentional (as manifested merely in consciousness), but in terms that incorporate both of these spheres of bodily action.[16] However, in a note to his unfinished work, *The Visible and Invisible*, Merleau-Ponty writes: "The problems posed in Ph.P. [*Phenomenology of Perception*] are insoluble because I start there from the 'consciousness'-'object' distinction."[17] The mind-body separation was certainly not taken naively nor was it regarded as a trivial matter in *Phenomenology of Perception*. In fact, one of Merleau-Ponty's main endeavors was to blur this traditional dichotomy, establishing the poles merely as points of reference to differentiate one's thought from them, and casting them as edge-points to delineate an intermediary realm.[18]

Still, Merleau-Ponty acknowledges that he failed to create a new point of departure for philosophical inquiry that transcended the dichotomy of consciousness and object, mind and world, and that was not ultimately based on consciousness. As he writes in another note: "The problems that remain after this first description, [*Phenomenology of Perception*] are due to the fact that in part I retained the philosophy of 'consciousness'" (*VI*, 183). This dramatic shift in Merleau-Ponty's thought has been extensively discussed and debated.[19] Suffice it to say that this change represents something far more substantial than a simple replacement of concepts. Merleau-Ponty is in fact searching for a new philosophical language, a new ontology, which would structurally enable non-binary relations of subject and object in their deepest sense and would successfully transcend Cartesian dualism without falling into a too simplistic monism.

This shift, moreover, is not only a significant event in Merleau-Ponty's oeuvre but a new attitude that he indirectly assumes towards Husserl's thought. He tends not to directly criticize Husserl, which has sometimes led scholars to question the originality of his thought. Yet his very search for a new philosophical language indicates that Merleau-Ponty distanced himself from Husserlian thought. This search expresses his dissatisfaction with his own phenomenology of the body and his urge to develop a new terminology for speaking of carnality. It is also a recognition of the limits of Husserlian phenomenology, which, while identifying the lived body as a primary object of inquiry, remains "a philosophy of consciousness" and a prisoner to the traditional dichotomy of consciousness and world.[20] As he writes, "The whole Husserlian analysis is blocked by the framework of *acts* which imposes upon it the philosophy of *consciousness*" and, thus, he argues, "It is necessary, to take as primary, not the consciousness and its *Ablaufsphänomen* with its distinct intentional threads, but the vortex which this *Ablaufsphänomen* schematizes, the spatializing-temporalizing vortex (which is flesh and not consciousness facing a noema)" (*VI*, 244). Given his unequivocal criticism, in what way does the Husserlian example of the touching hands play such a significant role in Merleau-Ponty's late ontology as he himself claims?

HUSSERL AND OTHER PHENOMENOLOGISTS

The Ontological Rehabilitation of the Sensible—the Flesh

Husserl's example of the touching hands first appears in Merleau-Ponty's "The Philosopher and His Shadow" (1959), the only published work on Husserl's thought among his late writings.[21] Here, he claims that rationalist as well as empiricist approaches disregard a substantial part of the world's enormous richness by making the world "an idea" or "an aim" in order to solve the tension between pure mind (subject) and pure nature (object). The human body, he argues, can serve as a key factor in untangling this complication; it bears a relation to itself "which makes it the *vinculum* of the self and things." It does not take part in the dichotomy of absolute mind and transcendent nature, but rather serves as a vinculum, a connector, between these two "rival" components, which traditional philosophy has fruitlessly entangled in its efforts to establish their relations. This unique relation to itself is manifested in carnal reflexivity that is grounded, he explains, in the Husserlian example of the hands:

> [W]hat link is there between my body and me in addition to the regularities of occasional causality? There is a relation of my body to itself which makes it the *vinculum* of the self and things. When my right hand touches my left, I am aware of it as a "physical thing." But at the same moment, if I wish, an extraordinary event takes place: here is my left hand as well starting to perceive my right, *es wird Leib, es empfindet* [citing *Ideen II*, 145]. The physical thing becomes animate. Or, more precisely, it remains what it was (the event does not enrich it), but an exploratory power comes to rest upon or dwell in it. Thus I touch myself touching; my body accomplishes "a sort of reflection." In it, through it, there is not just the unidirectional relationship of the one who perceives to what he perceives. The relationship is reversed, the touched hand becomes the touching hand, and I am obliged to say that the sense of touch here is diffused into the body—that the body is a "perceiving thing" [*Ideen II*, 119: "*Empfindendes Ding*"], a 'subject-object' [*Ideen II*, 124: "*Das subjective Objekt*"]. (166)

What Merleau-Ponty discovers in this example is thus a constitutive event of the embodied self through tactile reflexivity. The right hand touches the left hand as a *subject* touches an *object*. Yet at that very moment, the feeling of the left hand as a physical thing is inverted and the left hand becomes animated; it starts to perceive the right hand, it can sense and explore it. The body touches and is being touched; the relations between the hands are reversed, crossed, and, consequently, the sense of touch is diffused into the body. This ability, according to Merleau-Ponty, is only "a sort of reflection," as he wishes to differentiate it from the traditional reflection of pure consciousness. In contrast to it, carnal reflection does not close upon itself hermetically since the body is open to the world in an almost structural, unmediated, pre-thematic way.

The sense of being touched and at the same time of being that which touches establishes the body as a "perceiving thing," a "subject-object." It is a "subject-object" but not in the sense of a simple juxtaposition of a subject *and* an object, nor of a subject *or* an object that has reversed its position—for these options of interpretation would fall under "the 'consciousness'-'object' distinction" (*VI*, 200) which Merleau-Ponty wishes to overcome. In other words, what needs to be underscored in Merleau-Ponty's understanding of the subject-object is precisely the connecting hyphen that appears between the two terms—that is, the carnal self occupies an intermediate realm, located so to speak within the hyphenated space that spans the subjective and the objective.

Still, how should we explain the manner in which the body's reflexive ability enables it to be the vinculum of self and things, subject and object? How does this happen? This is

HUSSERL AND OTHER PHENOMENOLOGISTS

precisely where Husserl's example of the touching hands becomes particularly pertinent for Merlau-Ponty, ultimately culminating in "an ontological rehabilitation of the entire sphere of the sensible" (*S*, 167).

The body, Merleau-Ponty writes, has the ability of

> [a] veritable touching of the touch, when my right hand touches my left hand while it is palpating the things, where the "touching subject" passes over to the rank of the touched, descends into the things, such that the touch is formed in the midst of the world and as it were in the things. (*VI*, 133–34)

Moreover,

> The enigma is that my body simultaneously sees and is seen. ... It sees itself seeing; *it touches itself touching; it is visible and sensitive for itself.* It is not a self through transparence, like thought, which only thinks its object by assimilating it, by constituting it, by transforming it into thought. *It is a self* ... through inherence of the one who sees in that which he sees, and *through inherence of sensing in the sensed*—a self, therefore, that is caught up in things, that has a front and a back, a past and a future. (emphasis added)[22]

What is emphasized in and through Merleau-Ponty's expanded paraphrases of Husserl's example is that the constitution of the self is not the subject's self-possession through assimilation of the things comprising its "outside" (a reassuring of one's self). Instead, it is a self that recognizes itself through reflexive touch, *as well as* by touching things and the world—one hand touches the other while it palpates what is tangible; it can touch the other hand touching, it "can turn its palpation back upon it" (*VI*, 141). This carnal self-recognition thus occurs within an extended reflexive circle that combines the two aspects of the Husserlian examples presented earlier: the example of the touching hands and the example of the body's ability to feel touch-sensations on or in the body while it touches an object. Thus, Self and things intertwine: "the touch is formed in the midst of the world and as it were in the things" (*VI*, 133–34). It is a "self-recognition," so to speak, which comes from an untraditional direction—not from the "inside"—from an intrinsic reflection, but from one's inhering within the things that one touches and sees, suggesting that the "subject" and the "thing" are *interdependent* and not separated.[23]

If the self is conceived as a site of the intertwining of "subject" and "object," wherein they can no longer be sharply distinguished, then we indeed face a completely different notion of things and world. The thing, the ob-ject—etymologically, what stands against, in front, opposite to—no longer faces the subject, and the world no longer faces the subject as an object to be examined. The Husserlian example thus implies that the ontology of the sensible, as traditionally perceived, needs a *rehabilitation*. It is a *re*-habilitation since the sensible is no longer construed in terms of the opposition between two separate substantive realms, an opposition that remains intact, even if, in different ontological frameworks, it takes on different forms.

Merleau-Ponty remarks to himself in a working note: "*Define* the mind as the *other side* of the body" (*VI*, 259). For him, having an *other side* means that the body can no longer be treated in objective terms or as something that inherently belongs to the soul. The "other side" of the body "*overflows* into it (*Ueberschreiten*), encroaches upon it, is hidden in it—and at the same time needs it, terminates in it, is *anchored* in it." These complex and dynamic relations form a dense, thick realm of depth and movement, within which "[t] here is a body of the mind, and a mind of the body and a chiasm between them." In this respect, Merleau-Ponty offers an altogether different sense of the *sensible*, whose core lies in the body's capacity for tactile reflectivity, as Husserl argued: the body's ability to touch and explore itself and things and simultaneously to feel that touching and exploring from within. "The essential notion for such philosophy," Merleau-Ponty writes, "is that of the flesh, which is not the objective body, nor the body thought by the soul as its own (Descartes), which is the sensible in the twofold sense of what one senses and what senses" (*VI*, 259).

Flesh [Fr. *chair*] is a dynamic intermediate realm of constant chiasmic movement between the sensing and the sensed. More generally, it is the interlacing of what is perceived to be general and anonymous, of "what is touched," with what is perceived to be singular and active, "what one touches." Flesh is thus like a Möbius strip in which one side turns into the other, and so Merleau-Ponty names it "reversible," as in Husserl's example of the hands touching each other. As a result, both body and thing are interwoven in an intentional fabric, which, from now on, is carnal and partakes of the same fabric as one's body (*S*, 167). The thing perceived is grasped *literally* "in person": "in the flesh," as Merleau-Ponty emphasizes, and that flesh of what is perceived is "a type of being, a universe with its unparalleled 'subject' and 'object,' the articulation of each in terms of the other" (*S*, 167).

The question, however, is in what sense can this rehabilitation of the sensible be seen as *ontological*? At first glance, flesh remains, in a way, the indivisible mélange of *subject-object*. The heart of the matter has not dramatically shifted. Yet the hyphen between subject and object no longer suffices, so to speak, for Merleau-Ponty who searches for a notion that would utterly transcend that dichotomy: "We must not think [of] the flesh [as] starting from substances, from body and spirit—for then it would be the union of contradictories—but we must think it, as we said, *as an element, as the concrete emblem of a general manner of being*."[24] Flesh, for Merleau-Ponty is thus, "a type of being" (*S*, 167), an "element" (*VI*, 147), functioning in the primordial sense attached to water, air, earth, and fire. Take, for instance, the element of water in Thales, for whom it is neither an *eidos* nor something present in its material form within things. Water serves as the origin of life, of nature, of beings and, at the same time, it is also the essence of all these things—their source of growing, developing—their power of life. As such, like water, flesh grounds the nascence of things, their most primal origin and, at the same time, their unique carnal existence.[25] And like water, flesh is the most general form of being, standing at the heart of every worldly thing.[26] It is, thus, as Françoise Dastur writes, "a new name for the being of every being, a new determination of the common essence of things,"[27] and yet, this "common essence" is used by Merleau-Ponty in an idiosyncratic manner, for unlike the conventional notions of essence, flesh is carnal, dynamic, and relational.

We see that the Husserlian example of the hands treasures, for Merleau-Ponty, the discovery of the chiasmic, tactile relations between the world and the subject. And, thus, it holds the potential for the ontological rehabilitation of the sensible into flesh, as well as for overturning notions of things and world and what is meant by subjectivity. While Merleau-Ponty's concept of flesh is a general element of being, its most refined manifestation appears in the reflexivity that he terms "human flesh," which is also why he adopts the Husserlian example of the constitution of the human body. Human flesh is a unique phenomenon in which the general structure of flesh culminates since reversibility and reflexivity can occur only within the human. The flesh of the world, on the other hand, "is not self-sensing (*se sentir*) as is my flesh—it is sensible and not sentient" (*VI*, 250). Moreover, although not effortlessly accessible, human flesh is the only form of flesh with the potentiality to recognize the structure of flesh—the structure of oneself, of things and of the world.

HUSSERL AND OTHER PHENOMENOLOGISTS

The Husserlian example of the touching hands thus becomes the prototype of embodied subjectivity, emphasizing the intertwining and the chiasm between activity and passivity, "subject" and "object." Merleau-Ponty in fact dramatically extends the example into an ontology grounded in *aesthetics* in its etymological sense of the term: an ontology of flesh whose core is the sensible. It is an ontology that its basic structure is not pure and static, but rather a vibrant, sensuous movement of encroachment and chiasm of "the sensible in the twofold sense of what one senses and what senses" (*VI*, 259).

Husserl's Unthought-of Element

The significance of the works of a philosopher is expected, according to Merleau-Ponty, to be wholly *positive* and thus "susceptible to an inventory which sets forth what is and is not in those works." But, as he insists, "this is to be mistaken about works and thought" (*S*, 159-60). Instead, a philosopher's thought does not unravel in an entirely positive manner but rather reveals itself through a complex apparatus similar to how the world reveals itself, through "reflections, shadows, levels, and horizons between things." These things "mark out by themselves the fields of possible variation in the same thing and the same world" (*S*, 159–60). Similarly, "the works and thought of a philosopher are also made of certain articulations between things said." These articulations are gathered from the shadows, reflections, and horizons *of his thought*, that is, by what has been understood by what the philosopher said and wrote and, not less importantly, by what he *did not* write: the things he did not directly think of but that his thinking provokes others to further think about—what Merleau-Ponty calls "*the unthought-of element*" in his work. These articulations are thus fragile, for they can be destroyed if we subject them to analysis or treat them as "*objects of thought*." We can remain faithful to them, and find them without distorting them only by *thinking again*. However, by "thinking" Merleau-Ponty does not mean the traditional sense that consciousness possesses "the objects of thought"; rather, he proposes that these "things said" be used to create a realm that enables us to think about what has not yet been thought or expressed (*S*, 160).

Merleau-Ponty's concept of thinking is one where thought is constantly evolving: a thinking that is always open to new thoughts arising from its own thought, from the thoughts of others, and from the unthought-of elements, and calls for further thinking. Thinking or, perhaps, creative thinking, is thus not the ability to create something new from nothing, but to form a new thought from what is already given, and to do so from what is apparently positive, but never completely is. It is a form of thinking that takes the unthought-of-element of one's thought a step further, pulling it onward, and creating positive aspects along with new, unthought-of elements of its own.

"At the end of Husserl's life," Merleau-Ponty writes "there is an unthought-of element in his works which is wholly his and yet opens out on something else" (*S*, 159–60). That "something else," I suggest, is the phenomenological ontology of the sensible that transcends Husserl's own phenomenology. Merleau-Ponty finds in Husserl's example of touching hands the hidden grains of thought that, though were not directly thought and given, provoke him to think further, and, thus, these seeds are instances of the "unthought-of element" in Husserl's work.[28] By using Husserl's example of the hands as his starting point he delineates a new intermediate realm that enables him to think what has not yet been thought and developed in Husserl's work, but that is present there in an implicit, non-positive way. This

HUSSERL AND OTHER PHENOMENOLOGISTS

interpretive undertaking started off and developed, as we saw, into an *aesthetic* ontology of flesh, which Merleau-Ponty offered as a new, non-binary, philosophical language. It is a movement of thinking that turns invisible elements that have not yet been thought of into visible, thought-of elements, while at the same time it opens up new, unthought-of horizons of its own to emerge and to be further thought of with wonder.

Notes

1. On Merleau-Ponty's reading of Husserl, see, among others, Dan Zahavi, "Merleau-Ponty on Husserl: A Reappraisal," in *Merleau-Ponty's Reading of Husserl*, ed. Ted Toadvine and Lester Embree (Dordrecht: Kluwer Academic Publishers, 2002), 3–30; Renaud Barbaras, "Perception and Movement: The End of the Metaphysical Approach," in *Chiasms: Merleau-Ponty's Notion of Flesh*, ed. Fred Evans and Leonard Lawlor (Albany, NY: State University of New York Press, 2000), 77–88; Arthur David Smith, "The Flesh of Perception: Merleau-Ponty and Husserl," in *Reading Merleau-Ponty: On* Phenomenology of Perception, ed. Thomas Baldwin (New York: Routledge, 2007), 1–22; and Ted Toadvine, "Leaving Husserl's Cave? The Philosopher's Shadow Revisited," in *Merleau-Ponty's Reading of Husserl*, 71–95.
2. Ted Toadvine, "Merleau-Ponty's Reading of Husserl: A Chronological Overview," in *Merleau-Ponty's Reading of Husserl*, 270.
3. This subject is widely discussed, see, for instance, Sara Heinämaa, "From Decisions to Passions: Merleau-Ponty's Interpretation of Husserl's Reduction," in *Merleau-Ponty's Reading of Husserl*, 127–48; Taylor Carman, "The Body in Husserl and Merleau-Ponty," *Philosophical Topics* 27 (1999): 205–26; and Scott L. Marratto, *The Intercorporeal Self* (New York: State University of New York Press, 2012).
4. Maurice Merleau-Ponty, "The Philosopher and His Shadow," in *Signs*, trans. Richard C. McCleary (Evanston, IL: Northwestern University Press, 1964), 167; hereafter cited a *S* in the text.
5. Edmund Husserl, *Ideas Pertaining to a Pure Phenomenology and to a Phenomenological Philosophy: Second Book*, trans. Richard Rojcewicz and André Schuwer (Dordrecht: Kluwer Academic Publishers, 1980), 152; hereafter cited in the text.
6. Merleau-Ponty addresses this example already in *Phenomenology of Perception* (1945) in "The Experience of the Body and Classical Psychology," the second section of "The Body," the first part of the book, in which he outlines Husserl's view of double sensation in his discussion of different views of the human body.
7. In "The Philosopher and His Shadow" (1959), in "Eye and Mind" (1961), the last work published in his lifetime, and in his unfinished book *The Visible and the Invisible* (1959–61). I believe this should be read in light of Merleau-Ponty's renewed thinking about his major work *Phenomenology of Perception*, and his future projects.
8. Françoise Dastur, "World, Flesh, Vision," in *Chiasms: Merleau-Ponty's Notion of Flesh*, ed. Fred Evans and Leonard Lawlor (Albany, NY: State University of New York Press, 2000), 23.
9. Merleau-Ponty borrows this term from Husserl's unpublished writings; see *Phenomenology of Perception*, trans. Colin Smith (London: Routledge & Kegan Paul, 1962), 159.
10. Dermot Moran, *Introduction to Phenomenology* (London: Routledge & Kegan Paul, 2000), 423.
11. Dastur, "World, Flesh, Vision," 23.
12. Maurice Merleau-Ponty, *Themes from the Lectures at the Collège de France, 1952–1960* (Evanston, IL: Northwestern University Press, 1970), 76–77.
13. Taylor Carman, "The Body in Husserl and Merleau-Ponty," 206.
14. Maurice Merleau-Ponty, *The Prose of the World*, trans. John O'Neill (Evanston, IL: Northwestern University Press, 1973), 139.
15. Merleau-Ponty, *Phenomenology of Perception*, 70.
16. Martin C. Dillon, *Merleau-Ponty's Ontology* (Bloomington, IN: Indiana University Press, 1988), 131.

HUSSERL AND OTHER PHENOMENOLOGISTS

17. Maurice Merleau-Ponty, *The Visible and the Invisible*, trans. Alphonso Lingis (Evanston, IL: Northwestern University Press, 1968), 200; hereafter cited as *VI* in the text.

18. Some scholars, however, have criticized Merleau-Ponty on this point. Renaud Barbaras, for instance, claims that although Merleau-Ponty wanted to break away from the language of realism or intellectualism, he remained a prisoner to their terminology. Renaud Barbaras, *The Being of the Phenomenon: Merleau-Ponty's Ontology*, trans. Ted Toadvine and Leonard Lawlor (Bloomington, IN: Indiana University Press, 2004), 6.

19. On this shift in Merleau-Ponty's thought, see, among others, Barbaras, "Perception and Movement: The End of the Metaphysical Approach," 77–88 ; Dastur, "World, Flesh, Vision," 23–49; Wayne Froman, "Alterity and the Paradox of Being," in *Ontology and Alterity in Merleau-Ponty*, ed. Galen. A. Johnson and Michael. B. Smith (Evanston, IL: Northwestern University Press, 1990), 98–110; Claude Lefort, "Body, Flesh," in *Merleau-Ponty and the Possibilities of Philosophy: Transforming the Tradition*, ed. B. Flynn et al. (Albany, NY: State University of New York Press, 2009), 275–92; Wayne Froman, "The Blind Spot" in *Merleau-Ponty and the Possibilities of Philosophy: Transforming and Tradition*, 155–65; Jacques Taminiaux, "Phenomenology in Merleau-Ponty's Late Work," in Jacques Taminiaux, *Dialectic and Difference: Finitude in Modern Thought*, ed. James T. Decker and Robert. Crease (Atlantic Highlands, NJ: Humanities Press, 1985), 115–29, esp. 126. There is, for example, a tension between different approaches: while M. C. Dillon argues that Merleau-Ponty's late writings are adumbrated in his earlier works, Barbaras sees in them a complete rupture with the earlier works.

20. As Carman writes in "The Body in Husserl and Merleau-Ponty": "[I]t is precisely this conceptual dualism, this idea that consciousness and reality are separated by an 'abyss of meaning,' that prevents Husserl from acknowledging the body as the original locus of intentional phenomena in perceptual experience. ... To put it bluntly, as Husserl does, 'all sensings belong to my soul (*Seele*), everything extended to the material thing' (*Id II*, 150)" (209).

21. Toadvine, "Merleau-Ponty's Reading of Husserl: A Chronological Overview," 270.

22. Merleau-Ponty, "Eye and Mind," 162.

23. For Merleau-Ponty, unlike for Husserl, reflexivity in the visual realm is immediate and as important as tactile reflexivity for the constitution of the self. Although I cannot elaborate on this point here, we see that the Husserlian example touches on an essential element of humanity that can be extended, according to Merleau-Ponty, to the visual realm as well.

24. Which will lead us again, as noted, to insoluble problems: "The problems posed in Ph.P. [*Phenomenology of Perception*] are insoluble because I start there from the 'consciousness'-'object' distinction" (*VI*, 200).

25. This tension between the search for the origin and the essence of Being, which accompanied Merleau-Ponty's thinking from the very start, is manifested in his writings on painting. While in "Cézanne's' Doubt" (1942) painting serves as a key for unveiling the nascence point, in "Eye and Mind," for example, Merleau-Ponty is more concerned with unraveling the richness of Being through the medium of painting.

26. The notion of *flesh* often does not stand on its own in *The Visible and the Invisible*, but appears in phrases such as "flesh of being" (88), "flesh of the world" (84, 142, 255, 267, 271), "flesh of the visible" (119), "flesh of things"(133, 193), and even "flesh of time" (111).

27. Dastur,"World, Flesh, Vision," 33.

28. Merleau-Ponty quotes *Der Satz vom Grund*, where Heidegger argues that the power of the un-thought-of element in a work is in direct proportion to its greatness. Martin Heidegger, *Der Satz vom Grund* (Pfullingen: Verlag Gunther Neske, 1957), 123–24; English translation: *The Principle of Reason*, trans. Reginald Lilly (Bloomington, IN: Indiana University Press, 1991), 71.

Husserl and Jacob Klein

Burt C. Hopkins

Department of Philosophy, Seattle University, Seattle, WA, USA

ABSTRACT

The article explores the relationship between the philosopher and historian of mathematics Jacob Klein's account of the transformation of the concept of number coincident with the invention of algebra, together with Husserl's early investigations of the origin of the concept of number and his late account of the Galilean impulse to mathematize nature. Klein's research is shown to present the historical context for Husserl's twin failures in the *Philosophy of Arithmetic*: to provide a psychological foundation for the proper concept of number (*Anzahl*), and to show how this concept of number functions as the mathematical foundation of universal (symbolic) arithmetic. This context establishes that Husserl's failures are ultimately rooted in the historical transformation of number documented in Klein's research, from its premodern meaning as the unity of a multitude of determinate objects to its modern meaning as a symbolic representation with no immediate relation to a concrete multiplicity. The argument is advanced that one significant result of bringing together Klein's and Husserl's thought on these issues is the need to fine-tune Husserl's project in *The Crisis of European Sciences and Transcendental Phenomenology* of de-sedimenting the mathematization of nature. Specifically, Klein's research shows that "a 'sedimented' understanding of numbers" "is superposed upon the first stratum of 'sedimented' geometrical 'evidences'" uncovered by Husserl's fragmentary analyses of geometry in the *Crisis*. In addition then to the task of "the intentional-historical reactivation of the origin of geometry," recognized by Husserl as intrinsic to the reactivation of the origin of mathematical physics, Klein discloses a second task, that of "the reactivation" of the "complicated network of sedimented significances" that "underlies the 'arithmetical' understanding of geometry."

Introduction

The first "Klein" typically associated with Edmund Husserl is the mathematician Felix Klein (1849–1925), whose final years at Göttingen overlapped with all but two of the years Husserl spent there (1901–15). No reference to Felix Klein's namesake, Jacob Klein (1899–1978)[1] exists in Husserl's published and unpublished work.[2] The first public

HUSSERL AND OTHER PHENOMENOLOGISTS

connection between Husserl and Jacob Klein occurs in 1940, with the publication of Klein's article "Phenomenology and the History of Science" in *Philosophical Essays in Memory of Edmund Husserl*.[3] This article is noteworthy above all for two reasons. One, it is the first discussion in the literature of Husserl's posthumously published essays "Die Frage nach dem Ursprung der Geometrie als intentional-historisches Problem"[4] and "Die Krisis der europäischen Wissenschaften und die transzendentale Phänomenologie. Eine Einleitung in die phänomenologische Philosophie."[5] Two, despite Klein's sympathetic presentation of Husserl's phenomenology and appreciation of the consistency of Husserl's late turn to historical reflection with his earlier thought, Klein critically departs from "Husserl's 'intentional-historical' analysis of the origin of mathematical physics" (PHS, 79). At the very point in the *Crisis* where he praises Husserl's "amazing piece of historical 'empathy,'" Klein purports "to give a general outline of that actual historical development" behind the origin of mathematical physics and with that of the origin of "modern consciousness."

Klein situates the "actual" historical development in question within the context of Husserl's statements about Galilean science in the *Crisis*, having first extracted from Husserl's analysis of the concepts of 'history' and 'tradition' in "The Origin of Geometry," what Klein refers to as the phenomenological problem of "intentional history."[6] Klein's account of this development presents it in terms of "a 'sedimented'[7] understanding of numbers" (PHS, 84), which he maintains "is superposed upon the first stratum of 'sedimented' geometrical 'evidences'" uncovered by Husserl's fragmentary analyses of geometry in the *Crisis*. In addition, then, to the task of "the intentional-historical reactivation of the origin of geometry" (83), recognized by Husserl as intrinsic to the reactivation of the origin of mathematical physics, Klein recognizes a second task, that of "the reactivation" (84) of the "complicated network of sedimented significances" that "underlies the 'arithmetical' understanding of geometry." According to Klein, Husserl's analyses in the *Crisis* noted this network[8] but did not pursue the task of its reactivation, a task that Klein also argues is crucial for the reactivation of "the 'sedimented history' of the 'exact' nature" constructed by mathematical physics.

Three scholarly curiosities are connected with Klein's presentation of the actual historical development of the exact science of mathematics involved in the origin of modern physics. Each of these is crucial for understanding not only the relation of his thought to Husserl's but also that thought's heretofore unrecognized importance for Husserlian phenomenology's foundational aspirations in the philosophy of mathematics. The first concerns the fact that Klein presents the reactivation of the sedimented arithmetical evidences as a "task," whereas it had in fact already been accomplished by Klein himself (in two long articles published in 1934 and 1936[9]) precisely along the lines of the "actual" development leading to the origin of mathematical physics that he sketched in PHS. Klein's neglect (in PHS) in mentioning his own earlier work on this topic in relation to Husserl's is mirrored by the fact that he altogether neglects to mention Husserl in that work. Thus the second curiosity about the relation of Klein's thought to Husserl's is his silence about its relation to Husserl's phenomenology. As we shall see, given the topic of Klein's work—the transformation of the premodern concept of number into its modern 'symbolic' concept—reference to Husserl's work on the concept of number in the *Philosophy of Arithmetic* and of symbolic cognition in both that work and his *Logical Investigations* would seem to have been natural. Indeed, this has been pointed out by two among the very few scholars aware of the phenomenological horizon of Klein's work.[10]

HUSSERL AND OTHER PHENOMENOLOGISTS

The third curiosity concerns the speculation that the *Crisis*'s "Galileo section might have resulted from a reported visit during this period [sometime in 1934] by Husserl's friend and former student Alexandre Koyré, who published his monumental *Etudes Galiléenes* in 1940."[11] This speculation is fueled by "The striking similarity between Husserl's and Koyré's interpretation of the significance of Renaissance science." However, until recently it has remained unknown that the basic ideas behind Koyré's Galileo research most likely had their origin in Klein's thought and research. Karl Schuhmann publicly called attention in 1997 to Koyré's penchant for appropriating without attribution the ideas of others. Schuhmann notes that Koyré's book on Plato neglected to mention that the source of many of its ideas was Adolf Reinach's lecture course on Plato that Koyré had attended.[12] And a recently discovered interview with Klein's wife mentions that her husband, together with Leo Strauss and Koyré were together in Paris in the early 1930s, and that ideas Klein explained to Koyré ended up being published by Koyré without acknowledgment.[13] According to Klein's wife,

> Strauss was furious and didn't want to have anything more to do with Koyré. But instead of telling Koyré, "Why did you do that? I was present," he just didn't answer and didn't talk to him—simply mistreated him. ... Jasha [Klein's nickname] simply laughed, and said, "Well, I'm very glad that he got it."[14]

Klein's ideas most likely concerned[15] "the elaboration of a study of Galileo's physics and its relation to Plato, Aristotle, and Archimedes,"[16,17] which Klein planned to develop after he completed (in the spring of 1934) the two already mentioned long articles titled "Die griechische Logistik und die Entstehung der Algebra."[18]

Foundational Problems in the Philosophy of Arithmetic

Husserl's first philosophical problem was that of the foundation of the concept of number, where number is understood to be the answer to the question: how many? His formulation of this problem, in turn, had two dimensions. The first concerned the problem of accounting for the objective unity of the most basic numbers, that is, those with which we count. The second concerned accounting for the manner in which these numbers provide the logical foundation for the higher, symbolic numbers, including those employed in universal analysis. The issue behind the first foundational problem is the following. Each number with which we count is composed as the unity of a multiplicity, beginning with the unity of the least multiplicity, the number 'two'. Given that the unity of each number cannot be accounted for on the basis of the individual qualities proper to the items in the multitude composing the multiplicity of which the number is the unity, the problem that presents itself is how to account for the unity of number in question. The issue behind the second foundational problem is the following. Granted the mathematical-foundational role of the most basic numbers, the general concept of which is captured by the Euclidean definition of number as "a multitude composed of units," the problem that presents itself is how to account for the 'numerical' significance of the following 'kinds' of numbers: those that are either too large to permit the direct apprehension—all at once—of the multitude of discrete units that are proper to it, or those that are functionally irreducible to the concept of number as a multitude of units (e.g., negative numbers, irrational square roots, etc.).

Husserl's investigation of the problem of number in his first major work, *Philosophy of Arithmetic*, operates within a terminological universe that moves between the "presentation" (*Vorstellung*) and "concept" of its subject matter, and does so in a manner that distinguishes between "authentic" or "proper" (*eigentlich*) instances of each. Thus, and most crucially, Husserl distinguishes the "proper concept" of number as "the unity of a multitude of units" from the "proper presentation" of number as the amount of units a single act of consciousness can apprehend discretely all at once. Moreover, number itself in Husserl's investigation has neither the status of a concept nor of a presentation, but rather precisely that of the concrete unity of a multiplicity of units, of discrete items either perceived or thought. The concrete unity in question here is not 'conceptual', where concept is understood, as Husserl understands it, in terms of the quality shared by objects having a common meaning. This is the case because the status of the unity proper to the numerical unity of the perceived or thought discrete items that compose a given number is not that of a common quality belonging to that number qua the number that it is; rather, it is that of the belonging together of exactly so many concrete units *as the one* number that it is. For example, Socrates and Hippias are each one, and both together two: their amount as two is not predicated of them individually but only collectively. This state of affairs gives rise to the question of the origin of the collective unity manifest here, since it cannot originate in the predicative qualities of the individuals that are unified collectively. Likewise, the concrete numerical unity in question here does not have the status of being a presentation, because as Husserl understands it, presentational unity is manifestly a psychological content, not an objective or logical one. Thus while the concept of number, in the sense of number "in general," signifies for Husserl the unity of a multiplicity of units, its species are the natural numbers beginning with the number two, which as mentioned comprises the least multiplicity.

Had Husserl's first work not lacked philosophical maturity, it would have consistently maintained the distinction between the conscious presentation of a multitude of units as a unity and the general concept of the unity of a multitude of units, that is, the distinction between the proper presentation of number and its proper concept. In addition, the distinction between a number concept, say, the concept of 'five'—the general concept of five (fiveness)—and the number 'five'—the concrete unity of any one of the unlimited arbitrary 'one and one and one and one and one' units that falls under this general concept—would have been maintained. Clearly, however, it was Husserl's intention to maintain these distinctions, beginning with the most important one behind which lies his first work's major discovery, namely, that that which falls under the proper concept of number, to wit, the concrete unity of a multitude of units, is *not* a concept but precisely a multitude of units. Thus, 5+7=12 does not signify that the concept 'five' plus the concept 'seven' is identical or otherwise equivalent to the concept 'twelve' but rather it signifies that the 'five' units composed by the *number* five's unity and the 'seven' units composed by the *number* seven's unity, when combined, make up the 'twelve' units composed by the *number* twelve's unity. Moreover, Husserl clearly intended to maintain the philosophical distinction between the proper concept of number in general as the unity of a multitude of units and the proper presentation of the units signified by a number in an act of consciousness. For instance, the empirical limitation of human consciousness to be barely able to entertain in a single act more than three discrete units should in no way impinge upon the validity of the general concept of number as the unity of a multitude of units. Therefore, the inability of consciousness to apprehend the totality of five hundred units in a single act has absolutely no *mathematical* significance in relation to the proper content of the concept of the number five hundred being exactly the unity of a multitude composed of five hundred units.

HUSSERL AND OTHER PHENOMENOLOGISTS

It was also Husserl's intention, however, to account for the objective status of the unity of a number's multiplicity on the basis of the conscious act of combining the units in the multitude composed by the number. Owing to this unity's irreducibility to the properties of the units so combined, its "collective" status clearly cannot be accounted for on the basis of the appeal to qualities possessed by the units. Hence Husserl attempted in the *Philosophy of Arithmetic* to account for its origin in an act of inner reflexion that abstracts the collective unity of the assemblage (*Inbegriff*) of units united in a multiplicity from the act of "collective combination" in which the assemblage is initially composed. This attempt, however, was misguided, and recognized (after the *PA*'s publication) by Husserl himself as such. As he himself would put it, "from the reflexion on acts" of collecting "the concept of collecting... is all that can result"—not the concept of the unity of the collection.[19] The problem Husserl was trying to resolve—that of the origin of the collective unity proper to number—however, was not misguided. Moreover, it's important to note that what was misguided in Husserl's appeal to "psychological reflexion in Brentano's sense" to account for the unity of a collection, the concept of unity, and, finally, cardinal number, was not the logical psychologism Husserl criticizes in the *Logical Investigations*. That is, Husserl's position in the *PA* wasn't that collective unity is *really* psychological because that unity makes its appearance in psychological acts. As we've seen, Husserl's intention was to keep distinct both the presentation and the concept of number from number itself as the concrete unity of a multitude of units. Rather than reduce the objective unity of number to the psychological status of a presentation, Husserl's intention was clearly to account for the origin of that objective unity in the full recognition that its collective property renders it irreducible to the properties of the individual units that it unifies. Husserl's realization of the failure of the appeal to an abstraction from the act of combining units into a collection to account for the origin of that collective unity's objectivity therefore leaves intact the problem of that origin.

Another problem that the *PA's* method of psychological abstraction leaves unresolved is that of the objectivity of the unity of the units that make up each number. To number, as the determinate amount of a multitude of any arbitrary items whatever (e.g., a feeling, an angel, the moon, Italy), there belongs according to Husserl the formal-logical category of "the anything" (*Etwas*), in the exact sense that any arbitrary thing whatever, no matter what it is, can be combined into an arithmetic unity. Thus the units of number, in the precise sense of the combination of "'anything' and 'anything' and..." fall for Husserl under a formal logical category. As to the origin of this category, Husserl again appeals to psychological abstraction, this time from the act of presentation itself, which—qua act—he maintains is without individual content and thus suitable to account for the unrestricted scope of the category in question. Because the abstraction in question does not concern what is presented in the act of presentation but only the act itself, the 'anything' has for Husserl the status of a "negative" determination. What it determines is therefore not the individual content presented in a presentation but the very act presupposed by the presentation of any possible individual content. But, of course, the psychological appeal to the objective origin of this categorial determination in an act suffers in this case from the same psychologistic illegitimacy as in the similar appeal in the case of the objectivity of collective unity. Specifically, the abstractive reflexion directed to the manifold presentative acts in which determinate individual contents are given does not yield the materially indeterminate formal-logical category of the "*Etwas*" but only the materially empty concept of a determinate act of presentation.

HUSSERL AND OTHER PHENOMENOLOGISTS

The psychologism behind the *PA*'s response to the first dimension of the problem of the foundation of number is also related to that book's response to the second dimension of the problem of number's foundation. Or, more precisely, it is related to Husserl's initial approach to the problem of the origin of the numerical significance proper to the higher symbolic numbers, because Husserl eventually abandons that approach in the *PA*'s analyses. Husserl's initial approach to this second problem, as mentioned, is driven by the conviction that the proper concept of number, number as the unity of a multitude of units, provides the *mathematical* foundation for symbolic numbers. However, in the course of his analyses in the *PA* he came to realize that the rules that govern the symbolic calculus in universal analysis assume a complete autonomy from arithmetical *concepts*, as they function instead to stipulate the "rules of the game" governing the combination of sense perceptible signs. Indeed, by mathematical 'symbol' Husserl understands precisely the sense perceptible signs that compose the calculus, which as arbitrarily stipulated letters with no conceptual referent and therefore no meaning apart from the calculative rules that govern their manipulation, function in a manner that will be called "signitive" rather than conceptual. With this realization, the *PA*'s overarching project of accounting for the foundation of the higher symbolic numbers in the proper numbers is effectively abandoned by Husserl.

Husserl's initial account of the foundational role provided by proper numbers for symbolic numbers is based on the assumption that the general concept of each is the unity of a multiplicity of units. He characterizes the identity of concepts involved here in terms of the "logical equivalence"[20] of the objects falling under the concepts of each kind of number, that is, of the proper and symbolic numbers themselves, namely, the concrete presentation of the unity of a multiplicity of units. According to Husserl's (initial) view it is this logical equivalence that makes it possible for symbolic numbers to function as "surrogates" for the proper presentation of numbers and it is the task of the philosophy of arithmetic to account for this possibility. The surrogate function of symbolic numbers is bound up with the peculiar status of the signitive functioning of the sense perceptible sign in which the symbolic number is presented. Rather than represent an absent object, which in the case at hand is the unity of a determinate amount of units, the sign signifies the *idealized* possibility of presenting the unity of a multiplicity of units the totality of which exceeds the capacity of consciousness to intuit. Husserl's account of the idealization in question presents it as an extension of the perceptual acts that collectively combine sensible multitudes. He characterizes these acts in terms of the spontaneous emergence of a "figural moment" that presents sensibly the multitude's unity as a multiplicity that encompasses the items of the multitude beyond their partial intuition. Words like "file," "row," "flock," "gaggle," "covey," "heap" thus express "the existence of quasi-qualitative moments" (*PA*, 203) that can be grasped at once "as unified intuitions analogous to sense qualities" (209). These figural moments naturally function as *signs* "for the full process intended" (213), that is, for actually carrying out the psychical activity of collectively combining all the members in the multitude.

On this view, then, a symbolic number presents the idealized extension of the naturally occurring signs in the experience of collective combination, an extension that works equally well for the symbolic presentation of finite and infinite multitudes. In the latter case, the symbolic "number" functions to present "imaginary" arithmetic objects, as the impossibility in principle of a finite consciousness unifying an infinite multitude of units signals that the mathematical status of the symbolic presentation has entered the domain of the non-actual.

76

HUSSERL AND OTHER PHENOMENOLOGISTS

Husserl's account of symbolic numbers, of course, exemplifies his earlier mentioned inability to maintain crucial distinctions in his analyses. The most obvious case in point is the distinction between the concepts of proper and symbolic numbers and the presentation of such numbers. One result of this is the claim that the *arithmetical* function of symbolic numbers originates in the *psychological* limits of arithmetical cognition of large multitudes. Hence, following this line of analysis, the sense perceptible mathematical sign does not symbolize a kind of number but the extension of the mind's cognitive powers beyond its natural limits to combine collectively the content of the concept of proper number, viz., multitudes of units. In his later analysis, however, Husserl rejects this view of symbolic number, albeit on grounds other than its peculiar psychologism. These grounds concern what he comes to understand as the actual meaning of symbolic numbers in the algorithmic operations of universal arithmetic. Rather than function as "surrogates" for unities of multitudes of units, which is to say, rather than refer indirectly to what falls under the proper concept of number, numbers employed in the symbolic calculus have a symbolic function that is purely "signitive." According to Husserl, this means that the arithmetical meaning of the manipulation of the sense perceptible signs composing the symbolical calculus is not determined by arithmetical concepts but by the "rules of the game" stipulated for whatever operations are in question.

These rules, in turn, are presented in the *PA* as being generated on the basis of their algorithmic "parallelism" with the proper domain of numbers and the actual operations on those numbers. Husserl, however, does not unpack this idea in terms of that work's psychological or logical investigations. The result is what one astute commentator has referred to as a "gap" in Husserl's account of the "step" from the original domain of proper numbers to the domain of their symbolic representation and, beyond that, to the extension of the number domain itself beyond what is admitted in the original domain.[21] This extension includes the natural integers (thus includes "0" and "1") and "imaginary" numbers (negative numbers, irrational square roots, etc.). If that original domain of numbers is identified with the cardinal numbers,[22] the results of Husserl's investigation of the second foundational problem in the *PA* may be summed up as follows: initially guided by the conviction that the cardinal numbers provide the foundation for the algorithm constitutive of the rules of calculation determinative of universal arithmetic, Husserl's discovery of the autonomy of the symbols employed by the latter, from both direct references to concepts and indirect references to multitudes of units, compelled the abandonment of his original conviction. Husserl's letter to Carl Stumpf in 1890, before the *PA* was complete, confirms this summary. In it Husserl relates that "[t]he view by which I was still guided in the elaboration of my *Habilitationsschrift*, to the effect that the concept of cardinal number forms the foundation of universal arithmetic, soon proved to be false." This means, among other things, that "[b]y no clever devices, by no 'inauthentic presenting', can one derive negative, rational, irrational, and the various sorts of complex numbers from the concept of cardinal number." Universal arithmetic, rather, "finds application to the cardinal numbers (in 'number theory'), as well as to ordinals, to continuous quantities, and to n-dimensional manifolds (time, space, color, force, continua, etc.)."[23]

Husserl goes on to relate how, with the realization that "no common concept underlies these various applications of arithmetic," he had to confront the question about its content, about its "conceptual objects," and why he had to reject his original supposition that this content is intrinsically conceptual. That is, he had to reject his initial view that to all of the signs of universal arithmetic there correspond, "at least potentially" (159/15), "designated concepts" (160/15). The view that a "system of signs and operations with signs can replace a system of concepts and operations with judgments, where the two systems run rigorously parallel," only holds (within the context of mathematics) in the case of "ordinary arithmetic [*gemeinen Rechenkunst*]" (159/14). Thus, for instance, if arithmetic "deals with discrete magnitudes, then 'fractions', 'irrational numbers', imaginary numbers and, in the case of cardinal numbers for example, also the negative numbers, lose all sense" (160/15). This is the case because the signs for these numbers, in contrast to the signs that refer to the concepts proper and to discrete magnitudes, are "representatives of 'impossible' concepts." But rather than have to get clear about "how operations of thought with contradictory concepts could lead to correct theorems," which is what Husserl relates he originally tried to do, he came to realize that "through the calculation itself and its rules (as defined for those fictive numbers), the impossible falls away, and a genuine equation remains." Therefore, the system of *arithmetica universalis* "is not a matter of the 'possibility' or 'impossibility' of concepts," but "an accomplishment of the signs and their rules" (160/16). Universal arithmetic is, therefore, "no science, but a part of *formal* logic," which Husserl defines here "as a technique of signs (etc., etc.)" and designates "as a special—and one of the most important—chapters of logic as the technology of knowledge." Husserl also adds, very significantly, that "these investigations appear to push toward important reforms in logic, and that he knows "of no logic that would even do justice to the possibility of an ordinary arithmetic [*gemeinen Rechenkunst*]" (161/17).

Historical Context of the Foundational Problems in the *Philosophy of Arithmetic*

Husserl's discovery of the systematic discontinuity between (1) proper numbers and conceptual objects, and (2) the algorithmic system of operations on signs is tantamount to the realization that neither the proper concept of number—the unity of a multitude of units—nor the proper numbers themselves—any of the unlimited concrete unities of "one and one and. ..."—are capable of forming the foundation for 'universal arithmetic' (symbolic mathematics). And this is where Klein's account of the actual development of the mathematics inseparable from the origin of mathematical physics comes in, as it shows that the premodern concept of number as *Anzahl*—the positive natural numbers beginning with 'two'—undergoes a radical transformation in Vieta's establishment of the algebra that lies at the basis of modern mathematics and modern science. This transformation involves the 'formalization' of number that substitutes for the ideal numerical entities of Greek arithmetic (the unity of determinate amounts of multitudinous units) their symbolic expressions. Because the resulting universal and symbolic mathematics rests on the formalized understanding of number, number as *Anzahl* is in principle incapable of forming the foundation of the new mathematics. Thus Klein's account of the conceptual independence of modern universal and symbolic mathematics from number understood as *Anzahl* tracks Husserl's realization that universal arithmetic does not have its foundation in the proper concept of number and that which falls under that concept. Indeed, the similarity noted here is what is behind Caton's and Miller's characterization of Klein's research in terms of its employing the *a priori* possibilities uncovered in Husserl's systematic investigations for the study of the actual history of mathematics.

HUSSERL AND OTHER PHENOMENOLOGISTS

Despite this similarity, however, there are two fundamental differences between Husserl's and Klein's accounts of these issues, of which Klein was no doubt aware. The first concerns that which is responsible for the universality of the units of non-formalized numbers (proper numbers in Husserl's sense and the premodern *Anzahlen* in Klein's sense). The second concerns the character of the initial indirect relation of symbolic numbers to the concrete unity of the multitude of units characteristic of non-formalized numbers.

Regarding this first difference, we have seen that for Husserl the arithmetic universality of proper numbers has its basis in the formal-logical category of the 'anything' (*Etwas*). Husserl accounts for the capacity of the units of proper numbers to function as variables, such that any arbitrary object whatever may enter into a relation with each unit and be combined in a number, on the grounds that each of these units is itself an extension of and therefore a concrete object that falls under the formal concept of the 'anything'. For Klein, however, the units of *Anzahlen* are not formal-logical but ontological, in the precise sense of their conception as sensibly independent units of thought. For Plato, as for Aristotle, arithmetical universality has its ground in the conviction they share that what is numbered in theoretical arithmetic are units that do not have any sensible qualities and therefore are only accessible to thought. These thought-objects—*noêta*—are the true objects of counting. Rather than present logical concepts under which individual objects fall, *noêta* themselves are the true objects responsible for arithmetic's formality, that is, for number's unrestricted capacity to count any kind of object. Aristotle's dispute with Plato, according to Klein, was not over the pure status of the true objects of arithmetic treated by theoretical arithmetic, but rather over the origin of these objects. Indeed, for Klein the philosophical significance of Aristotle's account of their origin in the *abstraction* (literally, *subtraction*) of all sensible qualities from things until all that remains is their *quality* of being one, only comes to the fore when its status as a critical alternative to the origin of *noêta* found in Plato is considered. This is the case, because for Klein Plato's account of the exclusively *intelligible* origin of *noêta* brings with it the presupposition that the foundational unit of theoretical arithmetic as well as the unity of arithmetical and eidetic multitudes cannot be derived from sensible beings.

The second difference between Husserl and Klein, that regarding the relation of symbolic number to number as a multitude of units, has its basis in their radically different accounts of the symbolic number's origin. We have seen that for Husserl, prior to abandoning the conviction of the foundational role played by cardinal numbers in universal arithmetic, the property responsible for a number being 'symbolic' was manifest in its peculiar "surrogate" function: rather than simply "representing" the totality of the units composing a multitude that is too large to be apprehended by a single conscious act, what made a number 'symbolic' for Husserl was its idealizing extension of the natural sign (the figural moment) made manifest in the perceptual experience of collective combination. The signitive function of that sign, both in the original perceptual experience and in its idealizing extension, involves its association with the possibility in principle of extending any partial intuition of multitudes too large to be apprehended in a single act of collective combination, to other units composing the partially intuited multitude in question.

For Klein, however, what makes a number 'symbolic' is *not* its peculiar surrogate function in relation to the perceptual experience of collective combination or any other experience originating in perception. As shall be discussed in detail below, what makes a number symbolic is its presentation—in a completely determinate intuitable mark—of the indeterminate meaning of the *concept* of a determinate multitude or of multitude in general. Thus, for

79

HUSSERL AND OTHER PHENOMENOLOGISTS

instance, the non-symbolic number five, that is, any multitude of units whose exact amount is 'five', is symbolically expressed as the general concept of '5', that is, "fiveness," which as a concept is manifestly *not* something multitudinous—as it is intuited as the cipher '5'— and therefore is only indirectly related to the multitude of units composing any arbitrary non-symbolic number five. For Klein, as again we shall see in detail below, the step from this symbolic expression of 'five' to the symbolic expression of any number whatever, the variable "a," is but a short one. For the determination of the sense perceptible mark 'a' as a symbol arises with its expression of the general concept of any number, that is, the general concept of a multiplicity as such. Finally, we shall also see that the shift in number represented by either their symbolic expression as *Zahlen* or as number in general originates for Klein in the transformation of the basic unit employed by the arithmetic art of calculation. This transformation moves from the unity of determinate amounts of the units composing *actual* multitudes to the *concepts* as such of *possible* multitudes.

These differences between Husserl's and Klein's understanding of the 'units' that compose non-symbolic numbers and the origin and meaning of symbolic numbers are, I submit, behind the first two scholarly curiosities mentioned above. For Klein to have called attention to the priority of his reactivation of the sedimented understanding of numbers constitutive of scientific modernity in *GMT* over Husserl's research in this area would have immediately invited questions about Klein's silence in that work about Husserl's systematic investigations of very similar phenomena. There can be no doubt that Klein was aware of Husserl's investigations when he wrote *GMT*. In PHS Klein writes that "Husserl's logical researches amount in fact to a reproduction and precise understanding of the 'formalization' which took place in mathematics (and philosophy) ever since Vieta and Descartes paved the way for modern science" (70). Of course, the key qualifier here is "amount in fact." In the remainder of this discussion of Husserl and Klein, I will endeavor to show two things. One, that Klein's researches into the sedimentation of number effectively establish that despite Husserl's monumental "rediscovery" of the non-conceptual and non-presentational *being* of *Anzahlen*, his account of the foundation of their universality remains formal-logical and thus cut off from the true philosophico-mathematico problem of this universality's foundation. Two, that Klein's account of the origin of symbolic numbers in the transformation of the art of calculation effectively establishes that there is a lingering psychologism in Husserl's mature attempts to account for the constitution of the formal-logical unity presupposed by modern mathematics, a transformation that for Husserl supposedly occurs on the basis of "modifications" traceable back to perceptual experience.

In Klein's view, then, the modern understanding of the basic element of arithmetic— number in the sense of *Zahl*—is inseparable from the historical origin of François Viète (Latin: Vieta) of Fonenay's invention of the "Analytic Art (*Artem Analyticen*)" for Princess Mélusine (Catherine of Parthenay) in 1591.[24] According to Klein, to this day this "art" functions as the *sine qua non* for the formalization that makes modern mathematics possible and therefore composes its *foundation*.[25]

Klein's research shows that Vieta presented his analytical art as "the new algebra" and took its name from the ancient mathematical method of "analysis," which he understood to have been first discovered by Plato and so named by Theon of Smyrna. Ancient analysis is the 'general' half of a method of discovering the unknown in geometry, the other half, "synthesis," being 'particular' in character. The method was defined by Theon like this: analysis is the "'taking of the thing sought as granted and proceeding by means of what follows

80

HUSSERL AND OTHER PHENOMENOLOGISTS

to a truth that is uncontested." Synthesis, in turn, is "'taking the thing that is granted and proceeding by means of what follows to the conclusion and comprehension of the thing sought." The transition from analysis to synthesis was called "conversion," and depending on whether the discovery of the truth of a geometrical theorem or the solution ("construction") to a geometrical problem was being demonstrated (ἀπόδειξις), the analysis was called respectively "theoretical" or "problematical."[26]

Klein presents Vieta's innovation to involve the understanding of a novel form of arithmetical analysis found in the recently rediscovered third-century AD text (titled simply *Arithmetic*) of Diophantus of Alexandria as a procedure that is completely parallel to geometrical analysis. This permitted Vieta to treat the sought after and therefore unknown numbers—understood as unities of multitudes of units—as already granted in their *species*. By the *species* of numbers he followed Diophantus' designations in his *Arithmetic*, that is, square, cube, square-times-cube, and cube-times-cube. To the species of each of these unknown and therefore indeterminate quantities as well as to the species of every known quantity, Vieta assigned what he called an "everlasting and very clear symbol" taken from the alphabet (vowels to the known and consonants to the unknown).[27] This allowed both the *possibility* of there being given a determinate amount of units (i.e., a number in the premodern and therefore non-formalized sense of the 'unity of a multitude') to be apprehended in a manner that functioned as if it were *actually* given, and it also allowed known numbers to be expressed by their species. Following this, Klein maintains that the arithmetical need for an analogue to the second part of the geometrical method of analysis, the theoretical or problematic conversion of the synthesis that proved a *particular* theorem or solved a *particular* problem, was dispensed with by Vieta. This made possible for the first time the "analytic"—that is, the indeterminate and therefore 'general'—solution to arithmetical problems. Klein presents three significant results as following from Vieta's innovation: One, the geometrical distinction between the kind of object presented in a theorem and in a problem falls away, such that in the analytic art theorems are equated with problems and with this the synthetic distinction between the "theoretical" and "problematical" dissolves. Two, the exclusive calculation with the *species* of known and unknown numbers made possible by Vieta's analytic art, what he terms "*logistice speciosa*," is employed by him in the service of "pure" algebra and therefore applies indifferently to finding unknown numbers and unknown geometrical magnitudes. And three, because the *logistice speciosa* has but a small interest in the determinate results of the solutions to its calculations—what Vieta terms the "*logistice numerosa*"—the artful procedure of Vieta's analytic method is conceived as a general auxiliary method whose purpose is not to solve problems singly but to solve the problem of the general ability to solve problems. Characterized by Vieta as "the art of finding, or the finding of finding," the general analytic is an *instrument* in the realm of mathematics analogous to the sense in which Aristotle's *Prior and Posterior Analytics* are presented as an *organon* in the realm of all possible knowledge. In this regard, Vieta's conclusion to his *Analytic Art* is telling: "the analytic art... appropriates to itself by right the proud problem of problems, which is: TO LEAVE NO PROBLEM UNSOLVED."[28]

Husserl recognized Vieta's method as marking the appearance of "that 'formalization' or algebraization" which "distinguishes subsequent formal 'analysis' from all material mathematical disciplines."[29] This is consistent with Klein's view that Vieta's formalization is coincident with the invention of the mathematical formula and the first modern axiom system, whereby the syntactical rules of mathematical analysis "define" the object to which they

81

apply. But for Klein it is also coincident with the transformation of both the mode of being of the foundational concept of arithmetic—number—and with this the transformation of the mode of being of the objects of mathematics in general, together with the transformation of the process of abstraction that generates the formal concepts operative in the system of knowledge in general.

Klein therefore presents Vieta's innovation as containing three interrelated and interdependent aspects. One, there is its *methodical* innovation of making calculation possible with both known and unknown indeterminate (and therefore 'general') numbers. Two, there is its *cognitive* innovation of resolving mathematical problems in this general mode, such that its indeterminate solution allows arbitrarily many determinate solutions based on numbers assumed at will. And, three, there is its *analytic* innovation of being applicable indifferently to the numbers of traditional arithmetic and the magnitudes of traditional geometry.

For Klein, the significance of this first innovation is the *formalization* of number and thus of its concept, such that number no longer signifies what it did in Greek arithmetic and in mathematics generally prior to Vieta's innovation, a "multitude composed of units." But, rather, number now signifies the *concept* of such a multitude in the case of known numbers and the *concept* of a multitude as such (or in general) in the case of unknown numbers. Behind this crucial distinction for Klein between a 'multitude' and the 'concept' of a multitude is the fundamental ontological difference between a determinate multitude of items and the concept of such a multitude: the being of the former is multitudinous, that is, more than one; the being of the latter is singular and therefore precisely not multitudinous. Klein maintains that this formalization of number and of its concept can be grasped neither by Aristotelian abstraction nor by Platonic dialectic.[30] This is because, as *formalized*, number is: (1) neither the product of the abstraction that yields the unit that functions to measure a multitude of items, as it is for Aristotle; nor (2) the Ideal unity of such a multitude that is grasped by dialectical thought as being irreducible to the items it unifies once the sensible suppositions of the mathematicians are left behind, as it is for Plato. Rather, for Klein, number in Vieta is the result of the conceptual process of ascending from the mind's unmediated and therefore direct relation to multitudes of items to its relation to its own apprehension of this unmediated and direct relation while simultaneously identifying these two modes of relation. This simultaneous identification of heterogeneous 'relations', namely of (1) the real relation to a multitude of concrete things, and (2) the cognitive relation to the concept of this multitude, is exhibited by the meaning assigned by Vieta both to ordinary number signs and to his algebraic letters. And it was exhibited and therefore manifest for him as it is (according to Klein) for us every time a sense perceptible letter is intuited *as*—and not simply as *signifying*—the general concept in question—whether that concept be of this or that number, for instance, *the concept of any 'two' in general*, or the *concept of any 'number' in general*. That is, for Klein, numerical symbols are not signs with a reference to concepts or objects that are other than the sense intuitable mark taken for the "number" or variable in question, as, for example, '2' or 'a'. It is Klein's original, and profoundly challenging, claim that what is manifest in this intuition of *at once* a sensible mark and a general concept is precisely Vieta's invention of the mathematical *symbol*. The claim is original because prior to Klein's research, the difference between non-formal and formal numbers, to the extent it was noticed at all, was attributed to different degrees in abstractness. It is challenging, because the numerical ontological difference to which Klein is calling attention remains invisible so long as it is approached exclusively from the conceptual level that takes the formalization of number in question for granted. That is, so long as 'number' is self-evidently thought in terms of 'formal' (or, better, 'formalized') concepts, the ontological distinction between the multitudinous being of a concrete multitude of items and the non-multitudinous being of the singular concept of a multitude will be lost on thought.

According to Klein, a mathematically foundational problem follows from the analytic innovation of Vieta's method that concerns the derivation of the syntactical rules that govern the axiom system and establish the systematic context that defines the indeterminate objects to which they apply. Vieta established these rules on the basis of the "*logistice numerosa*" and thus in calculations with determinate amounts of monads, which is to say, in calculations with the "natural" and therefore non-symbolic numbers dealt with by ancient Greek arithmetic. This is what allows letter signs with no numerical properties to nevertheless have a numerical significance in the *logistice speciosa* and in the new algebra for which it is the foundation. Vieta, however, conceptualizes these multitudes composed of units at the *same time* from the perspective of their symbolic presentation, giving rise to the symbolic expression, barely visible today, of the intrinsically non-symbolic *Anzahlen*.[31]

As we have seen, Husserl's attempt to ground the logical objectivity of the concept of number employed in the symbolic calculus of universal analysis in the psychological phenomenon of "collective combination" ended in self-acknowledged failure. However, as already hinted above, Husserl's later works never managed to resolve either of the mathematical problems that the *PA* failed to resolve psychologistically, namely, that of the foundation of the unity of the collective unity constitutive of proper numbers along with the constitution of the formal-logical unity constitutive of symbolic numbers.[32] The common view that the pure logic developed in Husserl's *Logical Investigations* and, more specifically, that the descriptive phenomenological foundation of this logic in categorial intuition is capable of providing logical foundations for both of these mathematical unities is, I believe, misguided.

In the case of the foundation of the "collective unity" of pre-formalized numbers, the categorial distinction between logical 'species' and their 'instances' merely substitutes one philosophically unsuitable solution—psychologism—for another one—logicism. This is the case because so long as the 'collective unity' of a multitude is held to have its foundation in the *concept* of the 'species' of that multitude, the problem of the unity of a non-conceptual manifold is in no way resolved but simply shifted to a higher level. That is, it's shifted to the problem of providing the foundation for the conceptual unity of the manifold presupposed in the extension of the concept of 'species' (or the logically equivalent concept of class) supposedly providing the foundation of the unity of the original manifold. Thus with respect to the problem at hand, to say as, for instance, Jan Patočka says in following Husserl's *Logical Investigations* and in thinking thus that he is resolving it, that "the number five is not my counting to five, nor someone else's counting, nor is it my or some else's conceptualization of five; it is a *species*, a generality, an *ideality* which is realized or given in the individual *instance* of a class of five members,"[33] doesn't resolve the issue. And, again, it doesn't do so because the foundation of the unity of the manifold that instantiates the "class of five members" is in no way provided but simply presupposed as unproblematically given by the unity of the *class* in this account.[34]

83

Symbolic Abstraction

In the case of the formal-logical concept presupposed by the symbolic concept of number, the "anything whatever" (*Etwas überhaupt*) that is the presupposition behind the indeterminate generality presupposed by the various domains of non-proper numbers cannot be generated by an "abstractive" emptying of the "material" content from categories, as Husserl claims. Because the "material" in question is the unity of a multitude of units, the metaphor of "emptying" is clearly not pertinent to the transformation of the concept of number that occurs in Vieta's analytic art with the substitution of the 'concept' of multiplicity for the direct reference to its concrete givenness. Indeed, Klein appeals to the medieval distinction between first and second intentions to clarify what he terms the "symbolic abstraction" responsible for the generation of the formal-logical concept of indeterminate generality, that is, for Husserl's "anything whatever," at stake in Vieta's symbolic expression of number. Klein's clarification unpacks Descartes's philosophical attempt to understand the origin of the novel mode of being that belongs to the symbolic number concept, because according to Klein Descartes's attempt was the first, as well as the last such attempt in the philosophical tradition. In Klein's view, this attempt appealed to the power of the imagination to assist the pure intellect in making visible to it (the pure intellect), as a "symbol," the indeterminate object that it has already abstracted from its own power of knowing determinate numbers. As already mentioned, abstraction in Aristotle presupposes definite beings that are intelligible in terms of common qualities, the latter being "lifted off" the former in accordance with a process that is more logical than psychological; abstraction in Descartes presupposes definite beings but not their intelligibility, in the case at hand their "intelligibility" as so many beings. Rather, Descartes's abstraction works upon the mind's act of knowing a multitude of units, separating out the mind's own conceiving of that multitude, which it immediately makes objective. The mind turns and reflects on its own knowing when it is directed to the idea of number as a multitude of units, and, in so doing, it no longer apprehends the multitude of units directly, in the "performed act" (*actus exercitus*) and thus as object of its first intention, but rather indirectly, in the "signified act" (*actus signatus*), as object of its second intention. Thus, notwithstanding the fact that what is being conceived by the intellect is a multitude of units, the intellect's immediate apprehension of its own conceiving as something, as one and therefore as a being, has the effect of transforming the multitude belonging to the number into a seemingly independent being, albeit a being that is only a "rational being" (*ens rationis*). To repeat: this "rational being" is the result of the intellect—and not, as in Husserl's analysis, the result of the idealization of a tendency intrinsic to the perceptual experience of collective combination. Thus Descartes's account of the intellect secondarily (in reflection) intending a thing already conceived before, and intending it insofar as it has been conceived, is radically different from Husserl's account of the process of idealization overcoming the mind's finitude with respect to its capacity to apprehend large multitudes. When the rational being is then "grasped *with the aid of the imagination* in such a way that the intellect can, in turn, take it up as an object in the mode of a 'first intention', we are dealing with a *symbol*."[35]

The relevance of Klein's presentation of Descartes's account of abstraction to Husserl's is twofold. On the one hand, it establishes Descartes's historical precedent for the problem of accounting for the origin of the formalization of categorial meaning. On the other hand, it discloses that Husserl's account of formalizing abstraction presupposes that which it

HUSSERL AND OTHER PHENOMENOLOGISTS

is intended to account for: the materially indeterminate meaning of the formal category 'anything whatever'.

Abstraction for Descartes is therefore characterized by Klein as "symbolic," because the "concept" (*Begriff*) that it yields is manifestly not something that is lifted off the intelligible qualities of things but rather is something whose very mode of being is inseparable from the following: (1) the intellect's pure—by "pure" is meant completely separate from the things it apprehends—grasping of its own power to apprehend these qualities themselves; and (2) this power itself being apprehended as an object whose mode of being is nevertheless akin to the very things that its mode of being separates itself from. Klein stresses that the "kinship" between the power of apprehension proper to the "pure" intellect and that which is effectively foreign to it (i.e., the things possessing the intelligible qualities that are apprehended by the "pure" intellect's power) is established by making this power "visible." The "kinship" in question pertains not to visibility per se but to that between each individual thing in a multitude and each individual symbol, since each is graspable as the object of a "first intention." The algebraic letter "signs" of Vieta or the "geometric" figures of Descartes are what accomplish this. They are what—in the language of the Schools—allow the object of a second intention to be apprehended as the object of a first intention, and are therefore "symbols." The indeterminate or general object yielded in "symbolic abstraction" is neither purely a concept nor purely a "sign," but precisely the unimaginable and unintelligible identification of the object of a second intention with the object of a first. This identification is "unimaginable" because "images" properly—both for the ancient Greeks and for Descartes—refer to either particular objects of first intentions or to their particular "common qualities."[36] The identification between second and first intentional objects is "unintelligible" because for "natural" predication, to say that a concept is both general and particular "at the same time" is nonsensical.

Klein's account of this peculiar identification of first and second intentional objects therefore represents a first step in unpacking the "'sedimented' understanding of numbers" (PHS, 84) that he maintains "is superposed upon the first stratum of 'sedimented' geometrical 'evidences'" uncovered by Husserl's fragmentary analyses of geometry in the *Crisis*-texts. Thus, in addition to the phenomenological task of "de-sedimenting" the symbolic occlusion of the non-formalized spatial dimension of the life-world identified by Husserl in Galileo's geometrical mathematization of nature, Klein identifies the related task of de-sedimenting the symbolic occlusion of the life-world's concrete multiplicity in Vieta's algebraic formalization of natural numbers.

The analytical philosopher of science Ernst Nagel's critical comments on Klein's "Phenomenology and the History of Science" in his 1941 review of *Philosophical Essays in Memory of Edmund Husserl* provide an instructive occasion to conclude our consideration of Husserl and Klein.[37] They do so by allowing us to address the unintelligibility to natural predication of the symbolic expression of modern mathematics within the context of the third scholarly curiosity characteristic of Klein's relation to Husserl noted above. That curiosity, recall, concerned Klein's indirect role as the source of Husserl's account of Galileo's geometrically mathematizing impulse. After granting that Klein's paper "raises by implication the important question to what extent and in what sense genetic analysis is relevant to the understanding of scientific concepts," Nagel concludes "it is not clear how the psychological (or phenomenological) analysis which Dr. Klein suggests does bear upon the nature and history of geometry or how it contributes to the solution of the concrete problems connected with the use of geometry in the natural sciences." Nagel's lack of clarity has its source in what he sees as Klein's agreement with Husserl "that to be intelligible an object must be understood in terms of its 'constitutive origins' and its 'intentional genesis.'" The problem with this for Nagel is that it places the impossible demand of having to "be at least the demi-urge in order to know anything," because as he understands "Dr. Klein's position, it is only in so far as we grasp the method by which we are supposed to construct or 'constitute' objects that we can really be at home with them intellectually" (303).

Nagel's criticism is informed by the understandable yet misguided presupposition that the aim of phenomenology's "genetic analysis" of scientific concepts is to enhance our understanding of their meaning for contemporary science on the basis of an investigation of their meaning in the science antedating ours. The latter meaning, while out of date, is nevertheless enlisted in the service of contributing to the clarification of our contemporary concepts. Nagel cites "the writings of such men as Mach and Duhem" as exemplifying "[t]hat a historical-genetic account of science can be illuminating and clarifying." This presupposition is of course understandable, since the prevailing philosophical understanding of natural science in the 1930s as well as today takes it for granted that its method and results provide knowledge of "true" nature, or what amounts to the same thing, the "true" knowledge of nature. It is misguided, however, because phenomenology's genetic analysis of historical meaning cannot be characterized without further ado as the straightforward investigation of historically datable 'concepts' against the backdrop of the a priori assumption that those with the most recent date are necessarily ontologically superior. Husserl's key methodical term in this context, "reactivation," is crucial for understanding what is at stake in Husserl's *Crisis*-texts' appeal to 'history'. The history at issue in those texts, for Husserl, is "intentional" in the precise sense of the layers of meaning whose methodically reflective exposure provides foundational evidence for the constitution of the very meaning of the most recently dated concepts, for instance, of their meaning proper to an exact science such as geometry. As presented by Husserl in the *Crisis*-texts, the method behind these reflections aspires not to the grandeur fitting only the demi-urge but rather to the recovery of the integrity of knowledge in the face of the crisis precipitated by knowledge's peculiar naturalization, and, indeed, its naturalization made possible on the foundation of the symbolic formalization of the mathematics employed by modern mathematical physics.

Given Klein's indirect, albeit seminal, role in the Galilean focus of Husserl's *Crisis* writings, it is no accident that he was not only the first but also that he remains to this day the only thinker to have grasped the peculiar phenomenological significance of Husserl's late turn to historical reflection, and in the case at hand, to historical reflection on the origin of an exact science like geometry. The significance at stake here may be succinctly characterized in terms of the following insight. That to the reactivation of the sedimentation of a historically prior "conceptuality" (*Begrifflichkeit*), belonging to a science in the constitution of its historically later conceptuality, there corresponds, in the case of the exact sciences of analytic geometry and universal analysis, two things: (1) the rediscovery of that prior conceptuality; and (2) the disclosure of the latter conceptuality's ontological status as "a symbolic disguise concealing the original 'evidence' and the original experience of things" (PHS, 84).

HUSSERL AND OTHER PHENOMENOLOGISTS

Notes

1. Jacob Klein was born in 1899 in Libau, Russia (which was then in Courland and a part of the Russian Empire and which is now a part of Latvia), educated there, and in Belgium and Germany (1922 Ph.D. Marburg University). He attended Heidegger's lectures in Marburg (1924–28) and studied with Max Planck and Erwin Schrödinger at the Institute for Theoretical Physics in Berlin (1928–29) before emigrating to the United States in 1938 to escape the Nazis. He was a personal friend of Edmund Husserl's family. He taught at St. John's College Annapolis, Maryland, from 1938 until his death in 1978.

2. A letter from Husserl's wife Malvine to her daughter Elisabeth (26 March 1937) mentions a "Klein" whom the editor of Husserl's letters, Karl Schuhmann, identifies as "Der Altphilologe Jacob Klein (geb. 1899)." *Edmund Husserl. Briefwechsel*, vol. IX, ed. Karl Schuhmann (in cooperation with Elisabeth Schumann), 487. (The reference concerns Klein's written communication to Malvine expressing his positive assessment of a publication by Jakob Rosenberg, husband of Elisabeth.) According to Klein's wife, Klein "visited old Husserl in 1919 in Freiburg—he wanted to study with Husserl. He went to Freiburg and visited Husserl. ... But he couldn't study with Husserl because he couldn't get a room there, because it was 1919. All the boys came back from the war, and they had preference, so he went to Marburg. Old Husserl said, 'Well, you study with my old friend Natorp'" (Else [Dodo] Klein, page 14 of a transcript of a tape recording [the original tape recording is apparently lost] among Klein's papers, which are housed in St. John's College Library, Annapolis, Maryland; hereafter cited as "Interview."

3. Jacob Klein, "Phenomenology and the History of Science," in *Philosophical Essays in Memory of Edmund Husserl*, ed. Marvin Farber (Cambridge, MA: Harvard University Press, 1940), 143–63; reprinted in Jacob Klein, *Lectures and Essays*, ed. Robert B. Williamson and Elliott Zuckerman (Annapolis, MD: St. John's Press, 1985), 65–84; hereafter cited in the text as PHS. All citations from this text reflect reprinted pagination. Klein's contribution was a late addition to the volume. In a letter to Klein dated 10 November 1939, Marvin Farber, editor of *Philosophical Essays in Memory of Edmund Husserl*, invited him to submit a paper to the volume. He wrote that Husserl's son Gerhart "has written to me about your ability to have a paper ready for the E. H. memorial volume within a week, or very soon thereafter," and that "unusual circumstances... make it possible at this late date to consider another paper." In a letter to Farber dated 12 November 1939, Klein wrote: "Although the time is very short I can get the article written before the deadline. I shall be grateful to you, if you can extend the time limit to the end of November." Farber eventually extended the deadline to 5 December, in response to Klein's telegram on 27 November 1939 to Farber requesting an extension. In his letter to Farber of 12 November, Klein described his proposed paper as follows:

   "The subject of my paper would be something like Phenomenology and History with special reference to the History of science. I have in mind the *Philosophica* essay which you mention in your letter and, in addition, Husserl's article "Die Frage nach dem Ursprung der Geometrie als intentional-historisches Problem" published in the *Revue internationale de philosophie* (Janvier 1939). (It goes without saying that I should have to refer to other publications of Husserl as well.)

   I should like to add that my intention is not to give simply a commentary on those texts but also to examine the notion of History of science as such."

   All of the correspondence referred to and cited above may be found among Klein's papers, which are housed in the St. John's College Library in Annapolis. I wish to express my thanks to Mr. Elliot Zuckerman, the literary executor of Klein's estate, for permission to cite from Klein's correspondence.

4. First published in the *Revue internationale de Philosophie* 1, ed. Eugen Fink (1939): 203–25. English translation, "The Origin of Geometry," in *The Crisis of European Sciences and Transcendental Phenomenology*, trans. David Carr (Evanston, IL: Northwestern University Press, 1970), 370; hereafter cited as "OG" with English page references. Fink's typescript of Husserl's original, and significantly different, 1936 text (which is the text translated by

HUSSERL AND OTHER PHENOMENOLOGISTS

Carr) was published as Beilage III in *Die Krisis der europäischen Wissenschaften und die transzendentale Phänomenologie. Eine Einleitung in die phänomenologische Philosophie*, ed. Walter Biemel, Husserliana VI (The Hague: Nijhoff, 1954; 1976).

5. First published in *Philosophia* 1 (1936): 77–176. The text of this article is reprinted as §§1–27 of the text edited by Biemel, cited in the previous note; hereafter cited as *Crisis*.

6. Klein's article makes repeated references to "Husserl's notion of 'intentional history'" (PHS, 70; cf. 72–74, 76, 78, 82). However, Klein's consistent use of quotation marks when referring to the expression "intentional history" is misleading, since he and not Husserl was its originator.

7. "Sedimentation" is an important concept that Husserl introduced in his last writings to indicate the status of meaning formations that are no longer present to consciousness but that nevertheless can still be made accessible to it. This status pertains both to the temporal modification of the experience of meaning formations and the role that passive understanding plays in the apprehension of the meaning of concepts and words. In either case, it is sometimes possible to render the sedimented formations present to consciousness again in a process called 'awakening'. In the case of the passive understanding of meaning formations, because it does not reproduce the cognitive activity that originally produced their meaning, Husserl contends that the original meaning becomes diminished and in some sense forgotten. Insofar as the original meaning has not completely disappeared, however, it can still be "awakened" by phenomenological reflection. In the *Crisis* Husserl attempts to 'awaken' the original cognitive activity that gave rise to the meaning formations constitutive of Euclidean geometry, meaning formations that he maintained are "sedimented" in Galileo's project of mathematizing nature.

8. Klein, PHS, 84. Klein refers to *Crisis*, 44–45, where Husserl discusses the "arithmetization of geometry" and the consequent automatic "emptying of its meaning" as "the geometric signification recedes into the background as a matter of course, indeed drops out altogether" (44).

9. See Jacob Klein, "Die griechische Logistik und die Entstehung der Algebra," *Quellen und Studien zur Geschichte der Mathematik, Astronomie und Physik*, Abteilung B: *Studien* 3.1 (1934): 18–105 (Part 1), and 2 (1936): 122–35 (Part 2); English translation: *Greek Mathematical Thought and the Origin of Algebra*, trans. Eva Brann (Cambridge, MA: MIT Press, 1969; reprint, New York: Dover, 1992); hereafter cited in the text as *GMT*.

10. Hiram Caton, "Review of Jacob Klein's *Greek Mathematical Thought and the Origin of Algebra*," *Studi Internationali di Filosofia* 3 (1971): 222–26. In his review of the English translation of Klein's articles, Caton remarked upon Klein's "failure to cite Husserl as the source of his Husserlian terminology" (225), that is, the terminology of the "theory of symbolic thinking" and the "concept of intentionality." It is Caton's contention that precedence for both of these should go to Husserl. In the case of the former, he appeals to Husserl's "remarkably similar theory in the *Logische Untersuchungen* (vol. 2/1, par. 20)." In the case of the latter, he points to how, "by citing the scholastic Eustachias as illustrating the sources of the thinking of Vieta and Descartes," Klein "ingeniously capitalizes on... [the] genealogy" of intentionality, which Husserl took "from Brentano, who in turn took it from medieval logic."

    J. Philip Miller, *Numbers in Presence and Absence: A Study of Husserl's Philosophy of Mathematics* (The Hague: Nijhoff, 1982). He writes: "Although Husserl's own analyses [i.e., in *Philosophy of Arithmetic*] move on the level of a priori possibility, Klein's work shows how fruitful these analyses can be when the categories they generate are used in studying the actual history of mathematical thought" (132).

    As we shall see below, however, the relationship between Klein's analyses of natural and symbolic numbers and Husserl's is more complex than either Caton or Miller is aware. One consequence of this is that the common assumption behind Caton's and Miller's remarks here—that Husserl and Klein understand *exactly* the same thing when it comes to these kinds of numbers and their relationship—cannot withstand critical scrutiny.

11. David Carr, "Translator's Introduction," *Crisis*, xix n. 7. This publication date of Koyré's book is incorrect; it was published in Paris in 1939.

HUSSERL AND OTHER PHENOMENOLOGISTS

12. Karl Schuhmann, "Alexandre Koyré," in the *Encyclopedia of Phenomenology* (Dordrecht: The Netherlands, 1997), 391, referring to Alexandre Koyré, *Introduction à la lecture de Platon* (Paris: Gallimard, 1945).

13. Klein's wife mentions the dates as "'31, or '32" (14).

14. Else Klein, "Interview," 14. Edmund Husserl's daughter Elisabeth (Ellie) Rosenberg, one of Klein's students in a 1933 Plato seminar he taught, invited him to visit her brother Gerhart in Kiel. Klein accepted the invitation, and soon became friends with the extended Husserl family and Gerhart's wife, Else (Dodo) ("Interview," 17). (Gerhart Husserl divorced Else in 1948; she and Klein were married in 1950 ["Interview," 9].)

15. Klein's wife's memory that the ideas concerned "something from one of the [Plato's] dialogues" is clearly confused, since Koyré's Plato book, based on lectures he gave in Cairo in 1940, was published in 1945. However, two articles containing parts of *Etudes Galiléenes* had already appeared in 1937: "Galilée et l'expérience de Pise," in *Annales de l'Université de Paris* 12 (1937): 441–53; "Galilée et Descartes," in *Travaux du IXᵉ Congrés international de Philosophie* 2 (1937): 41–47, which makes it much more than likely that it is they that contain the unacknowledged ideas borrowed from Klein reported by his wife.

16. Curtis Wilson, "Preface" to *Essays in Honor of Jacob Klein* (Annapolis, MD: St John's College Press, 1976), ii. Wilson, whose source for this information was most likely Klein himself, reports that Klein was engaged in this study from1935 to 1937 while a fellow of the Moses Mendelssohn Stiftung zur Förderung der Geisteswissenschaften. Klein's status as a Jew led to his exile from Germany in 1937 and the impossibility of continuing his Galileo studies during those turbulent times. See also Klein's letter to Leo Strauss, 9 November 1934, in *Leo Strauss Gesammelte Schriften*, Bd. 3, ed. Heinrichand Wiebke Meier (Stuttgart/Weimar: J. B. Metzler, 2001), 521, in which he discusses his plans to publish a study on Galileo, Aristotle's *de coelo* and Archimedes; and Klein's letter to Krüger, 13 February 1930: "Als Habilitationsschrift würde ich in zwei Monaten eine Arbeit über Galileis Dialog im Verhältnis zum *de coelo* und *Timaios* fertigsgeotellen." ["For my qualifying thesis I would complete in two months a work about Galileo's dialogue in relation to *de coelo* and *Timaeus*."]

17. Recently Dermot Moran (*Husserl's Crisis of the European Sciences and Transcendental Philosophy: An Introduction* [Cambridge: Cambridge University Press, 2012]), and Rodney Park r following him ("The History Between Koyré and Husserl," forthcoming, in *Hypotheses and Perspectives within History and Philosophy of Science: Homage to Alexandre Koyré,s 1964–2014*, ed. Raffaele Pisano, Joseph Agassi, and Daria Drozdova [Berlin: Springer]) have suggested, contrary to Carr's suggestion that Husserl's Galileo section may be the result of a visit by Koyré in 1934, that the evidence points rather to Husserl being the source of Koyré's interest in Galileo. On the one hand, Moran points out, "Reinhold Smid has shown (*HUA*, 24.il n.2) that Koyré's last visit with Husserl was in July 1932, prior to the appearance of Koyré's studies on Galileo that began to appear in artilce form from 1935 on" (72). Smid, moreover, also quotes Ludwig Landgrebe, who reported that he met Koyré in Paris in 1937 and Koyré told him he was "very much in agreement with the Galileo interpretation in the *Crisis*" (*HUA*, 24.il n.2). On the other hand, Moran speculates that "Husserl's interest in Galileo's use of geometry was most probably influenced by Jacob Klein, who had published a number of works on the origins of Greek geometry between 1934 and 1936" (72–73). Parker, in addition, cites Aaron Gurwitsch, who "recalls that Koyré once remarked that, 'even though Husserl was not a historian by training, by temperament, or by direction of interest, his analysis provides the key for a profound and radical understanding of Galileo's work. He submits [Galilean] physics to a *critique*, not (once again be it said) a criticism'" (3, ms). Parker also relates that "Gurwitsch points out that some of the preparatory studies for the *Crisis* date from the late 1920s, perhaps referring to texts dealing with the 'Mathematisierung der Natur' written in 1926, and notes also that 'some of the relevant ideas can be found, at least in germinal form, as early as 1913'" (24, ms).

This evidence, however, is not only inconclusive but also in one instance flawed. Regarding the chronology, we've already seen that Klein's wife reports 1931 or 1932 as the dates in Paris that Koyré absorbed Klein's ideas. These dates, then, are consistent with the date Smid (following Karl Schuhmann) reports Koyré last visited Husserl, July 1932. Moran's suggestion that Klein's articles on the origins of Greek geometry (which are dated 1934 and 1936 but actually were published together in 1936 in a single volume) most probably influenced Husserl's understanding of Galileo is very problematic. This is the case because the focus of the articles in question is *not* geometry but the transformation of the ancient Greek concept of number that occurred with the invention of modern algebra. Neither Greek geometry nor Galileo are thematically treated in Klein's articles. (See note 10 above, for bibliographic information on the German originals of the articles and their English translation by Eva Brann.) In addition, Gurwitsch's claim that the preparatory studies for the *Crisis* date from the 1920s and before, and Parker's singling out in particular Husserl's texts on the mathematization of nature in 1926, do not establish that Husserl's appreciation of Galileo's role in the establishment of modern mathematical physics and the mathematization of nature in these texts is sufficient to account for his account of Galileo's role in the mathematization of the life-world in the *Crisis*, together with Husserl's presentation of the Greek mathematical context of Galileo's mathematization in this account. In fact, close study of these texts discloses the basis for the opposite conclusion, namely, the *Crisis*'s account of the reinterpretation of Euclidean geometry that is sedimented in Galileo's mathematization of nature is unprecedented in Husserl's pre-*Crisis* discussions of Galileo and the mathematization of nature. Finally, neither Koyré's expression of appreciation for (to Gurwitsch) or agreement with (to Landgrebe) Husserl's critique of Galileo in 1937 rules out the possibility that Koyré's appropriation of Klein's ideas about the relation of Galileo's physics to ancient Greek mathematics influenced Husserl in their 1932 meeting. It's clear that Koyré's appreciation and agreement relate to the aspect of Husserl's analysis that goes beyond their historical presentation of Galileo, that is, to their phenomenological dimension, regarding which he of course could not have influenced Husserl.

18. Oskar Becker, whose article "The Theory of Odd and Even in the Ninth Book of Euclid's *Elements*" appeared in the same journal that Klein's first article appeared in, refers therein to Klein's article as "a very important work." *Quellen und Studien zur Geschichte der Mathematik, Astronomie und Physik*, Abteilung B: *Studien* 3.1 (1934): 533–53.

19. "Entwurf einer 'Vorrede' zu den *Logischen Untersuchungen* (1913), ed. Eugen Fink, in *Tijdschrift voor Philosophie* (1939): 106–33; English translation, *Introduction to the Logical Investigations*, trans. Philip J. Bossert and Curtis H. Peters (The Hague: Martinus Nijhoff, 1975), 127 (German page number, which is reproduced in the English translation.)

20. Husserl holds that, "Two concepts are logically equivalent when each object of the one is also an object of the other, and conversely. That, for the purposes of our interests in forming judgments, symbolic presentations can surrogate, to the furthest extent, for the corresponding authentic presentations rests upon this circumstance" (*PA*, 194, my emphasis).

21. Ulrich Majer, "Husserl and Hilbert on Completeness: A Neglected Chapter in Early Twentieth Century Foundations of Mathematics," *Synthese* 110 (1997): 41–44.

22. Insofar as for Husserl proper numbers begin with the least multiplicity ('two') and cardinal numbers begin with '1', this identification is not without its problems. See Majer, "Husserl and Hilbert on Completeness," 42.

23. "Husserl an Stumpf, ca. Februar 1890," in Edmund Husserl, *Briefwechsel*, Band I, ed. Karl Schuhmann (Dordrecht: Kluwer, 1994), 158. English translation, "Letter from Edmund Husserl to Carl Stumpf," in Edmund Husserl, *Early Writings in the Philosophy of Logic and Mathematics*, trans. Dallas Willard (Dordrecht: Kluwer, 1994), 13; hereafter cited in the text as "Stumpf Letter," with page numbers referring to the original and the English edition, respectively.

24. Francisci Vietae, *In Artem Analyticem* (sic) *Isagoge*, Seorsim excussa ab opere restitute Mathematicae Analyseo, seu, Algebra Nova (*Introduction to the Analytical Art*, excerpted as a separate piece from the *opus* of the restored Mathematical Analysis, or *The New Algebra* [Tours, 1591]). English translation, f *Introduction to the Analytic Art*, trans. J. Winfree Smith, appendix to Jacob Klein, *Greek Mathematical Thought and the Origin of Algebra*, trans. Eva Brann (Cambridge, MA: MIT Press, 1968); hereafter cited in the text as *Analtyic Art*.

HUSSERL AND OTHER PHENOMENOLOGISTS

25. See Jacob Klein, *GMT*, and Burt C. Hopkins, *The Origin of the Logic of Symbolic Mathematics: Edmund Husserl and Jacob Klein* (Bloomington, IN: Indiana University Press, 2011); hereafter cited as *Origin*.

26. Vietae, *Analytic Art*, 320.

27. Vietae, *Analytic Art*, 340.

28. Vietae, *Analytic Art*, 353 (capitals in original).

29. Edmund Husserl, *Formale und transzendentale Logik* (The Hague: Nijhoff, 1974); English translation, *Formal and Transcendental Logic*, trans. Dorion Cairns (The Hague: Nijhoff, 1969), 48; page numbers refer to the original, and are included in the English translation.

30. In Klein's view, the prevalent attempt to capture the difference between the ancient and modern concepts of number in terms of the latter's greater "abstractness" falls short of the mark of the difference in question, which, as we have seen, cannot be measured in terms of degrees of abstraction but only in terms of the transformation of the basic unit of arithmetic from a determinate multitude to the *concept* of such a multitude.

31. Vieta's conceptualization of numbers grasped as *Anzahlen*, that is, determinate amounts of units, at the same time from the conceptual level of their symbolic formulation, is the historical precedent behind Husserl's conviction that in the case of ordinary arithmetic the system of signs and operation with signs runs "rigorously parallel" to the "system of concepts and operation with judgments" (*Stumpf Letter*, 159/14). As we have seen, the symbolic level of conceptualization initiated by Vieta treats the *concepts* of determinate multitude of units (e.g., two units, three units, etc.) as numerically equivalent with their non-conceptual multitudes. Thus, the "number two" is conceptualized as the general concept of 'two', which is to say, 'twoness', while at the same time the numeral '2' is identified with the (non-conceptual) number itself, viz., the determinate multitude of two units. This formulation of *Anzahlen* from the conceptual level of their symbolic formulation is what, according to Klein, is responsible for what is now the matter of fact identification of ordinary (cardinal) numbers with their signs (numerals). Thus the systematic parallelism between symbolically and conceptually conceived numbers appealed to by Husserl *presupposes* rather than accounts for the symbolic expression of *Anzahlen*; this is the case because what falls under the 'concepts' that are expressed by the system of symbolically employed signs on Husserl's view are not "determinate amounts of units" (*Anzahlen*) but the self-identical and therefore manifestly non-multitudinous general concepts (the individuated species) of the cardinal numbers or the general concept of being a cardinal number as such.

32. Burt C. Hopkins, "Husserl's Psychologism, and Critique of Psychologism, Revisited," *Husserl Studies* 22 (2006): 91–119.

33. Jan Patočka, "The Philosophy of Arithmetic," in *An Introduction to Husserl's Phenomenology*, ed. James Dodd, trans. Erazim Kohák (Chicago, IL: Open Court, 1996), 35.

34. See Klein, *Origin*, chap. 32.

35. Klein, *GMT*, 208.

36. Indeed, it is for this reason that Descartes, on Klein's view, stresses the "power" of imagination, and not the imagination's "images," to assist the pure intellect in grasping the completely indeterminate concepts that it has separated from the ideas that the imagination offers it, because these ideas are precisely "determinate images"—and therefore, intrinsically unsuitable for representing to the intellect its indeterminate concepts. The imagination's power, however, being indeterminate insofar as it is not limited to any particular one of its images, is able to use its own indeterminateness to enter into the "service" of the pure intellect and make visible a "symbolic representation" of what is otherwise invisible to it, by facilitating, as it were, the identification of the objects of first and second intentions in the symbol's peculiar mode of being. The imagination's facilitation involving, as it were, its according its "power" of visibility to the concept's invisibility.

37. Ernest Nagel, "Review of *Philosophical Essays in Memory of Edmund Husserl*, ed. Marvin Farber, *The Journal of Philosophy* 38.11 (22 May 1941): 301–6.

A Tale of Two Schisms: Heidegger's Critique of Husserl's Move into Transcendental Idealism

George Heffernan

Philosophy Department, Merrimack College, North Andover, MA, USA

ABSTRACT

The history of the early phenomenological movement involves a tale of two schisms. The Great Phenomenological Schism originated between 1905 and 1913, as many of his contemporaries, for example, Pfänder, Scheler, Reinach, Stein, and Ingarden, rejected Husserl's transformation of phenomenology from the descriptive psychology of his *Logical Investigations* (1900/1901[1]) into the transcendental idealism of his *Ideas I* (1913). The Phenomenological-Existential Schism started between 1927 and 1933, as with *Being and Time* (1927) Heidegger moved away from Husserl's transcendental phenomenology of consciousness toward an ontological analytic of existence. Yet these schisms were not unrelated developments. Closely following the documentary evidence to determine the exemplary nature of Heidegger's critique of Husserl's move into transcendental idealism, this essay establishes the inextricable linkage between the Great Phenomenological Schism and the Phenomenological-Existential Schism.

Introduction: The Relationship between the Two Schisms

It is generally accepted that there were two schisms in the early phenomenological movement. The first, the Great Phenomenological Schism, originated between 1905 and 1913, as many of his younger contemporaries, for example, Alexander Pfänder (1870–1941), Max Scheler (1874–1928), Adolf Reinach (1883–1917), Edith Stein (1891–1942), and Roman Ingarden (1893–1970), rejected Edmund Husserl's transformation of phenomenology from the descriptive psychology of his *Logical Investigations* (1900/1901[1]) into the transcendental idealism of his *Ideas for a Pure Phenomenology and Phenomenological Philosophy, First Book: General Introduction to Pure Phenomenology* (1913). The second, the Phenomenological-Existential Schism, started between 1927 and 1933, as with *Being and Time* (1927) Martin Heidegger (1889–1976) moved away from Husserl's transcendental phenomenology of consciousness toward an ontological analytic of human existence (*Dasein*) as the way to an interpretation of the question of the meaning of Being (*Sein*). It is also generally accepted that the first schism is less well known than the second.

HUSSERL AND OTHER PHENOMENOLOGISTS

This essay is about neither the first schism nor the second schism per se but rather about the relationship between the two. It indicates that there is not only undeniable underlapping but also overwhelming overlapping between the two schisms and that the chronological distinction between them is not as sharp as the standard dating implies. It suggests that the first schism anticipated the second and the second recapitulated the first, so that, although the first could have occurred without the second, the second would not have happened as it did without the first. This interpretation leads to the conclusion that the schism between descriptive psychology and transcendental phenomenology is the proper horizon on which to understand the schism between Husserl's phenomenology of consciousness and Heidegger's hermeneutics of existence. The historical evidence for this interpretation is circumstantial but compelling, for there is considerable temporal continuity between the two schisms. First, the Great Phenomenological Schism continued far into the time of the Phenomenological-Existential Schism, and the first schism did not abruptly erupt with *Ideas I*, since Husserl had practiced the method of phenomenological reduction in the "Seefelder Manuscripts on Individuation" (1905–1909) and clarified it in *The Idea of Phenomenology* (1907).[1] Further, the second schism had begun during the time of the first, which was starting rather than stopping in 1913. Finally, positing a dichotomy between the two developments obscures the continuity between them. One need only examine the exemplary evidence in the case of the special break between Husserl and Heidegger to see that the break must be understood both as a process and as an event.

The essay focuses on the philosophical evidence, for there is a remarkable coincidence between the issues that separated Husserl and the early phenomenologists and the ones that divided him and Heidegger. A short list of these issues includes but is not exhausted by the realism-idealism debate, the critique of the nature of reflection and the method of reduction, the argument for the existence of the transcendental ego, the problem of the existence of the external world, the function of intentionality, and, above all, the relationship between descriptive phenomenology and transcendental idealism.[2] These topical coincidences indicate that, as the Great Phenomenological Schism is *not only* about the philosophical differences between Husserl and Pfänder, Scheler, Reinach, Stein, Ingarden, and other phenomenologists, *but also* about those between Husserl and Heidegger, so the Phenomenological-Existential Schism too is *not only* about the philosophical differences between Husserl and Heidegger, *but also* about those between Husserl and Pfänder, Scheler, Reinach, Stein, Ingarden, and other phenomenologists. Many philosophers in the early phenomenological movement were perplexed at the primacy, suggested by Husserl, of theory over practice, reflection over action, logic over ethics, essence over existence, eternity over history, science over life, objects over things, or, in a word: *Bewusstsein* over *Dasein*. They were concerned that the methodical performance of the transcendental reduction and the rigorous focus on "thoughts as thoughts" (*noemata*) did not lead *toward* but rather led *away from* "the things themselves" (*die Sachen selbst*), resulting in a loss of access to their Being (*Sein*).

A fateful interpersonal connection between the Great Phenomenological Schism and the Phenomenological-Existential Schism lies in the fact that Husserl first placed his hopes for the future of phenomenology in Pfänder, a pivotal figure in the first schism. Eventually, however, Husserl came to regard Pfänder as "bogged down" in "ontologism" and "realism" because he neglected the idealistic transformation of Husserlian phenomenology.[3] Then Husserl transferred his hopes, again only temporarily, to Heidegger, the leading figure in the

HUSSERL AND OTHER PHENOMENOLOGISTS

second schism. Ironically, Husserl later confessed his error of judgment about Heidegger, his philosophy, and his character to none other than Pfänder.[4] Tragically, Reinach had fallen for his *Vaterland* in the Great War on November 16, 1917, and could not succeed Husserl at Freiburg.[5]

Thus the essay seeks an answer to the question: How can the Great Phenomenological Schism and the Phenomenological-Existential Schism illuminate one another philosophically? These schisms were, after all, not unrelated developments. Closely following the documentary evidence to determine the exemplary nature of Heidegger's critique of Husserl's move into transcendental idealism, this essay establishes the inextricable linkage between the Great Phenomenological Schism and the Phenomenological-Existential Schism.

An "Average" Account of the Relationship between Husserl and Heidegger

In the sense in which Heidegger uses the words in *Being and Time*,[6] there is an *average*, *everyday*, and *vague* understanding of the relationship between Husserl and Heidegger. "One can say" (*man kann sagen*),[7] in "idle talk" (*Gerede*),[8] something like this: Edmund Husserl (1859–1938) precedes and prepares the way for Martin Heidegger (1889–1976). Husserl is Heidegger's teacher, and Heidegger is Husserl's student. They are first mentor and mentee, then master and apprentice, and finally collaborators and colleagues. Gradually they develop not only a friendship but also a family-ship, with Husserl as a kind of father-figure and Heidegger as a kind of filius-figure. Heidegger dedicates *Being and Time* to Husserl (1926), who publishes it in his *Yearbook for Philosophy and Phenomenological Research* (1927) and arranges for Heidegger to succeed him to his chair at the University of Freiburg (1928). But then something, one knows not exactly what, happens. At first imperceptibly and at length unmistakably, their relationship unravels. Although it is hard to identify any event as the one that finalizes the break, the breakdown as a process can be dated to 1927–1933. There can be no doubt that a pivotal point is the failed attempt by Husserl and Heidegger to compose together an article on phenomenology for the Encyclopaedia Britannica (1927–1928). When Heidegger arrives in Freiburg as his successor, he breaks off professional contact with Husserl (1928). On April 6–7, 1933, Husserl, a Jew, is "vacated," along with all "non Arian" civil servants, from his university position by discriminatory National Socialist legislation, while Heidegger becomes the rector of the University of Freiburg on April 21, 1933, and joins the N.S.D.A.P. on May 1, 1933. On May 27, 1933, Heidegger delivers his morally ambiguous rector's address, "The Self-Assertion of the German University," leading one observer to remark that by the end of the speech 'one did not know whether one should read the Pre-Socratics or march with the Storm Troopers.'[9] When Husserl dies in 1938, Heidegger, pleading illness, does not attend his funeral. Rumors arise about the relationship between them, the most notable of which is that Heidegger was "a potential murderer" because he forbade Husserl access to the Philosophy Faculty at the University of Freiburg.[10] This would be the *average*, *everyday*, and *vague* "understanding" of the relationship between these two thinkers. It is superficial and requires scrutiny.

Heidegger's Account of His Relationship with Husserl

The evidence for a *final* break between Husserl and Heidegger between 1927 and 1933 is convincing. Yet the evidence for an *early* break between 1913 and 1927 is also persuasive.

HUSSERL AND OTHER PHENOMENOLOGISTS

It is circumstantial but compelling. The key to understanding the relationship between Husserl and Heidegger is the paradigm shift from viewing the publication of *Being and Time* only as the *terminus a quo* of their break to seeing it also as a *terminus ad quem*. In fact, the publication of Husserl's *Ideas I* (1913) had as much to do with their break as did the appearance of Heidegger's *Being and Time* (1927). There were two phases in the process of their break, the years 1913–1927 and the years 1927–1933. To date, the focus has been too much on the second time frame and too little on the first. A balanced judgment attributes appropriate weight to the earlier time frame and to the later.

Properly understood, Heidegger's "My Way Into Phenomenology" (1963/1969) is the key to understanding his relationship to and break with Husserl.[11] The obvious problems with Heidegger's account are that it was written long after the events that it records, that it is Heidegger's account only and not also Husserl's, and that for personal and professional reasons Heidegger has an interest in putting the best face on his past break with his former promoter. Also, the essay dates from around the time of Heidegger's "Spiegel Interview," which has long been recognized as revisionist.[12] Finally, the essay is not so much a philosophical dialogue with Husserl as a professional tribute to Hermann Niemeyer, the publisher of such foundational works of phenomenology as Husserl's *Logical Investigations* and *Ideas I*, as well as Heidegger's *Being and Time* (92). It is a very brief history of phenomenology from the perspective of the House of Niemeyer. Therefore one should, of course, be skeptical of the accuracy of Heidegger's account. Independent investigation shows, however, that other evidence from other sources strongly corroborates the account, which is then consistent with that other evidence. This also holds for Heidegger's other statements pertaining to his relationship to and break with Husserl. The following reading focuses on the evidence in "My Way" that is relevant to the question about the relationship between the Great Phenomenological Schism and the Phenomenological-Existential Schism.

Heidegger begins "My Way" by recounting the familiar path marks of his earliest philosophical development. He reports that since 1907, when he was still in the Gymnasium, Brentano's dissertation *On the Manifold Meaning of Being according to Aristotle* (1862)[13] was the "staff and rod" of his "first awkward attempts to penetrate into philosophy" (81). In 1908, his last year in the Gymnasium, Heidegger also read Braig's *On Being: Outline of Ontology* (1896),[14] which presented long passages from Aristotle, Aquinas, and Suarez, as well as "the etymology of words for the basic ontological concepts" (81–82). In the winter of 1909–1910, Heidegger began his academic studies in the Faculty of Theology at the University of Freiburg, and, having made time for the study of philosophy, as well as having learned "from philosophical journals" that Husserl's "way of thinking" was "determined" by Brentano's, he had the two volumes of the First Edition of Husserl's *Logical Investigations* (1900/1901) on his desk from the start (the theologians were apparently not very interested in it) (81). From the beginning of "My Way," Heidegger makes it clear that, from his "first attempts to penetrate into philosophy" on, his question was not about *being* but about *Being* (81): "If being [*das Seiende*] is said in manifold senses, then what is the leading basic meaning? What is Being [*Sein*]?" Thus Heidegger's question was not Husserl's, which was about consciousness (*Bewusstsein*).

Heidegger reports that his attitude toward Husserl's philosophy was ambivalent from the beginning. On the one hand, he expected from Husserl's *Logical Investigations* "a decisive aid" in the questions stimulated by Brentano's book (82). On the other, his effort to find an answer to his own question about Being with the help of Husserl's work was "in vain,

95

HUSSERL AND OTHER PHENOMENOLOGISTS

because, as [he] only very much later learned, [he] was not searching in the right way" (82). Yet Heidegger remained so fascinated by Husserl's *Logical Investigations* that he "read in [the work] again and again in the following years," but "without gaining sufficient insight into what fascinated" him (82). Husserl's work emanated "magic," but Heidegger's understanding of phenomenology was "limited and vacillating" (82). In 1911, Heidegger gave up his theological studies, and, in 1912, began his philosophical studies under Heinrich Rickert (1863–1936), a leading Neo-Kantian known for his work in theory of knowledge (82–83).[15]

According to Heidegger, it was his turn toward the transcendental philosophy of knowledge of Rickert, and especially of his pupil Emil Lask (1875–1915), whose works exhibited the influence of Husserl's *Logical Investigations*,[16] that "forced [him] anew to work through Husserl's work" (83). Although he does not mention it in "My Way," Heidegger submitted, in 1913, his doctoral dissertation, "On the Doctrine of Judgment in Psychologism,"[17] under Artur Schneider (1876–1945) as director and Rickert as reader. There he acknowledged the importance of Husserl's contribution to the battle against logical psychologism, the position, dominant in German thought at the time, that not philosophy but psychology is the proper science not only of the acts of thinking but also of the objects of thought as well as of the judgments that express them in logic.[18] Yet "the repeat attempt" to work through Husserl's *Logical Investigations* also remained "unsatisfactory" because Heidegger could not overcome "the chief difficulty of how the manner of thinking that called itself 'phenomenology' was to be carried out" (83). The main concern, Heidegger says, resulted from the "ambiguity" of Husserl's work that showed itself "at first glance" (83). The problem was, or *is*, that the first volume of the *Logical Investigations, Prolegomena to Pure Logic*,[19] refutes psychologism in logic by demonstrating that the doctrines of thought and knowledge cannot be based on psychology, whereas the second volume, *Investigations into Phenomenology and Theory of Knowledge*,[20] contains the descriptions of the acts of consciousness that are essential for the structure of knowledge (83). To Heidegger, the second volume, which was three times longer than the first, seemed to represent psychology, and Husserl, with his phenomenological descriptions of the phenomena of consciousness, seemed to have "relapsed" into the psychologism that he had refuted in the first volume (83).[21] This seemed to him to hold especially for the analyses of "intentional experiences and their 'contents'" in the Fifth Investigation (83). Yet, Heidegger asked, if such "a gross error" could not be attributed to Husserl's work, then what are the phenomenological descriptions of the acts of consciousness supposed to represent (83)? What is supposed to be special about phenomenology if it is neither psychology nor logic (83)? Is it supposed to be a new, important, discipline in philosophy (83–84)? Heidegger reports that he "could not disentangle these questions," that he "remained without knowing what to do or where to go," and that at the time he "could hardly even formulate the questions with the clarity with which they are expressed" in "My Way" (84).

Heidegger distinguishes carefully between *now* and *then* in his account, so as not to project into the past insights that he possesses in the present. Thus there emerges here, *in the years between 1909 and 1913*, a first level of ambivalence on Heidegger's part with respect to Husserl's work. So Heidegger's initial attitude of hesitancy and uncertainty toward Husserl's phenomenology is generated by what he perceives as the "ambiguity" in the relationship between the first volume of the *Logical Investigations* and the second. A second level of ambiguity soon follows on Husserl's part, evoking a second level of ambivalence on Heidegger's.

HUSSERL AND OTHER PHENOMENOLOGISTS

In "My Way," Heidegger initially reports that "the year 1913 brought an answer" to his questions (84). Yet he immediately indicates that the publication of Husserl's *Ideas for a Pure Phenomenology and Phenomenological Philosophy, First Book: General Introduction to Pure Phenomenology*[22] in that year introduced a new level of ambiguity for him, which led to a higher degree of ambivalence on his part. Heidegger describes Husserl's "pure phenomenology" thus:

> "Pure phenomenology" is the "fundamental science" of the philosophy that is shaped by that phenomenology. "Pure" means: "transcendental phenomenology." Yet the "subjectivity" of the knowing, acting, and valuing subject is posited as "transcendental." Both terms, "subjectivity" and "transcendental," show that "phenomenology" consciously and decidedly moved into the tradition of modern philosophy, but in such a way that "transcendental subjectivity" attains a more original and universal determination through phenomenology. Phenomenology retained the "experiences of consciousness" as its thematic realm, but now in the systematically planned and secured investigation of the structure of the acts of experience together with the investigation of the objects that are experienced in those acts with respect to their objectivity. (84)

Here Heidegger says that phenomenology "moved into" (*einschwenken*: "to swing into") modern transcendental philosophy. He poses the question of whether this new approach by Husserl provided the answers to the old questions that Heidegger saw raised by the *Logical Investigations*. Given that it is clear from his account in "My Way" that Heidegger does not answer this question affirmatively, it must be understood that Husserl's move from the descriptive phenomenology of the *Logical Investigations* to the transcendental phenomenology of *Ideas I* only served to create for Heidegger another, second, level of ambiguity, leading to another, second, sense of ambivalence on his part. His hesitation and vacillation gradually assume the character of skepticism and rejection.

That this is Heidegger's reaction becomes clear from the fact that he declines to affirm that Husserl's *Ideas I* represented progress in the phenomenological project of attaining "the things themselves," but rather testifies that he and other phenomenologists remained more interested in the *Logical Investigations* than in *Ideas I*. This happened even as, Heidegger relates, Husserl introduced another, a third, source of ambiguity. In the attempt, namely, to assign to the *Logical Investigations*, which, as Heidegger puts it, "had remained, so to speak, philosophically neutral" with respect to the transcendental turn, "a systematic place in the universal project of a phenomenological philosophy," Husserl published the work in a second, revised, edition in 1913 (84). Yet this action introduced a complication within the complication, because only the *Prolegomena* and Investigations I–V were published in the Second Edition of that year, even as Investigations I–V were subjected to various levels of revisions ranging from those which left "obscurities," "errors," and "shortcomings" standing (I) to those which underwent "a very thorough-going revision" (III) and "deep-reaching revisions" (V) (84). In the "Preface" to the Second Edition of the work, Husserl, articulating his vision for the relationship between the *Logical Investigations* and the new work, conceded "the impossibility of raising the old work wholly and completely to the level of *Ideas*," explained his "maxims for revision," and claimed that "in the last investigation the level of *Ideas* [had] essentially been reached."[23] In the case of Investigation VI, "the most important one with respect to phenomenology" (as both Husserl and Heidegger note), however, Husserl did not want to make any compromises, so he withheld its revised version until 1921 in order to introduce a series of new chapters to it (84).[24]

97

HUSSERL AND OTHER PHENOMENOLOGISTS

Even before examining the third level of ambivalence on his part, it should be clear that Heidegger demurs at the development of Husserl's phenomenology from the *Logical Investigations* to *Ideas I*.[25] Instead of acknowledging the validity of "the obvious idea often encountered at that time," that is, that in the year 1913 "a new direction had come about within European philosophy," namely, "phenomenology," Heidegger challenges the correctness of this view with a rhetorical question (85): "Who would have wanted to deny the correctness of this statement?" Yet Heidegger *both does and did* this, for he says that "such a historical miscalculation" failed to account for "what had happened with 'phenomenology', that is, already with the *Logical Investigations*," that "Husserl's own programmatical explanations and methodological presentations rather strengthened the misunderstanding that through 'phenomenology' a beginning of philosophy was claimed which denied all previous thinking," and that this fact "remained unspoken, and can hardly even be rightly expressed today," that is, in 1963 (85). Putting it beyond doubt that he declined to make "the transcendental turn" of Husserl in 1913, Heidegger states simply (85): "Even after *Ideas for a Pure Phenomenology* was published, I was still captivated by the never-ceasing spell that emanated from the *Logical Investigations*." "The spell," Heidegger continues, "brought about anew an unrest unaware of its own reason, although it made one suspect that it came from the inability to attain the act of philosophical thinking called 'phenomenology' simply by reading the philosophical literature" (85). Indeed, "the philosophical literature" to be read now included Husserl's *Ideas for a Pure Phenomenology and Phenomenological Philosophy*! There can hardly be a clearer statement by Heidegger that he was one of the first phenomenologists to balk at Husserl's transformation of descriptive phenomenology into transcendental philosophy with its inevitable move into transcendental idealism.

Heidegger proceeds to report that "[his] perplexity decreased slowly and [his] confusion dissolved laboriously only after he was able to encounter Husserl personally in his workshop" (85). Husserl had arrived in Freiburg in 1916 as the successor to Rickert, who had succeeded Wilhelm Windelband (1848–1915) at Heidelberg. Yet again Heidegger gives with one statement and takes away with another, for he clarifies what he claims to have learned from Husserl (86): "Husserl's teaching took place in the form of a step-by-step training in phenomenological 'seeing', which at the same time demanded that one relinquish the untested use of philosophical knowledge, but also that one give up introducing the authority of the great thinkers into the conversation." The inference is that either Husserl is "a great thinker" and his "authority" cannot be "introduced into the conversation," or he is not and it can be. The clearer it became to Heidegger, however, that "the growing familiarity with phenomenological seeing was fruitful for the interpretation of the Aristotelian writings," the less he was able "to separate [himself] from Aristotle and the other Greek thinkers" (86). Although he adds that he "could not immediately see what decisive consequences the renewed turn to Aristotle" would have for his way into phenomenology, it later became clear to Heidegger that it would lead him away from Husserl's new idea of a transcendental phenomenology of consciousness and its contents and toward a phenomenological hermeneutics of practical life.[26] Without mentioning that he became Husserl's assistant in 1919 (on January 21), Heidegger reports that, "teaching and learning himself in the proximity of Husserl since 1919," he "practiced phenomenological seeing" and tried out "a transformed understanding of Aristotle in a seminar" (86). With this combination of phenomenology and hermeneutics, his "interest leaned anew toward the *Logical Investigations*, above all, toward the Sixth Investigation of the First Edition" (86). Heidegger says that the distinction

98

HUSSERL AND OTHER PHENOMENOLOGISTS

between sensuous and categorial intuition worked out in that investigation "revealed itself to [him] in its scope for the determination of the 'manifold meaning of being'" (86).

Now the indicated three levels of ambiguity on Husserl's part and the corresponding three levels of ambivalence on Heidegger's part fall into place. The third level of ambiguity on Husserl's part emerges in full and generates a whole new level of ambivalence on Heidegger's part. Referring to the relevance of the distinction between sensuous and categorial intuition for an understanding of the question about the manifold meaning of being, Heidegger says that, "for this reason," "we," "friends and pupils" of Husserl, "asked the master again and again" to republish the Sixth Investigation, which had become difficult to obtain (86). Yielding to their pressure, so to speak, Husserl published the Second Edition of the Sixth Investigation "in the old form" and "only in some sections essentially improved" in 1921.[27] Yet Heidegger reports that Husserl made a point of stating that he did this only for "the friends of the present work," and that in doing so he was also saying that "he himself could no longer really be on friendly terms with the *Logical Investigations* after the publication of the *Ideas*" (86).[28] According to Heidegger, "the passion and effort of [Husserl's] thought at the new location of his academic activity [Freiburg] had more than ever turned toward the systematic development of the program presented in *Ideas*" (86–87). Yet Heidegger and other pupils remained fascinated with the *Logical Investigations*, especially the Sixth Logical Investigation, in their respective First Editions, that is, without the questionable efforts of Husserl to raise them to the level of *Ideas*.

From then on, Heidegger reports, Husserl "observed [him] in a generous fashion, but basically in disagreement, as [he] worked on the *Logical Investigations* weekly in special workgroups with older students" (87).[29] According to Heidegger, it was "above all the preparation for this work" that was "fruitful" for him, and in it, he says, he learned "one thing," first as "a presentiment" and then as "a founded insight" (87): "What takes place for the phenomenology of the acts of consciousness as the manifestation of the phenomena themselves is thought even more originally by Aristotle and in all Greek thinking and existence as Ἀλήθεια [aletheia], as the unconcealed-ness of what-is present, its being revealed, its showing itself." As a result, Heidegger states, what the phenomenological investigations have found anew as "the supporting attitude of thought" proves to be "the fundamental characteristic feature of Greek thinking, if not indeed of philosophy as such" (87). Evidently, Heidegger had discovered "a [new] great thinker," Aristotle, and "introduced" his "authority into the conversation."[30] Indeed, between becoming Husserl's assistant (1919) and publishing *Being and Time* (1927), Heidegger confided to Löwith that he was seriously considering "whether [he] should withdraw [his] Arist[otle]" because, if he published a book indicating his thinking in this direction, "the old man" would "probably" notice that he was "wringing his neck" and "it [would be] over with the succession" in Freiburg—only to add that "[he] could not help [himself]," so that he would, at least for a time, keep going in the same direction.[31] The reference is to the fact that in the fall of 1922 Heidegger had sketched the outline of a book on Aristotle, to appear in Husserl's *Yearbook* after 1923, that would lay out his own "hermeneutics of facticity" or "phenomenology of life."[32] In a research report on the work, Heidegger praises Husserl's *Logical Investigations* as a radical "breakthrough" in phenomenological research, but criticizes the notion that phenomenology should be nothing more than 'conceptual analysis'.[33] He also makes it clear that for him phenomenology is not analysis of consciousness and its contents but investigation of "*human existence*" and its "character of Being."[34] Defined by the shift from the old Husserlian concentration on *Bewusstsein* to a new Heideggerian focus on *Dasein*, the planned work on Aristotle anticipated "the phenomenological hermeneutics of the facticity"[35] of factical life in *Being and Time*, by which it was eventually superseded.

Concluding the section in "My Way" on his relationship to and break with Husserl, Heidegger reports that, the more he saw the connection between the manifestation of the phenomena in the phenomenological sense and the unconcealed-ness of what-is present in the Greek sense, the more pressing for him became the question (87): "Whence and how is it determined what must be experienced as 'the thing itself' according to the principle of phenomenology? Is it consciousness and its objectivity, or is it the Being of beings in its unconcealed-ness and concealment?" In answering the first question with a second question, a rhetorical one implying a clear disjunction, Heidegger indicates that Husserl and he were giving different answers to the same question. In this way, Heidegger says, he was brought to "the path of the question of Being," "enlightened by the phenomenological attitude" and "troubled anew but now differently from before" by the questions that had originally emerged from Brentano's dissertation on being according to Aristotle (87). Yet "the way of questioning," he says, became "longer than suspected" and required "many stops, detours, and wrong paths" (87). Heidegger concedes that his first attempts in his early lectures at Freiburg and Marburg to make way along "the way of questioning" only show the way indirectly (87).[36]

As Husserl moved away from the *Logical Investigations* toward *Ideas*, because he became increasingly interested in transcendental analyses of the contents, that is, the acts and the objects, of consciousness as such, so Heidegger moved away from *Ideas* back to the *Logical Investigations*, in their First Edition, because he considered them more fruitful and useful in his search for an answer to the question about the meaning of Being as inspired by Aristotle and the Greeks and as recapitulated by Brentano.[37] From the beginning to the end of Heidegger's involvement with phenomenology and his encounters with Husserl, he was focused on investigating *Sein* in terms of *Dasein*, whereas Husserl remained fixated on investigating *Sein* in terms of *Bewusstsein*. There can be no doubt that Heidegger viewed the transformation of descriptive phenomenology into transcendental phenomenology accompanied by transcendental idealism as performed in Husserl's *Ideas for a Pure Phenomenology and Phenomenological Philosophy* as a "wrong path" and that he did this at the time at which it happened.

In contrast to his rich description of his relationship with and break with Husserl, Heidegger's remarks on *Being and Time* in "My Way" are cursory in that they are restricted to a few basic facts about the publication of the work. Yet registering this part of the story is crucial for understanding the place of Heidegger's path of philosophizing in the history of the two schisms. Heidegger records that one day in the Winter Semester of 1925/1926 the dean of the Faculty of Philosophy of the University of Marburg (Max Deutschbein [1876–1949]) entered his office to inquire whether he had "a suitable manuscript" for publication (87–88). On August 5, 1925, the faculty at Marburg had ranked Heidegger first as proposed *professor ordinarius* to succeed Nicolai Hartmann (1882–1950). On January 27, 1926, the Prussian Minister of Science, Art, and National Education in Berlin, Carl Heinrich Becker (1876–1933), however, had rejected their request "on the grounds that [he] had not published anything for the last ten years" (88). Now, Heidegger says, it was time to "hand long-guarded work," namely, *Being and Time*, "over to the public" (88). Yet only after a second rejection by the ministry (on November 25, 1926), and the publication of the work

HUSSERL AND OTHER PHENOMENOLOGISTS

itself (in April, 1927), was Heidegger finally named ordinary professor in Marburg (on October 19, 1927) (88). He soon left for Freiburg (1928).

The bureaucratic absurdity of the situation can easily obscure the philosophical point that, because he had published nothing between the appearance of *The Doctrine of Categories and Meaning of Duns Scotus*,[38] his *Habilitationsschrift* (dedicated to Rickert),[39] in 1916 and the dean's inquiry in the winter of 1925/1926, the publication of *Being and Time* in 1927 generated the lasting but misleading impression that Heidegger's new work was the beginning of his break with Husserl, whereas it was, for all philosophical and practical purposes, the end.[40] In "My Way," Heidegger regards the appearance of *Being and Time* as anti-climactic for the rise and fall of his relationship with Husserl. With respect to the connection between the question about the relationship between Husserl and Heidegger and the question about the relationship between the Great Phenomenological Schism and the Phenomenological-Existential Schism, it is significant that Heidegger does not mention the phenomenological reduction in his observations on the phenomenological method of investigation in *Being and Time*,[41] that he praises Husserl's *Logical Investigations* globally but his *Ideas I* locally,[42] and that he consistently seeks *Sein* not through *Bewusstsein* but through *Dasein*. Finally, and decisively, one must understand the pivotal paragraph of *Being and Time* in this regard (§ 43: *Dasein*, Worldliness, and Reality) as a critique of transcendental idealism—as Husserl did.[43]

In "My Way," then, Heidegger is not reinterpreting the past in the light of the future that has become the present. Rather, he is simply telling it like, he thinks, it was—*so, wie es gewesen* (Ranke). Thus "My Way Into Phenomenology" is the narrative of Heidegger's path away from Husserl's move into transcendental idealism. This source, though composed in 1963 and retouched in 1969, is not only internally coherent but also externally consistent with what is known of Heidegger's development between his study of Husserl's *Logical Investigations* and his reading of his *Ideas I*. The ambiguities in Husserl's three philosophical moves, (1) from the first volume to the second volume of the *Logical Investigations*, (2) from the *Logical Investigations* to *Ideas for a Pure Phenomenology and Phenomenological Philosophy I*, and (3) from the First Edition of the *Logical Investigations* to the Second Edition of the work, combined to convince Heidegger that he preferred not to have phenomenology transformed into transcendental idealism. Heidegger was intrigued by the questions that the *Logical Investigations* raised but he did not think that *Ideas I* provided the answers. He suggests that the move from the earlier work to the later represents not progress toward but regress away from "the things themselves."[44] Thus Heidegger's early break with Husserl is part of the Great Phenomenological Schism and pre-dates the Phenomenological-Existential Schism. Heidegger's "My Way" shows that he is such a key figure in these developments because he straddles both sides of both schisms.

Corroborating Evidence for Heidegger's Account

At first, of course, Heidegger's "My Way" may seem like an attempt after the fact to put distance between himself and Husserl before the fact. As shown, however, Heidegger's essay has a strong claim to represent an accurate account of their drifting and breaking apart. The early break between Husserl and Heidegger is corroborated not only by Heidegger's own narrative but also by a long list of contemporary sources, especially their correspondence. After reviewing the corroborating evidence, one may wonder whether Husserl and Heidegger were ever philosophically close.

101

HUSSERL AND OTHER PHENOMENOLOGISTS

One should follow the evidence. In 1917, a year after Husserl's arrival in Freiburg in 1916,[45] Heidegger tells his wife, Elfride, that he cannot accept Husserl's phenomenology as a "finality" because in terms of its "approach" and its "goal" "it is [...] too narrow and [too] bloodless," whereas "life is too rich and too great," so that someone who is *only* a logician" in search of "the absolute" cannot find "the liberating *way*" to "a shaping of relativities."[46] In 1919, Heidegger writes about "historical consciousness" and "life" à la Dilthey to Husserl's daughter, Elisabeth, saying that, "whether our life, in taking shape, really lives its historical living," "everything depends on the fact that it itself *is*," but not on "the theoretical observation of this possibility" and not on "reflection *on it*."[47] In 1919, Heidegger writes to Elfride that, although "with many more horizons and problems" he is "above and beyond [Husserl]," he has chosen "cooperation" with him because "personal" considerations are less important than "scientific" and "practical" ones.[48] In 1920, he describes to her how they are "on the way to a genuine, simple, and elementary grasping of life," but how he is "separated" by "worlds" from Husserl with a "great contrast" between them, so that he must, "solely in order to preserve us materially," get along with him "without violent conflict."[49]

These statements, combined with his account of his way into phenomenology, indicate that long before 1927–1931, and even longer before 1933–1934, Heidegger was critical of Husserl's phenomenology, and that his philosophical critique was connected to his rejection of his former mentor's turn from phenomenology as descriptive psychology in the *Logical Investigations* (1900/1901[1]) to phenomenology as transcendental idealism in *Ideas for a Pure Phenomenology and Phenomenological Philosophy* (1913) (81–90).[50]

Yet Heidegger did not express his concerns about Husserl and his new phenomenology only to his wife. In early 1923, Heidegger writes to Löwith that he has "burned and destroyed" Husserl's *Ideas* in his seminar, and that, looking back to the *Logical Investigations*, he has come to "the conviction that Husserl was never a philosopher, not even for one second of his life."[51] In the summer of 1923, Heidegger writes to Jaspers that Husserl "has become completely unglued [...] if he was ever 'in one piece'," that "he is speaking in such trivialities that one must pity him," that he "is living off the mission of 'the founder of phenomenology'," although "no one knows what that is," and that he "is beginning to suspect that people are not going along with him any longer."[52] In the spring of 1926, Heidegger reports to Jaspers that Husserl "finds the whole thing [*Being and Time*] disconcerting and 'no longer accommodates' it in the usual phenomenology," from which Heidegger infers that he is "de facto already further away" from Husserl than he thought.[53] In the winter of 1926, Heidegger writes to Jaspers that, if *Being and Time* is "written 'against someone'," then [it is] against Husserl," adding that Husserl "also saw that immediately" but "from the beginning stuck to the positive."[54]

For his part, Husserl had sensed the philosophical alienation between himself and Heidegger long before he alluded to it in his public lectures. During their failed attempt to co-author an article "Phenomenology" for the Encyclopaedia Britannica in 1927–1928,[55] it emerged that, whereas Husserl insists on a sharp separation of the pure transcendental ego and the natural human being, Heidegger rejects this egological approach as metaphysical and argues for the unity of the transcendental ego and the factical existence that is a human being.[56] For Husserl, *Bewusstsein* constitutes the *Sinn* of *Sein*; for Heidegger, *Sein* discloses its *Sinn* to *Dasein*. At the end of 1927, Husserl reports to Ingarden that "[he] had unfortunately not determined [Heidegger's] philosophical education" and that "[Heidegger] was apparently already peculiar as he studied [Husserl's] writings."[57] In 1928, as soon as

HUSSERL AND OTHER PHENOMENOLOGISTS

Heidegger arrives in Freiburg as his successor, he breaks off philosophical contact with Husserl.[58] In the summer of 1929,[59] after he had been repeatedly warned that Heidegger's phenomenology was critical of his own,[60] Husserl, given Heidegger's denials of such "nonsense," studied *Being and Time, Kant and the Problem of Metaphysics*,[61] and other works of his in order to arrive at "a sober and final position on the H[eidegger]ian philosophy,"[62] only to come to "the distressing conclusion that [he] had nothing to do with this H[eidegger] ian profundity, this ingenious unscientificality, that H[eidegger]'s open and hidden critique was based on gross misunderstanding, and that he was involved in the formation of a philosophical system of the kind which he [Husserl] had always considered it [his own] life's work to make forever impossible."[63] Thus Husserl lamented: "All the others already saw this long ago—only I did not."[64]

In 1930, Husserl reaffirms his transcendental turn in *Ideas* with an "Afterword,"[65] criticizing "philosophy of 'existence,'"[66] but not mentioning any "philosophers of existence" by name.[67] In 1931, in a public lecture entitled "Phenomenology and Anthropology,"[68] Husserl insists on the indispensability of the transcendental reduction as the starting-point of a methodologically sound phenomenological philosophy, and he sharply demarcates his own position from the approaches of *Dilthey* and *Scheler* by naming names.[69] Although he did not mention Heidegger by name in either place, people thought that they knew that Husserl meant him too, and Heidegger also thought that he was meant.[70] These events contributed to a public perception that the break between Husserl and Heidegger was *the* definitive moment of the Phenomenological-Existential Schism, whereas it was in fact *a* defining moment of the Great Phenomenological Schism. It is generally acknowledged that Heidegger rejected both "philosophy of existence" and "existentialism" as proper designations for his philosophy of Being.[71]

Husserl and Heidegger had, of course, drifted far apart in 1927–1931.[72] By 1933–1934, however, not only philosophical differences but also political divisions had presented themselves, as Husserl witnessed Heidegger's emerging National Socialism and increasing anti-Semitism.[73] On April 6, 1933, Husserl, with all "non-Arian" civil servants of Baden, was "vacated" from his university position by a measure of the regional *Reichskommissar*.[74] Husserl called this measure and the Reich-wide measure of April 7, 1933, the "Law for the Restoration of the Professional Civil Service" (*Gesetz zur Wiederherstellung des Berufsbeamtentums*), "the greatest personal injury of [his] life."[75] Yet the Ministry of Culture of Baden cancelled ("with reservations") the measure with respect to Husserl on April 28, the cancellation was confirmed on July 20, and the Rector Heidegger signed the cancellation on July 28.[76] On January 15, 1936, however, Husserl was finally stripped of his teaching license (*venia legendi* or *Lehrbefugnis*), effective retroactively to December 31, 1935.[77] These developments, accompanied by Husserl's struggles with fate and Heidegger's lack of solidarity,[78] brought the final end to what Husserl bitterly recalled as "this supposed philosophical friendship between souls."[79] Husserl saw a direct correlation between the rise of Heidegger's commitment to National Socialism and anti-Semitism and the decline and fall of their relationship.[80] At the end, Heidegger, pleading illness, declined to attend Husserl's funeral on April 29, 1938, a "human failure" for which he later (in 1950) apologized, with a note and a bouquet of flowers, to Husserl's widow.[81] The political division had rendered the philosophical break between Husserl and Heidegger irreversible.

Originally Husserl had said of Heidegger that, "whatever becomes of him," "it will be something of great value."[82] He thought of Heidegger as a "splendid human being"

HUSSERL AND OTHER PHENOMENOLOGISTS

("Prachtmensch")[83] and as "[his] student and future collaborator," to whom the founder of phenomenology could entrust the future of phenomenology.[84] He accepted *Being and Time* into his *Yearbook for Philosophy and Phenomenological Research* and "joyfully" read page-proofs for its publication (1926).[85] In turn, Heidegger dedicated *Being and Time* to Husserl "in reverence and friendship" (1927).[86] Even as they struggled against the inevitable in the fall of 1927, Heidegger called Husserl "dear fatherly friend," and Husserl called Heidegger "dear friend."[87] Recommending him as being "among the most significant philosophical teachers of our time,"[88] Husserl had Heidegger listed alone ("unico loco") as successor to his chair at the University of Freiburg (1928).[89] Even after they had ended their philosophical relationship, they still had sporadic social contact. For example, Husserl invited Heidegger to his home for a "philosopher's tea" on June 22, 1930, and for the fiftieth anniversary of his own doctorate on January 23, 1933 (one week before Hitler was named chancellor), and Heidegger accepted both invitations.[90]

It is understandable, then, how Heidegger could write in 1946, in an essay that would be published in 2000, that he had "*from the beginning and always stood outside the philosophical position of Husserl in the sense of a transcendental philosophy of consciousness.*"[91] All along, Heidegger says, he had sought neither to find "a new direction within phenomenology" nor to achieve "the new," but rather, vice versa, "to think the essence of phenomenology more originally [than Husserl], in order, in this way, to lead it back to its own affiliation with Western philosophy."[92] Husserl anticipated Heidegger's assessment of his own originality, having told Natorp in 1922 that Heidegger's "manner of seeing and working phenomenologically, and the field of his interests itself—none of this is merely taken over from me, but rather capable of standing on its own in its own originality."[93] Thus Heidegger's *Being and Time* is not only the starting point of one schism but also the end point of another schism. Husserl's *Ideas I* is the *terminus a quo* of the Great Phenomenological Schism in general, but Heidegger's *Being and Time* is the *terminus ad quem* of the same schism between these two thinkers in particular. It is commonly supposed that *Being and Time* is the *terminus a quo* of the Phenomenological-Existential Schism, but this cannot be so without further ado, because Heidegger wants to have nothing to do with philosophy of existence and existentialism.

The map of his path of thinking that Heidegger lays out in "My Way" is corroborated by what he says about his relationship to and deviation from Husserl in his posthumously published *Black Notebooks*.[94] In statements from the 1940s, what Heidegger says about Husserl's philosophical approach is far more critical than anything that he says about it in "My Way." He says, for example, that Husserl, clinging to "the principle 'to the things themselves'" at the cost of "the thinking of the things themselves," "knows nothing of and even resists" the idea of "the turning of thinking to Ἀλήθεια [aletheia] as an essential feature of Being itself in the sense of presence."[95] Heidegger juxtaposes Husserl's "Afterword to *Ideas*" and "Philosophy as Rigorous Science," on the one hand, and his *Logical Investigations*, on the other.[96] According to Heidegger, the earlier work was a start in the right direction of "thinking the experience of Ἀλήθεια [aletheia] out of the experience of the forgotten-ness of Being," but the later works do not continue in that direction.[97] For Heidegger, the *Logical Investigations*, which risked "the step into seeing" against "empty argumentation" and "historical assertion," secure Husserl's "place in history," whereas it is "precisely this" that "his mere proponents and propagandists do not want to see."[98] For Heidegger, "the false admiration" for Husserl's "later philosophy" makes him look, "against his will," "ridiculous" and like "a bungler."[99] Heidegger counts *Ideas for a Pure Phenomenology and Phenomenological Philosophy I*, together with the "Afterword" and the *Logos*-Article, as parts of Husserl's "later philosophy."[100] Under these circumstances, Heidegger says, he "passed" Husserl "by," adding that this was "a painful necessity."[101] Although he indicates that his essays since *Being and Time* are "the most worthy testimony" to what he owes Husserl, Heidegger emphasizes that he "learned from him and testified to his way by virtue of the fact that [he] did *not* remain his follower, which [he] also never was."[102] In closing, Heidegger suggests that one could have recognized his role in what is now regarded as the Great Phenomenological Schism if one had consulted his "lectures" as "testimonies" to his thinking.[103] This further corroborates Heidegger's observation in "My Way" on the role of his early Freiburg and Marburg lectures in the development of his thinking leading to *Being and Time* (87).

Conclusion: The Links between the Two Schisms

While there is undeniable underlapping between the Phenomenological-Existential Schism between Husserl and Heidegger from 1927 to 1933 and the Great Phenomenological Schism between Husserl and Pfänder, Scheler, Reinach, Stein, and Ingarden from 1913 to 1926, there is also overwhelming overlapping between the schism between Husserl and Heidegger from 1917 to 1927 and the schism between Husserl and the other phenomenologists from 1913 to 1926. The Great Phenomenological Schism between Husserl and those phenomenologists who, like Pfänder, Scheler, Reinach, Stein, and Ingarden, did not follow him into transcendental idealism preceded and prepared the Phenomenological-Existential Schism between Husserl and Heidegger, and it is necessary to understand the theme of the latter against the horizon of the former. With respect to the connection between the relationship between Husserl and Heidegger and the relationship between the Great Phenomenological Schism and the Phenomenological-Existential Schism, this means that these phenomena are distinct but inseparable, that they played out in such a way that Heidegger's early phenomenological break with Husserl anticipated his later phenomenological-existential break with him, and that the latter recapitulated the former. Thus the break between Husserl and Heidegger intersects with the Great Phenomenological Schism and the Phenomenological-Existential Schism, and therein lies its exemplary significance.

Following his suggestion, one can reinforce this interpretation with a selection from Heidegger's lectures at Freiburg from 1919 to 1923 and at Marburg from 1923 to 1928 (87).[104] In the Spring Semester of 1919, Heidegger argues that a philosophy committed to "the general dominance of *the theoretical*" or even "the primacy of the theoretical," which Husserl's transcendental phenomenology is, may reach "the things themselves" as "objects," but it cannot capture the human experience of historical life in a surrounding world.[105] In the Winter Semester of 1919/1920, Heidegger asks, regarding Husserl's definition of "philosophy as rigorous science" in his *Logos*-article of 1911, "what is left then" of "the ideals of phenomenology as rigorous research."[106] In the Winter Semester of 1920/1921, Heidegger proposes that Husserl's phenomenology take a turn toward "the historical."[107] In the Winter Semester of 1921/1922 and the Summer Semester of 1922, Heidegger, orienting himself decreasingly on Husserl and increasingly on

HUSSERL AND OTHER PHENOMENOLOGISTS

Aristotle, develops his "phenomenology of life" and his concept of philosophy as the analysis of "the facticity of factical life."[108] In the Summer Semester of 1923, Heidegger applies the concept of facticity to existence (*Dasein*), urges his listeners to make the hermeneutical turn in phenomenology, and suggests that Husserl, despite his "decisive contributions," did not.[109] In the Winter Semester of 1923/1924, Heidegger criticizes Husserl for being 'fixated on consciousness and blind for life' ("Cartesianism"), so that he fails to pose the question of the *Sein* of *Bewusstsein*.[110] In the Summer Semester of 1925, Heidegger faults Husserl for absolutizing the scientific ideals of the mathematical and natural sciences to the detriment of the *Geisteswissenschaften* and for favoring the theoretical to the neglect of the existential.[111] In the Winter Semester of 1925/1926, Heidegger questions the foundation of Husserl's critique of psychologism, namely, the rigorous distinction between the real act of judging and the ideal content of judgment, which, according to Heidegger, defines truth as an ideal character of being but does not clarify its really existent Being.[112] This evidence, too, indicates that Heidegger's early break with Husserl was the result of his rejection of phenomenology as redefined by *Ideas I*, and that the early break was a process in progress years before *Being and Time*.

The connections between Heidegger's philosophical critique of Husserl after his transformation of descriptive phenomenology into transcendental phenomenology and the philosophical criticisms of Husserl by Pfänder, Scheler, Reinach, Stein, and Ingarden are also evident. From Reinach's "Lecture on Phenomenology" (1914/1921),[113] through Pfänder's *Logic* (1921),[114] Scheler's "Idealism-Realism" (1927),[115] and Ingarden's "Remarks on the Problem 'Idealism-Realism'" (1929),[116] to Stein's *Finite and Eternal Being: Attempt at an Ascent to the Meaning of Being* (1931–1936),[117] these phenomenologists were pushing the limits of descriptive phenomenology as Husserl had redefined it with his move into transcendental idealism. If one also considers Stein's *On the Problem of Empathy* (1917),[118] Scheler's *The Position of the Human Being in the Cosmos* (1928),[119] and Pfänder's *The Soul of the Human Being* (1933),[120] as well as permits a reading of Heidegger's *Being and Time* as a philosophy of existence (Stein's critique of the work notwithstanding),[121] it becomes clear why Husserl misapprehended phenomenology as under assault by philosophical anthropology.

Finally, this interpretation of events is consistent with Husserl's distinction between topics that philosophy *must* treat and topics that transcendental phenomenology, with its rigorous method of transcendental reduction, *cannot* handle, that is, "limit or border problems of phenomenology."[122] Evidently Husserl believes that the *Grenzprobleme der Phänomenologie* include the question about the meaning of human life and the question about a meaningful human life.[123] It is not, of course, as if Husserl did not pose "the questions about meaning or meaninglessness of this entire human existence."[124] It is the case, however, that Heidegger did not think that these existential questions could be addressed in the transcendental-idealistic attitude of Husserl's *Ideas*.[125] At the end of "My Way," Heidegger states that "the time of phenomenological philosophy," certainly in the sense of Husserl's transcendental idealism, seems to be over, and suggests that "the matter of thinking," in his own sense, appears to be just beginning (90). Thus "My Way Into Phenomenology" is also the narrative of Heidegger's way out of phenomenology, as well as of how his decision to go his own way was originally occasioned by Husserl's move into transcendental idealism.

HUSSERL AND OTHER PHENOMENOLOGISTS

Acknowledgement

This is the revised version of a paper that was presented at the Fourth Annual Conference of the North American Society for Early Phenomenology, Universidad Nacional Autónoma de México, Mexico City, Mexico, June 3, 2015. I am grateful to Gregory Fried for his comments on the earlier version. An anonymous reviewer also contributed comments.

Notes

References to Husserl's works are to *Edmund Husserl: Gesammelte Werke* or *Husserliana* (*HUA*), vols. 1–42 (The Hague: Martinus Nijhoff, 1950–1987/Dordrecht: Kluwer Academic Publishers, 1988–2004/Dordrecht: Springer, 2004–). References to Husserl's correspondence are to *Edmund Husserl: Briefwechsel* (*BW*), vols. 1–10, ed. Karl Schuhmann with Elisabeth Schuhmann (Dordrecht: Kluwer Academic Publishers, 1994). References to Heidegger's works are to *Martin Heidegger: Gesamtausgabe* (*GA*), vols. 1–102 (Frankfurt am Main: Vittorio Klostermann, 1977–). All translations are the author's.

1. Husserl, *HUA*, 10.237–68, esp. 238, 253; *HUA*, 2.6–7, 9–12, 44–45, 48, 55–58, 60, 72.
2. Husserl, *Transzendentaler Idealismus: Texte aus dem Nachlass (1908–1921)* (*HUA*, 36), ed. Robin Rollinger with Rochus Sowa (Dordrecht: Springer, 2003).
3. Husserl, "Correspondence with Alexander Pfänder," *BW*, 2.129–86.
4. Husserl to Pfänder, 6 January 1931, *BW*, 2.178–86.
5. Husserl, "Correspondence with Adolf Reinach," *BW*, 2.187–208.
6. Heidegger, *Sein und Zeit* (Halle-an-der-Saale/Tübingen: Max Niemeyer, 1927/1977[14]), § 2. *Sein und Zeit* is in *GA*, 2, but the more reliable text is that of Niemeyer.
7. Heidegger, *Sein und Zeit*, § 27.
8. Heidegger, *Sein und Zeit*, § 35.
9. Karl Löwith, *Mein Leben in Deutschland vor und nach 1933: Ein Bericht* (orig. 1940), ed. Frank-Rutger Hausmann (Stuttgart: J. B. Metzler, 1986/2007[2]), 35.
10. Hannah Arendt and Karl Jaspers, *Briefwechsel 1926–1969*, ed. Lotte Köhler and Hans Saner (Munich: Piper, 1985), 79, 84, 99, 732. The exchange, clarifying a misunderstanding, is from 1946.
11. Heidegger, "Mein Weg in die Phänomenologie," in *Zur Sache des Denkens* (Tübingen: Max Niemeyer, 1988[3]), 81–90 (*GA*, 14.91–102). Page references to "Mein Weg" ("My Way") are given in parentheses in the text.
12. Heidegger, "Nur noch ein Gott kann uns retten" (Interview of 23 September 1966), *Der Spiegel* 23 (31 May 1976): 193–219; Karl Schuhmann, "Zu Heideggers *Spiegel*-Gespräch über Husserl," *Zeitschrift für philosophische Forschung* 32 (1978): 591–612; Lutz Hachmeister, *Heideggers Testament: Der Philosoph, der "Spiegel" und die SS* (Berlin: Propyläen/Ullstein, 2014[2]), 7–60, 283–310.
13. Franz Brentano (1838–1917), *Von der mannigfachen Bedeutung des Seienden nach Aristoteles* (Freiburg im Breisgau: Herder, 1862).
14. Carl Braig (1852–1923), *Vom Sein: Abriß der Ontologie* (Freiburg im Breisgau: Herder, 1896).
15. E.g., *Der Gegenstand der Erkenntnis: Einführung in die Transzendentalphilosophie* (Freiburg im Breisgau: Herder, 1895/1915[3]).
16. E.g., *Die Logik der Philosophie und die Kategorienlehre: Eine Studie über den Herrschaftsbereich der logischen Form* (Tübingen: J. C. B. Mohr, 1911) and *Die Lehre vom Urteil* (Tübingen: J. C. B. Mohr, 1912).
17. Heidegger, *Die Lehre vom Urteil im Psychologismus: Ein kritisch-positiver Beitrag zur Logik*, *GA*, 1.1–129.
18. Heidegger, *GA*, 1.5–6.
19. Husserl, *Logische Untersuchungen, Erster Band: Prolegomena zur reinen Logik* (orig. 1900/1913[2]) (*HUA*, 18), ed. Elmar Holenstein (The Hague: Martinus Nijhoff, 1975).
20. Husserl, *Logische Untersuchungen, Zweiter Band, Erster Teil und Zweiter Teil: Untersuchungen zur Phänomenologie und Theorie der Erkenntnis* (orig. 1901/1913[2]/1921[2]) (*HUA*, 19/1–2), ed. Ursula Panzer (The Hague: Martinus Nijhoff, 1984).

HUSSERL AND OTHER PHENOMENOLOGISTS

21. Husserl repudiated the charge of a "relapse into psychologism." Cf. "Entwurf einer 'Vorrede' zu den *Logischen Untersuchungen*" (orig. 1913), *HUA*, 20/1.279–80.

22. Husserl, *Ideen zu einer reinen Phänomenologie und phänomenologischen Philosophie, Erstes Buch: Allgemeine Einführung in die reine Phänomenologie* (*HUA*, 3/1–2), ed. Karl Schuhmann (The Hague: Martinus Nijhoff, 1976).

23. Husserl, *HUA*, 18.8–16.

24. Husserl, *HUA*, 19/2.533–36.

25. Heidegger associates Husserl's anti-Dilthey-ian "Philosophy as Rigorous Science" ("Philosophie als strenge Wissenschaft" [orig. 1911]: *HUA*, 25.3–62) not with the *Investigations* but with *Ideas*. Cf. "Mein Weg," 84–85.

26. Heidegger's last early lecture at Freiburg, in the Summer Semester of 1923, was "Ontology: Hermeneutics of Facticity": *GA*, 63 (*Ontologie: Hermeneutik der Faktizität*).

27. Heidegger says that the year was 1922, but that was the year in which the complete *Logical Investigations* were first published in the Second Edition. In the Foreword to the Second Edition of the Sixth Investigation (this Foreword was composed in 1920 and published in 1921) Husserl concedes that he was not able to fulfill his intention, which he had announced in the Foreword to the Second Edition of the *Logical Investigations* (this Foreword was composed and published in 1913), to raise at least the last investigation to the level of *Ideas I*. Cf. *HUA*, 18.8–15, esp. 11 and 15, and 19/2.533–34.

28. Husserl, *HUA*, 19/2.534.

29. Heidegger held Saturday morning private seminars on Husserl's Logical Investigations V and VI at Freiburg from the Winter Semester of 1920/1921 to the Summer Semester of 1923: *GA*, 17.328–29.

30. Heidegger held his first Freiburg lecture on Aristotle, "Phenomenological Interpretations on Aristotle: Introduction to Phenomenological Research," in the Winter Semester of 1921/1922 (*GA*, 61: *Phänomenologische Interpretationen zu Aristoteles: Einführung in die phänomenologische Forschung*). He continued with a Freiburg lecture of the same title in the Summer Semester of 1922 (*GA*, 62: *Phänomenologische Interpretation ausgewählter Abhandlungen des Aristoteles zu Ontologie und Logik/Im Anhang: Phänomenologische Interpretationen zu Aristoteles*). Seeking a position, Heidegger submitted his interpretations of Aristotle at Marburg in the fall of 1922. Having obtained the position at Marburg in 1923, Heidegger held his first Marburg lecture on Aristotle, "Basic Concepts of Aristotelian Philosophy," in the Summer Semester of 1924 (*GA*, 18: *Grundbegriffe der aristotelischen Philosophie*).

31. Heidegger to Karl Löwith, 8 May 1923, in *Heidegger-Handbuch: Leben–Werk–Wirkung*, ed. Dieter Thomä (Stuttgart: J. B. Metzler, 2013²), 40.

32. Heidegger, *GA*, 61.79–155.

33. Heidegger, *GA*, 62.364–65. Cf. Husserl, *HUA*, 18.8, and 19/1.5–29.

34. Heidegger, *GA*, 62.341–419.

35. Heidegger, *GA*, 62.365.

36. Thomä, *Heidegger-Handbuch*, 13–21 (Matthias Jung's study of Heidegger's Freiburg Lectures and other writings 1919–1923).

37. Thomä, *Heidegger-Handbuch*, 25–35 (Franco Volpi's study of Heidegger's recourse to the Greeks in the 1920s). Heidegger says he learned from Braig (1) the relevance of speculative theology for ontology and metaphysics and (2) the importance of Classical German idealism (Schelling and Hegel) as an alternative to Scholasticism. Cf. "Mein Weg," 81–82.

38. Heidegger, *Die Kategorien- und Bedeutungslehre des Duns Scotus*, *GA*, 1.131–353.

39. Heidegger thought that *De modis significandi* was by Duns Scotus, but Martin Grabmann showed that it was by Thomas of Erfurt. Cf. *HUA*, 17.54, where Husserl points this out.

40. The best study of the composition of *Sein und Zeit* is by Theodore Kisiel: *The Genesis of Heidegger's "Being and Time"* (Berkeley: University of California Press, 1993).

41. Heidegger, *Sein und Zeit*, § 7.

42. Heidegger, *Sein und Zeit*, 38, 47, 77, 166, 218, 363.

43. Roland Breeur, ed., "Randbemerkungen Husserls zu Heideggers *Sein und Zeit* und *Kant und das Problem der Metaphysik*," *Husserl Studies* 11 (1994): 3–63 (here 30–31).

HUSSERL AND OTHER PHENOMENOLOGISTS

44. Otto Pöggeler, *Der Denkweg Martin Heideggers* (Pfullingen: Günther Neske, 1983²), 67–80.

45. Husserl was named ordinarius on February 9 and moved to Freiburg on April 1, 1916. Cf. Karl Schuhmann, *Husserl-Chronik: Denk- und Lebensweg Edmund Husserls* (The Hague: Martinus Nijhoff, 1977), 199–200. The first correspondence between Husserl and Heidegger dates to May, 1916, and their first encounter to July 23, 1916. Cf. Husserl, *BW*, 4.127. The Husserl-Heidegger correspondence is in *BW*, 4.127–61.

46. Heidegger to Elfride, 27 May 1917, in *"Mein liebes Seelchen!" Briefe Martin Heideggers an seine Frau Elfride (1915–1970)*, ed. Gertrud Heidegger (Munich: Deutsche Verlags-Anstalt, 2005), 57.

47. Heidegger, "Brief Martin Heideggers an Elisabeth Husserl," 24 April 1919, *aut aut* 223–224 (1988): 6–11.

48. Heidegger to Elfride, 30 August 1919, in *"Mein liebes Seelchen!"*, 95–96.

49. Heidegger to Elfride, 4 January 1920, in *"Mein liebes Seelchen!"*, 103–4.

50. Pöggeler, *Der Denkweg Heideggers*, 67–80.

51. Heidegger to Löwith, 20 February 1923, in Thomä, *Heidegger-Handbuch*, 40.

52. Heidegger to Jaspers, 14 July 1923, in *Martin Heidegger/Karl Jaspers: Briefwechsel 1920–1963*, ed. Walter Biemel and Hans Saner (Frankfurt am Main: Vittorio Klostermann, 1990), 42.

53. Heidegger to Jaspers, 24 May 1926, in *Heidegger/Jaspers: Briefwechsel*, 64.

54. Heidegger to Jaspers, 26 December 1926, in *Heidegger/Jaspers: Briefwechsel*, 71.

55. Husserl, "Der Encyclopaedia Britannica Artikel" (1927–1928), *HUA*, 9.237–301.

56. Heidegger to Husserl, 22 October 1927, and Husserl to Heidegger, 8 December 1927, *BW*, 4.144–49; Husserl, *HUA*, 9.274–75; Walter Biemel, "Husserls Encyclopaedia-Britannica-Artikel und Heideggers Anmerkungen dazu," *Tijdschrift voor Philosophie* 12 (1950): 246–80; Heidegger to Löwith, 19 September 1921, in Thomä, *Heidegger-Handbuch*, 546.

57. Husserl to Roman Ingarden, 19 November 1927, *BW*, 3.234.

58. Thus Husserl to Dietrich Mahnke, 4/5 May 1933, *BW*, 3.491–502, esp. 493.

59. Schuhmann, *Husserl-Chronik*, 349.

60. And after hearing Heidegger's Inaugural Lecture at Freiburg, "Was ist Metaphysik?" (24 July 1929), *GA*, 9.103–22.

61. Heidegger, *Kant und das Problem der Metaphysik* (orig. 1929), *GA*, 3.1–318.

62. Breeur, "Randbemerkungen Husserls zu Heideggers *Sein und Zeit* und *Kant und das Problem der Metaphysik*," 3–63.

63. Husserl to Pfänder, 6 January 1931, *BW*, 2.180–84. Aside from Husserl to Mahnke, 4/5 May 1933 (*BW*, 3.491–502), this is the most important source for Husserl's view of the break with Heidegger.

64. Husserl to Pfänder, 6 January 1931, *BW*, 2.184.

65. Husserl, "Nachwort zu meinen *Ideen zu einer reinen Phänomenologie und phänomenologischen Philosophie*," *HUA*, 5.138–62, esp. 151–52, 154–55, 161.

66. Husserl, *HUA*, 5.138, 140.

67. In *Neue Wege der Philosophie: Geist–Leben–Existenz: Eine Einführung in die Philosophie der Gegenwart* (Leipzig: Quelle and Meyer, 1929), Fritz Heinemann characterized Heidegger as the "Hermeneutiker der Existenz" and his philosophy as "Phänomenologie der Existenz," a kind of "Existenzphilosophie" (370–91). "Philosophy of existence" is evident in Karl Jaspers, *Philosophie, Zweiter Band: Existenzerhellung* (Berlin: Springer, 1932). For a time, it was common to regard both Jaspers and Heidegger as engaging in *philosophy of existence*. Cf., e.g., Johannes Pfeiffer, *Existenzphilosophie: Einführung in Heidegger und Jaspers* (Leipzig: Felix Meiner, 1933).

68. Husserl, "Phänomenologie und Anthropologie," *HUA*, 27.164–81. Husserl presented the lecture in June, 1931, at the Kantgesellschaften in Frankfurt, Berlin, and Halle.

69. Husserl, *HUA*, 27.164 (Dilthey), 180 (Scheler, Dilthey).

70. Heidegger, "*Spiegel*-Gespräch" (September, 1966), 199. Heidegger learned of the contents of the lectures in part from newspaper reports. In *GA*, 97 (*Anmerkungen I–V* [*Schwarze Hefte 1942–1948*]), 462, Heidegger says that in public lectures in "1930/31" Husserl "took a position *against* [him] and rejected [his] work as un-philosophy," and adds that Husserl did the same in the "Afterword to *Ideas*" of "1930/31."

109

HUSSERL AND OTHER PHENOMENOLOGISTS

71. Heidegger, "Brief über den Humanismus" (orig. 1945) (Frankfurt am Main: Vittorio Klostermann, 1949/2010[11]) (cf. *GA*, 9.313–64); *GA*, 27.374; *GA*, 32.18; *GA*, 49, § 11b; Heidegger to Elisabeth Blochmann (1947), in *Martin Heidegger/Elisabeth Blochmann: Briefwechsel 1918–1969*, ed. Joachim Storck (Marbach am Neckar: Deutsche Schillergesellschaft, 1989), 93; Jaspers to Heidegger, 6 February 1949, in *Heidegger/Jaspers: Briefwechsel*, 168–71, 276–78; Helmuth Vetter, *Grundriss Heidegger: Ein Handbuch zu Leben und Werk* (Hamburg: Felix Meiner, 2014), 265–66. The designation of Heidegger's philosophy as "existentialism" ("existentialisme") is found in Jean-Paul Sartre's "L'existentialisme est un humanisme" (orig. 1946), ed. Arlette Elkaïm-Sartre (Paris: Gallimard, 1996), 26, 29; that of it as "philosophy of existence" ("Existenzphilosophie") is traceable to Heinemann's works.

72. Husserl, *Psychological and Transcendental Phenomenology and the Confrontation with Heidegger (1927–1931)*, ed. Thomas Sheehan and Richard Palmer (Dordrecht: Kluwer Academic Publishers, 1997), 1–32; Thomä, *Heidegger-Handbuch*, 35–44.

73. Husserl to Mahnke, 4/5 May 1933, *BW*, 3.491–502.

74. Schuhmann, *Husserl-Chronik*, 428.

75. Husserl to Gustav Albrecht, 1 July 1933, *BW*, 9.92.

76. Schuhmann, *Husserl-Chronik*, 429, 433.

77. Schuhmann, *Husserl-Chronik*, 472.

78. Elfride Heidegger to Malvine Husserl, 29 April 1933 (*BW*, 4.160–61), is no exception to the rule. Yet it is false that Rector Heidegger forbade Husserl entry to the University of Freiburg. Cf. Heidegger, "Letter to the Editor of *Der Spiegel*," 22 February 1966, *GA*, 16.639 (also *GA*, 97.462).

79. Husserl to Mahnke, 4 May 1933, *BW*, 3.493.

80. Husserl to Mahnke, 4 May 1933, *BW*, 3.493.

81. Heidegger to Malvine Husserl, 6 March 1950, *GA*, 16.443; Hugo Ott, *Martin Heidegger: Unterwegs zu seiner Biographie* (Frankfurt am Main: Campus, 1988), 167–68.

82. Husserl to Ingarden, 24 December 1921, *BW*, 3.215.

83. Husserl to Mahnke, 25 November 1925, *BW*, 3.451.

84. Husserl to Pfänder, 6 January 1931, *BW*, 2.181; Husserl to Ingarden, 19 November 1927, *BW*, 3.234.

85. Husserl to Fritz Kaufmann, 20 April 1926, *BW*, 3.347.

86. Heidegger, *Sein und Zeit*, v, 38.

87. Heidegger to Husserl, 22 October 1927, and Husserl to Heidegger, 8 December 1927, *BW*, 4.144, 148.

88. Husserl, Recommendation (draft), January (end), 1928, *BW*, 8.194–95.

89. Husserl to Heidegger, 21 January 1928, *BW*, 4.151; also *BW*, 3.457, 4.142.

90. Malvine Husserl to Elisabeth Rosenberg, 22 June 1930, and 25 January 1933, *BW*, 9.378, 416.

91. Heidegger, "Was ist das Sein selbst?" (12 September 1946), *GA*, 16.423 (emphasis added).

92. Heidegger, *GA*, 12.91.

93. Husserl to Paul Natorp, 1 February 1922, *BW*, 5.150.

94. Heidegger, "Schwarze Hefte," *GA*, 94–97.

95. Heidegger, *GA*, 97.442. The remarks on Husserl date from 1942–1948.

96. Heidegger, *GA*, 97.442; Husserl, "Philosophie als strenge Wissenschaft" (orig. 1911), *HUA*, 25.3–62; "Nachwort zu meinen *Ideen zu einer reinen Phänomenologie und phänomenologischen Philosophie*" (orig. 1930), *HUA*, 5.138–62.

97. Heidegger, *GA*, 97.442.

98. Heidegger, *GA*, 97.443.

99. Heidegger, *GA*, 97.443.

100. Heidegger, *GA*, 97.442.

101. Heidegger, *GA*, 97.462–63.

102. Heidegger, *GA*, 97.463.

103. Heidegger, *GA*, 97.463.

104. Heidegger, *GA*, 97.463.

105. Heidegger, *GA*, 56/57.73, 75, 87, 117.

HUSSERL AND OTHER PHENOMENOLOGISTS

106. Heidegger, *GA*, 58 (*Grundprobleme der Phänomenologie*: not *Die Grundprobleme der Phänomenologie*, Summer Semester Lectures at Marburg in 1927 [*GA*, 24]), 141.

107. Heidegger, *GA*, 60.31–65.

108. Heidegger, *GA*, 61.79–155.

109. Heidegger, *GA*, 63.16, 77.

110. Heidegger, *GA*, 17 (*Einführung in die phänomenologische Forschung*), 256, 267, 274–75.

111. Heidegger, *GA*, 20, § 4.

112. Heidegger, *GA*, 21.54, 58; *Sein und Zeit*, § 44.

113. Reinach, "Vortrag über Phänomenologie," in *Adolf Reinach: Sämtliche Werke* 1, ed. Karl Schuhmann and Barry Smith (Munich: Philosophia, 1989), 531–50.

114. Pfänder, *Logik*, in *Jahrbuch für Philosophie und phänomenologische Forschung* 4, 139–494e.

115. Scheler, "Idealismus-Realismus," in *Max Scheler: Gesammelte Werke* 9 (Bern: Francke, 1976), 183–342.

116. Ingarden, "Bemerkungen zum Problem 'Idealismus-Realismus,'" in *Festschrift E. Husserl zum 70. Geburtstag gewidmet* (*Ergänzungsband zum Jahrbuch für Philosophie und phänomenologische Forschung* 10 [1929]), 159–90.

117. Stein, *Endliches und ewiges Sein: Versuch eines Aufstiegs zum Sinn des Seins*, in *Edith Stein Gesamtausgabe* 11/12 (Freiburg im Breisgau: Herder, 2013²), 3–441.

118. Stein, *Zum Problem der Einfühlung*, ESG 5 (2010²), 1–136.

119. Scheler, *Die Stellung des Menschen im Kosmos*, MSGW 9, 7–72.

120. Pfänder, *Die Seele des Menschen* (Halle-an-der-Saale: Max Niemeyer, 1933).

121. Stein, "Husserls transzendentale Phänomenologie" (orig. 1931), ESG 9 (2014), 159–61, and "Martin Heideggers Existenzphilosophie" (orig. 1937), ESG 11/12 (2013²), 445–99.

122. On the term *Grenzprobleme* cf. Husserl, *HUA*, 39.875–76; *HUA*, 42.xix–cxv, xix, fn. 1.

123. *HUA*, 42 contains a text, No. 18 (1934?), in which Husserl mentions *Existenzphilosophie* but does not criticize it (228–35).

124. Husserl, *HUA*, 6.4; *HUA*, 29.104.

125. Heidegger to Husserl, 22 October 1927, and Husserl to Heidegger, 8 December 1927, *BW*, 4.144–49.

Bibliography

Alweiss, Lillian. "Between Internalism and Externalism: Husserl's Account of Intentionality." *Inquiry* 52 (2009): 53–78.

Arendt, Hannah, and Karl Jaspers. *Briefwechsel 1926–1969*. Edited by L. Köhler and H. Saner. Munich: Piper, 1985.

Barbaras, Renaud. "Perception and Movement: The End of the Metaphysical Approach." In *Chiasms: Merleau-Ponty's Notion of Flesh*, edited by F. Evans and L. Lawlor, 77–88. Albany, NY: State University of New York Press, 2000.

Barbaras, Renaud. *The Being of the Phenomenon: Merleau-Ponty's Ontology*. Translated by T. Toadvine and L. Lawlor. Bloomington, IN: Indiana University Press, 2004.

Biemel, Walter. "Husserls Encyclopaedia-Britannica-Artikel und Heideggers Anmerkungen dazu." *Tijdschrift voor Philosophie* 12 (1950): 246–80.

Braig, Carl. *Vom Sein: Abriß der Ontologie*. Freiburg im Breisgau: Herder, 1896.

Breeur, Roland, ed. "Randbemerkungen Husserls zu Heideggers *Sein und Zeit* und *Kant und das Problem der Metaphysik*." *Husserl Studies* 11 (1994): 3–63.

Brentano, Franz. *Von der mannigfachen Bedeutung des Seienden nach Aristoteles*. Freiburg im Breisgau: Herder, 1862.

Cairns, Dorion. "An Approach to Phenomenology." In *Philosophical Essays in the Memory of Edmund Husserl*, edited by M. Farber, 3–18. New York: Greenwood Press, 1968.

Carman, Taylor. "The Body in Husserl and Merleau-Ponty." *Philosophical Topics* 27 (1999): 205–26.

Caton, Hiram. "Review of Jacob Klein's Greek Mathematical Thought and the Origin of Algebra." *Studi Internazionali di Filosofia* 3 (1971): 222–26.

Dastur, Françoise. "World, Flesh, Vision." In *Chiasms: Merleau-Ponty's Notion of Flesh*, edited by F. Evans and L. Lawlor, 23–49. Albany, NY: State University of New York Press, 2000.

Derrida, Jacques. "Différance." In *Margins of Philosophy*, 3–27. Translated by A. Bass. New York: Harvester Wheatsheaf, 1982.

Derrida, Jacques. "Ousia and Grammé: Note on a Note from Being and Time." In *Margins of Philosophy*, 29–67. Translated by A. Bass. New York: Harvester Wheatsheaf, 1982.

Derrida, Jacques. "Speech and Phenomena." In *Speech and Phenomena and Other Essays on Husserl's Theory of Signs*, 3–104. Translated by D. Allison. Evanston, IL: Northwestern University Press, 1973.

Dillon, M. C. *Merleau-Ponty's Ontology*. Bloomington, IN: Indiana University Press, 1988.

Fitch, Frederic B. "Self-Reference in Philosophy." In *Contemporary Readings in Logical Theory*, edited by I. M. Copi and J. A. Gould. New York: The Macmillan Company, 1967.

Froman, Wayne. "Alterity and the Paradox of Being." In *Ontology and Alterity in Merleau-Ponty*, edited by G. A. Johnson and M. B. Smith, 98–110. Evanston, IL: Northwestern University Press, 1990.

Froman, Wayne. "The Blind Spot." In *Merleau-Ponty and the Possibilities of Philosophy: Transforming the Tradition*, edited B. Flynn, W. J. Froman, and R. Vallier, 155–65. Albany, NY: State University of New York Press, 2009.

Hachmeister, Lutz. *Heideggers Testament: Der Philosoph, der "Spiegel" und die SS*. Berlin: Propyläen/Ullstein, 2014.

HUSSERL AND OTHER PHENOMENOLOGISTS

Heidegger, Martin. *Anmerkungen I–V (Schwarze Hefte 1942–1948)*. In *GA*, 97, 1–528, 2015.

Heidegger, Martin. *Being and Time*. Translated by J. Macquarrie and E. Robinson. New York: Harper & Row, 1962.

Heidegger, Martin. "Brief Martin Heideggers an Elisabeth Husserl" (April 24, 1919). *aut* 223–24 (1988): 6–11.

Heidegger, Martin. *Die Grundprobleme der Phänomenologie* (1927). In *GA*, 24, 1–474, 1997.

Heidegger, Martin. *Die Kategorien- und Bedeutungslehre des Duns Scotus* (1915/1916). In *GA*, 1, 131–353, 1978.

Heidegger, Martin. *Die Lehre vom Urteil im Psychologismus: Ein kritisch-positiver Beitrag zur Logik* (1913/1914). In *GA*, 1, 1–129, 1978.

Heidegger, Martin. "Drei Briefe Martin Heideggers an Löwith." In *Zur philosophischen Aktualität Heideggers 2: Im Gespräch der Zeit*, edited by D. Papenfuss and O. Pöggeler, 27–39. Frankfurt am Main: Vittorio Klostermann, 1990.

Heidegger, Martin. *Einführung in die phänomenologische Forschung* (1923/1924). In *GA*, 17, 1–332, 2006.

Heidegger, Martin. *Grundbegriffe der aristotelischen Philosophie* (1924). In *GA*, 18, 1–418, 2002.

Heidegger, Martin. *Grundprobleme der Phänomenologie* (1919/1920). In *GA*, 58, 1–274, 1992.

Heidegger, Martin. *Kant und das Problem der Metaphysik* (1929). In *GA*, 3, 1–318, 2010.

Heidegger, Martin. *Martin Heidegger: Gesamtausgabe (GA)* (vols. 1–102). Frankfurt am Main: Vittorio Klostermann, 1977 ff.

Heidegger, Martin. *"Mein liebes Seelchen!" Briefe Martin Heideggers an seine Frau Elfride (1915–1970)*. Edited by G. Heidegger. Munich: Deutsche Verlags-Anstalt, 2005.

Heidegger, Martin. "Mein Weg in die Phänomenologie" (1963/1969). In *Zur Sache des Denkens*, 81–90. Tübingen: Max Niemeyer, 1988 (cf. *GA*, 14, 91–102, 2007).

Heidegger, Martin. "My Way into Phenomenology." In *On Time and Being*, 74–82. Translated by J. Stambaugh. New York: Harper, 1972.

Heidegger, Martin. "Nur noch ein Gott kann uns retten" (September 23, 1966). *Der Spiegel* 23 (May 31, 1976): 193–219.

Heidegger, Martin. "'Only a God Can Save Us': The *Spiegel* Interview (1966)." Translated by W. Richardson. In *Heidegger: The Man and the Thinker*, edited by T. Sheehan, 45–67. Piscataway, NJ: Transaction, 1981.

Heidegger, Martin. *Phänomenologische Interpretationen zu Aristoteles: Einführung in die phänomenologische Forschung* (1921/1922). In *GA*, 61, 1–204, 1994.

Heidegger, Martin. *Reden und andere Zeugnisse eines Lebensweges 1910–1976*. In *GA*, 16, 1–842, 2000.

Heidegger, Martin. *Sein und Zeit*. Tübingen: Max Niemeyer, 1967.

Heidegger, Martin. *Sein und Zeit*. Halle-an-der-Saale/Tübingen: Max Niemeyer, 1927/1977 (cf. *GA*, 2, 1–586, 1977).

Heidegger, Martin. *The Principle of Reason*. Translated by R. Lilly. Bloomington, IN: Indiana University Press, 1991.

Heidegger, Martin. "Über den Humanismus" (1945). Frankfurt am Main: Vittorio Klostermann, 1949/2010 (cf. *GA*, 9, 313–64, 1976/2004).

Heidegger, Martin. "Vom Wesen des Grundes." In *Wegmarken*, edited by Vittorio Klostermann, 21–71. Frankfurt am Main: Vittorio Klostermann, 1967.

Heidegger, Martin. "Was ist das Sein selbst?" (September 12, 1946). In *GA*, 16, 423–25, 2000.

Heidegger, Martin. "Was ist Metaphysik?" (1929). In *GA*, 9, 103–22, 1976/2004.

Heidegger, Martin, and Elisabeth Blochmann. *Briefwechsel 1918–1969*. Edited by J. Storck. Marbach am Neckar: Deutsche Schillergesellschaft, 1989.

Heidegger, Martin, and Karl Jaspers. *Briefwechsel 1920–1963*. Edited by W. Biemel and H. Saner. Frankfurt am Main: Vittorio Klostermann, 1990.

Heinämaa, Sara. "From Decisions to Passions: Merleau-Ponty's Interpretation of Husserl's Reduction." In *Merleau-Ponty's Reading of Husserl*, edited by T. Toadvine and L. Embree, 127–48. Dordrecht: Kluwer Academic Publishers, 2002.

HUSSERL AND OTHER PHENOMENOLOGISTS

Heinemann, Fritz. *Existenzphilosophie—lebendig oder tot?* Stuttgart: Kohlhammer, 1954.

Heinemann, Fritz. *Neue Wege der Philosophie: Geist–Leben–Existenz. Eine Einführung in die Philosophie der Gegenwart.* Leipzig: Queller und Meyer, 1929.

Heinemann, Fritz. "Was ist lebendig und was ist tot in der Existenzphilosophie?" *Zeitschrift für philosophische Forschung* 5 (1950): 3–24.

Hopkins, Burt. "Husserl's Psychologism, and Critique of Psychologism, Revisited." *Husserl Studies* 22 (2006): 91–119.

Hopkins, Burt. *The Origin of the Logic of Symbolic Mathematics: Edmund Husserl and Jacob Klein.* Bloomington, IN: Indiana University Press, 2011.

Husserl, Edmund. *Briefwechsel* (vol. 10). Edited by K. Schuhmann (in cooperation with E. Schumann). The Hague: Martinus Nijhoff, 1994.

Husserl, Edmund. *Cartesian Meditations: An Introduction to Phenomenology.* Translated by D. Cairns. The Hague: Martinus Nijhoff, 1960.

Husserl, Edmund. "Der Encyclopaedia Britannica Artikel" (1927–28). In *HUA*, 9, 237–301, 1968.

Husserl, Edumnd. "Die Frage nach dem Ursprung der Geometrie als intentional-historisches Problem." In *Revue internationale de Philosophie*, edited by E. Fink, 203–25. 1939. Fink's typescript of Husserl's original, and significantly different, 1936 text (which is the text translated in English) was published as Beilage III, in *Die Krisis der europäischen Wissenschaften und die transzendentale Phänomenologie. Eine Einleitung in die phänomenologische Philosophie*, edited by W. Biemel, *Husserliana* 6. The Hague: Martinus Nijhoff, 1954, 1976. English translation: "The Origin of Geometry." In *The Crisis of European Sciences and Transcendental Phenomenology.* Translated by D. Carr. Evanston, IL: Northwestern University Press, 1970.

Husserl, Edmund. *Die Idee der Phänomenologie: Fünf Vorlesungen* (1907). In *HUA*, 2, 1973.

Husserl, Edmund. "Die Krisis der europäischen Wissenschaften und die transzendentale Phänomenologie. Eine Einleitung in die phänomenologische Philosophie," *Philosophia* I (1936): 77v176. The text of this article is reprinted as §§ 1v27, *HUA*, 6.

Husserl, Edmund. *Edmund Husserl: Gesammelte Werke* or *Husserliana* (*HUA*) (vols. 1–42). The Hague: Martinus Nijhoff, 1950–1987/Dordrecht: Kluwer Academic Publishers, 1988–2004/New York: Springer, 2004 ff.

Husserl, Edmund. "Entwurf einer 'Vorrede' zu den Logischen Untersuchungen (1913)." *Tijdschrift voor Philosophie* 1 (1939): 106–33. English translation: *Introduction to the Logical Investigations.* Translated by P. J. Bossert and C. H. Peters. The Hague: Martinus Nijhoff, 1975.

Husserl, Edmund. "Entwurf einer 'Vorrede' zu den *Logischen Untersuchungen*" (1913). *Tijdschrift voor Filosofie* 1 (1939): 106–33, 319–39 (cf. *HUA*, 20/1, 272–329).

Husserl, Edmund. Erste Philosophie. In *Gesammelte Schriften* (vol. 6). Hamburg: Felix Meiner, 1992.

Husserl, Edmund. *Formale und transzendentale Logik.* The Hague: Martinus Nijhoff, 1974. English translation: *Formal and Transcendental Logic.* Translated by D. Cairns. The Hague: Martinus Nijhoff, 1969.

Husserl, Edmund. "Husserl an Stumpf, ca. Februar 1890." In *Briefwechsel* (vol. 1), edited by K. Schuhmann, 157–64. Dordrecht: Kluwer Academic Publishers, 1994. English translation: "Letter from Edmund Husserl to Carl Stumpf." In *Early Writings, Early Writings in the Philosophy of Logic and Mathematics*, 12–19. Translated by D. Willard. Dordrecht: Kluwer Academic Publishers, 1994.

Husserl, Edmund. *Husserliana Dokumente III: Briefwechsel* (10 vols.). Edited by K. Schuhmann with E. Schuhmann. Dordrecht: Kluwer Academic Publishers, 1994.

Husserl, Edmund. *Ideas I, General Introduction to Pure Phenomenology* (1913). Translated by W. R. Boyce Gibson. London: Routledge, 2012.

Husserl, Edmund. *Ideas Pertaining to a Pure Phenomenology and to a Phenomenological Philosophy: Second Book.* Translated by R. Rojcewicz and A. Schuwer. Dordrecht: Kluwer Academic Publishers, 1980.

Husserl, Edmund. *Ideas Pertaining to a Pure Phenomenology and to a Phenomenological Philosophy—First Book: General Introduction to a Pure Phenomenology.* Translated by F. Kersten. The Hague: Martinus Nijhoff, 1982.

HUSSERL AND OTHER PHENOMENOLOGISTS

Husserl, Edmund. *Ideen zu einer reinen Phänomenologie und phänomenologischen Philosophie, Erstes Buch*. Edited by R. Schuhmann. The Hague: Martinus Nijhoff, 1976.

Husserl, Edmund. *Ideen zu einer reinen Phänomenologie und phänomenologischen Philosophie, Erstes Buch: Allgemeine Einführung in die reine Phänomenologie* (1913). In *HUA*, 3/1–2, 1976.

Husserl, Edmund. *Logical Investigations* (vol. 1). Translated by J. Niemeyer Findlay. Edited by D. Moran. London: Routledge, 2001.

Husserl Edmund, *Logical Investigations* (vol. 2). Translated by J. N. Findlay. London: Routledge, 1970.

Husserl, Edmund. *Logische Untersuchungen*. In *Edmund Husserl, Gesammelte Schriften*, edited by U. Panzer (vols. 2–4). Hamburg: Felix Meiner Verlag, 1992.

Husserl, Edmund. *Logische Untersuchungen, Erster Band: Prolegomena zur reinen Logik* (1900/1913). In *HUA*, 18, 1975.

Husserl, Edmund. *Logische Untersuchungen: Untersuchungen zur Phänomenologie und Theorie der Erkenntnis* (1901/1913/1921). In *HUA*, 19/1–2, 1984.

Husserl, Edmund. *Logische Untersuchungen, Ergänzungsband, Erster Teil (Sommer 1913)*. In *HUA*, 20/1, 2002.

Husserl, Edmund. *Logische Untersuchungen, Ergänzungsband, Zweiter Teil (1893/94–1921)*. In *HUA*, 20/2, 2005.

Husserl, Edmund. *Méditations cartésiennes*. Translated by G. Peier and E. Levinas. Paris: Armand Colin, 1931.

Husserl, Edmund. "Nachwort zu meinen *Ideen zu einer reinen Phänomenologie und phänomenologischen Philosophie*" (1930). In *HUA*, 5, 138–62, 1971.

Husserl, Edmund. "Phänomenologie und Anthropologie" (1931). In *HUA*, 27, 164–81, 1989.

Husserl, Edmund. *Phänomenologische Psychologie*. Edited by W. Biemel. The Hague: Martinus Nijhoff, 1962.

Husserl, Edmund. "Philosophie als strenge Wissenschaft" (1911). In *HUA*, 25, 3–62, 1987.

Husserl, Edmund. *Philosophie der Arithmetik*. The Hague: Martinus Nijhoff, 1970.

Husserl, Edmund. *Philosophy of Arithmetic*. Translated by D. Willard. Dordrecht: Kluwer Academic Publishers, 2003.

Husserl, Edmund. *Psychological and Transcendental Phenomenology and the Confrontation with Heidegger (1927–1931)*. Edited and translated by T. Sheehan and R. Palmer. Dordrecht: Kluwer Academic Publishers, 1997.

Husserl, Edmund. "Seefelder Manuskripte über Individuation" (1905–7). In *HUA*, 10, 236–68, 1966.

Husserl, Edmund. *Späte Texte über Zeitkonstitution (1929–1934), Die C-Manuskripte*. Edited by D. Lohmar. Dordrecht: Springer Verlag, 2006.

Husserl, Edmund. (Wife of J. Klein), 14-page transcript of a tape recording [the original tape recording is apparently lost] among J. Klein's papers, which are housed in St. John's College Library, Annapolis, MD.

Husserl, Edmund. *The Idea of Phenomenology*. Translated by W. P. Alston and G. Nakhnikian. The Hague: Martinus Nijhoff, 1964.

Husserl, Edmund. *The Phenomenology of the Consciousness of Internal Time (1893-1917)*. Translated by J. Brough. Dordrecht: Kluwer Academic Publishers, 1991.

Husserl, Edmund. *Transzendentaler Idealismus: Texte aus dem Nachlass (1908–1921)*. In *HUA*, 36, 2003.

Husserl, Edmund. Unpublished manuscripts, B IV 12, B III 9. Cited with permission.

Husserl, Edmund. *Vorlesungen ber Ethik und Wertlehre 1908–1914*. In *HUA*, edited by U. Melle, 28. Dordrecht: Kluwer Academic Publishers, 1988.

Husserl, Edmund. *Zur Phänomenologie des inneren Zeitbewusstseins*. Edited by R. Boehm. The Hague: Martinus Nijhoff, 1966.

Ingarden, Roman. "Bemerkungen zum Problem 'Idealismus-Realismus.'" In *Festschrift E. Husserl zum 70. Geburtstag gewidmet (Ergänzungsband zum Jahrbuch für Philosophie und phänomenologische Forschung* 10), edited by Martin Heidegger, 159–90. Halle-an-der-Saale: Max Niemeyer, 1929.

Ingarden, Roman. *On the Motives which Led Husserl to Transcendental Idealism*. Translated by A. Hannibalsson. The Hague: Martinus Nijhoff, 1975.

HUSSERL AND OTHER PHENOMENOLOGISTS

Ingarden, Roman. "Über den transzendentalen Idealismus bei E. Husserl." In *Husserl et la Pensée Moderne—Husserl und das Denken der Neuzeit*, edited by Herman Leo van Breda and Jacques Taminiaux, 190–204. The Hague: Martinus Nijhoff, 1959.

Jaspers, Karl. *Philosophie, Zweiter Band: Existenzerhellung*. Berlin: Springer, 1932.

Kant, Immanuel. *Critique of Pure Reason*. Translated and edited by P. Guyer and A. Wood. Cambridge: Cambridge University Press, 1999.

Kenaan, Hagi. "Subject to Error: Rethinking Husserl's Phenomenology of Misperception." *International Journal of Philosophical Studies* 7 (1999): 55–67.

Kenaan, Hagi. *The Ethics of Visuality: Levinas and the Contemporary Gaze*. London: I.B. Tauris, 2013.

Kenaan, Hagi. "The Plot of the Saying." In *Etudes Phenomenologiques: Levinas et la phénoménologie* 22, 43–44. Brussels: Ousia, 2006.

Kisiel, Theodore. *The Genesis of Heidegger's "Being and Time."* Berkeley, CA: University of California Press, 1993.

Klein, Jacob. "Die griechische Logistik und die Entstehung der Algebra." In *Quellen und Studien zur Geschichte der Mathematik, Astronomie und Physik*, Abteilung B: *Studien* 3, no. 1 (1934): 18–105 (Part I), and no. 2 (1936): 122–235 (Part II). English translation: *Greek Mathematical Thought and the Origin of Algebra*. Translated by E. Brann. Cambridge, MA: MIT Press, 1969; reprint, New York: Dover, 1992.

Klein, Jacob. "Phenomenology and the History of Science." In *Philosophical Essays in Memory of Edmund Husserl*, edited by M. Farber, 143–63. Cambridge, MA: Harvard University Press, 1940; reprinted in *Jacob Klein, Lectures and Essays*. Edited by R. Williamson and E. Zuckerman, 65–84. Annapolis, MD: St. John's College Press, 1985.

Koyré, Alexandre. "Galilée et l'expérience de Pise." *Annales de l'Université de Paris* 12 (1937a): 441–53.

Koyré, Alexandre. "Galilée et Descartes." *Travaux du IXe Congrés international de Philosophie* 2 (1937b): 41–47.

Koyré, Alexandre. *Introduction à la lecture de Platon*. Paris: Gallimard, 1945.

Lask, Emil. *Die Lehre vom Urteil*. Tübingen: J.C.B. Mohr, 1912.

Lask, Emil. *Die Logik der Philosophie und die Kategorienlehre: Eine Studie über den Herrschaftsbereich der logischen Form*. Tübingen: J.C.B. Mohr, 1911.

Lefort, Claude. "Body, Flesh." In *Merleau-Ponty and the Possibilities of Philosophy: Transforming the Tradition*, edited by B. Flynn et al., 275–92. Albany, NY: State University of New York Press, 2009.

Levinas, Emmanuel. *Discovering Existence with Husserl*. Translated by R. A. Cohen and Michael B. Smith. Evanston, IL: Northwestern University Press, 1998.

Levinas, Emmanuel. *Entre Nous*. Translated by M. B. Smith and B. Harshav. New York: Columbia University Press, 2000.

Levinas, Emmanuel. *Ethics and Infinity: Conversations with Philippe Nemo*. Translated by R. A. Cohen. Pittsburg, PA: Duquesne University Press, 1985.

Levinas, Emmanuel. *Totality and Infinity: An Essay on Exteriority*. Translated by A. Lingis. Pittsburg, PA: Duquesne University Press, 1991.

Loidolt, Sophie. "A Phenomenological Ethics of the Absolute Ought: Investigating Husserl's Unpublished Ethical Writings." In *Ethics and Phenomenology*, edited by Mark Sanders and J. Jeremy Wisnewski, 9–38. Lanham, MD: Rowman & Littlefield, 2012.

Löwith, Karl. *Mein Leben in Deutschland vor und nach 1933: Ein Bericht* (1940). Edited by Frank-Rutger Hausmann. Stuttgart: J. B. Metzler, 1986/2007.

Majer, Ulrich. "Husserl and Hilbert on Completeness: A Neglected Chapter in Early Twentieth Century Foundations of Mathematics." *Synthese* 110 (1997): 37–56.

Marbach, Eduard. *Das Problem des Ich in der Phänomenologie Husserls*. The Hague: Martinus Nijhoff, 1974.

Marratto, Scott L. *The Intercorporeal Self*. New York: State University of New York Press, 2012.

Melle, Ullrich. "From Reason to Love." In *Phenomenological Approaches to Moral Philosophy: A Handbook*, edited by J. Drummond and L. Embree, 229–48. Dordrecht: Kluwer Academic Publishers, 2002.

HUSSERL AND OTHER PHENOMENOLOGISTS

Merleau-Ponty, Maurice. "Cézanne's Doubt." In *Sense and Non-Sense*, 9–25. Translated by H. Dreyfus. Evanston, IL: Northwestern University Press, 1964.

Merleau-Ponty, Maurice. "Eye and Mind." In *The Primacy of Perception*, edited by J. Edie, 159–92, Evanston, IL: Northwestern University Press, 1964.

Merleau-Ponty, Maurice. *Phenomenology of Perception*. Translated by C. Smith. London: Routledge & Kegan Paul, 1962.

Merleau-Ponty, Maurice. "The Philosopher and His Shadow." In *Signs*. Translated by R. C. McCleary. Evanston, IL: Northwestern University Press, 1964.

Merleau-Ponty, Maurice. *The Prose of the World*. Translated by J. O'Neill. Evanston, IL: Northwestern University Press, 1973.

Merleau-Ponty, Maurice. *Themes from the Lectures at the Collège de France, 1952–1960*. Evanston, IL: Northwestern University Press, 1970.

Merleau-Ponty, Maurice. *The Visible and the Invisible*. Translated by A. Lingis. Evanston, IL: Northwestern University Press, 1968.

Miller, J. Philip. *Numbers in Presence and Absence: A Study of Husserl's Philosophy of Mathematics*. The Hague: Martinus Nijhoff, 1982.

Mohanty Jitendra. "The Development of Husserl's Thought." In *The Cambridge Companion to Husserl*, edited by B. Smith and D. Woodruff Smith, 45–77. Cambridge: Cambridge University Press, 1995.

Moran, Dermot. *Husserl's Crisis of the European Sciences and Transcendental Philosophy: An Introduction*. Cambridge: Cambridge University Press, 2012.

Moran, Dermot. *Introduction to Phenomenology*. London: Routledge & Kegan Paul, 2000.

Moran, Dermot, and Joseph Cohen. *The Husserl Dictionary*. London: Bloomsbury, 2012.

Nagel, Ernst. "Review of Philosophical Essays in Memory of Edmund Husserl." Edited by M. Farber. *The Journal of Philosophy* 38 (1941): 301–6.

Nietzsche, Friedrich. *The Will to Power*. Translated by W. Kaufmann and R. J. Hollingdale. New York: Vintage Books, 1968.

Ott, Hugo. *Martin Heidegger: Unterwegs zu seiner Biographie*. Frankfurt am Main: Campus, 1988.

Parker, Rodney. "The History Between Koyré and Husserl." In *Hypotheses and Perspectives within History and Philosophy of Science: Homage to Alexandre Koyré 1964–2014*, edited by R. Pisano, J. Agassi, and D. Drozdova. Berlin: Springer (forthcoming).

Patočka, Jan. "The Philosophy of Arithmetic." In *An Introduction to Husserl's Phenomenology*, edited by J. Dodd, 19–40. Translated by E. Kohák. Chicago, IL: Open Court, 1996.

Pfänder, Alexander. *Die Seele des Menschen*. Halle-an-der-Saale: Max Niemeyer, 1933.

Pfänder, Alexander. *Logik*. In *Jahrbuch für Philosophie und phänomenologische Forschung* 4 (1921): 139–494e.

Pfeifer, Alexandra Elisabeth. "Ontological Phenomenology: The Philosophical Project of Hedwig Conrad-Martius." *Axiomathes* 18 (2008): 445–60.

Pfeiffer, Johannes. *Existenzphilosophie: Einführung in Heidegger und Jaspers*. Leipzig: Felix Meiner, 1933.

Pöggeler, Otto. *Der Denkweg Martin Heideggers*. Pfullingen: Günther Neske, 1983.

Reinach, Adolf. "Vortrag über Phänomenologie" (1914/1921). In *Adolf Reinach: Sämtliche Werke*, edited by K. Schuhmann and B. Smith, 1, 531–50. Munich: Philosophia, 1989.

Rickert, Heinrich. *Der Gegenstand der Erkenntnis: Einführung in die Transzendental-philosophie*. Freiburg im Breisgau: Herder, 1892/1915.

Sartre, Jean-Paul. *Being and Nothingness*. Translated by H. Barnes. New York: Washington Square Press, 1966.

Sartre, Jean-Paul. "Intentionality: A Fundamental Idea of Husserl's Phenomenology." Translated by J. Fell. *Journal of the British Society for Phenomenology* 1 (1970): 4–5.

Sartre, Jean-Paul. *L'existentialisme est un humanisme* (1946). Edited by A. Elkaïm-Sartre. Paris: Gallimard, 1996.

Sartre, Jean-Paul. *Sartre by Himself*. Translated by R. Seaver. New York: Urizen Books, 1978.

Sartre, Jean-Paul. *Situations IV*. Paris: Gallimard, 1964.

HUSSERL AND OTHER PHENOMENOLOGISTS

Sartre, Jean-Paul. *The Transcendence of the Ego*. Translated by F. Williams and R. Kirkpatrick. New York: Hill & Wang, 1960.

Sartre, Jean-Paul. *War Diaries*. Translated by Q. Hoare. New York: Pantheon, 1985.

Scheler, Max. *Die Stellung des Menschen im Kosmos* (1928), *MSGW*, 9, 7–72. Bern: Francke, 1976.

Scheler, Max. "Idealismus-Realismus" (1927). In *Max Scheler: Gesammelte Werke* (*MSGW*), 9, 183–242 (243–342). Bern: Francke, 1976.

Schutz, Alfred. "Sartre's Theory of the Alter-Ego." *Philosophy and Phenomenological Research* 9 (1948): 181–99.

Schmid, Richard. "Einleitung des Herausgebers', Die Krisis der Europäischen Wissenschaften und die Transzendentale Phänomenologie." In *Ergänzungsband Texte aus dem Nachlass 1924–1937*, edited by R. N. Smid. Dordrecht: Kluwer Academic Publishers, 1993.

Schuhmann, Karl. "Alexandre Koyré." In *Encyclopedia of Phenomenology*, edited by L. Embree, et al., 391–93. Dordrecht: Kluwer Academic Publishers, 1997.

Schuhmann, Karl. "Zu Heideggers *Spiegel*-Gespräch über Husserl." *Zeitschrift für philosophische Forschung* 32 (1978): 591–612.

Schuhmann, Karl, ed. *Husserl-Chronik: Denk- und Lebensweg Edmund Husserls*. The Hague: Martinus Nijhoff, 1977.

Smith, Arthur David. "The Flesh of Perception: Merleau-Ponty and Husserl." In *Reading Merleau-Ponty: On Phenomenology of Perception*, edited by T. Baldwin, 1–22, New York: Routledge, 2007.

Spiegelberg, Herbert. "How Subjective is Phenomenology?" In *Essays in Phenomenology*, edited by M. Natanson, 137–43. The Hague: Martinus Nijhoff, 1969.

Spiegelberg, Herbert. "Phenomenology of Direct Evidence." *Philosophy and Phenomenological Research* 2, no. 4 (1942): 427–56.

Spiegelberg, Herbert. *The Phenomenological Movement* (2 vols.). The Hague: Martinus Nijhoff, 1960.

Stawarska, Beata. "Defining Imagination: Sartre between Husserl and Janet." *Phenomenology and Cognitive Sciences* 4 (2005): 133–53.

Stawarska, Beata. "Memory and Subjectivity: Sartre in Dialogue with Husserl." *Sartre Studies International* 8 (2002): 94–111.

Stawarska, Beata. "Sartre and Husserl's *Ideen*: Phenomenology and Imagination." In *Jean-Paul Sartre: Key Concepts*, edited by S. Churchill and J. Reynolds, 12–32, Durham, NC: Acuman, 2013.

Stein, Edith. *Endliches und ewiges Sein: Versuch eines Aufstiegs zum Sinn des Seins* (1931–36). In *Edith Stein: Gesamtausgabe* (*ESGA*), 11/12, 3–441. Freiburg im Breisgau: Herder, 2013.

Stein, Edith. "Husserls transzendentale Phänomenologie" (1931). In *ESGA*, 9, 159–61. Freiburg im Breisgau: Herder, 2014.

Stein, Edith. "Martin Heideggers Existenzphilosophie" (1937). In *ESGA*, 11/12, 445–99. Freiburg im Breisgau: Herder, 2013.

Stein, Edith. *Zum Problem der Einfühlung* (1917). In *ESGA*, 5, 1–136. Freiburg im Breisgau: Herder, 2010.

Ströker, Elisabeth. *Husserl's Transcendental Phenomenology*. Stanford, CA: Stanford University Press, 1933.

Taminiaux, Jacques. "Phenomenology in Merleau-Ponty's Late Work." In Jacques Taminiaux, *Dialectic and Difference: Finitude in Modern Thought*, edited by J. T. Decker and R. Crease, 115–29. Atlantic Highlands, NJ: Humanities Press, 1985.

Thomä, Dieter, ed. *Heidegger Handbuch: Leben–Werk–Wirkung*. Stuttgart: J. B. Metzler, 2013.

Toadvine, Ted. "Leaving Husserl's Cave? The Philosopher's Shadow Revisited." In *Merleau-Ponty's Reading of Husserl*, edited by T. Toadvine and L. Embree, 71–95. Dordrecht: Kluwer Academic Publishers, 2002.

Toadvine, Ted. "Merleau-Ponty's Reading of Husserl: A Chronological Overview." In *Merleau-Ponty's Reading of Husserl*. Edited by T. Toadvine and L. Embree, 227–90. Dordrecht: Kluwer Academic Publishers, 2002.

Vetter, Helmuth. *Grundriss Heidegger: Ein Handbuch zu Leben und Werk*. Hamburg: Felix Meiner, 2014.

Vietae, François. *In Artem Analyticem (sic) Isagoge, Seorsim excussa ab opere restituate Mathematicae Analyseo, seu, Algebra Nova* (Introduction to the Analytical Art, excerpted as a separate piece from the

HUSSERL AND OTHER PHENOMENOLOGISTS

opus of the restored Mathematical Analysis, or The New Algebra), Tours 1591. English translation: *Introduction to the Analytic Art*. Translated by J. W. Smith, appendix to J. Klein 1969/1992.

Wilson, Colin. "Preface." In *Essays in Honor of Jacob Klein*, edited by S. Kutler. Annapolis, MD: St John's College Press, 1976.

Zahavi, Dan. "Intersubjectivity in Sartre's *Being and Nothingness*." *Alter* 10 (2002): 265–81.

Zahavi, Dan. "Merleau-Ponty on Husserl: A Reappraisal." In *Merleau-Ponty's Reading of Husserl*, edited by T. Toadvine and L. Embree, 3–30. Dordrecht: Kluwer Academic Publishers, 2002.

Index

Note: Page numbers followed by "n" denote endnotes

Anzahlen 78–80, 91n31
Aristotle 99–100, 106, 108n30; dispute with Plato 79; *Prior and Posterior Analytics* 81

Barbaras, Renaud 70n18
Becker, Carl Heinrich 100
Becker, Oskar 90n18
Being and Nothingness (Sartre) 37, 48, 57
Being and Time (Heidegger) 92, 94–5, 100, 101, 104

Cairns, Dorion 3–4, 14n2
Carman, Taylor 63, 70n20
Carr, David 88n11
Cartesian Meditations (Husserl) 20, 49; alter-ego and analogy 25; harmonious synthesis 24–5; intersubjective reduction 23–4; language in 22; Other's phenomenality 20–2
Caton, Hiram 88n10
Conrad-Martius, Hedwig 15n29
consciousness 18; ego and 56; freedom and 56–8; presence of Other and 21–2, 24; self-temporalizing 54; stream of 55; unity and individuality of 53–4
constitution 44n13; presence and 31–3; rationality and 33–4
contingency of reason 37–9
Crisis of European Sciences and Transcendental Phenomenology, The (Husserl) 72–3, 86
Critique of Pure Reason (Kant) 52

Dasein's kind of being 35–6, 38, 40
Dastur, Françoise 63, 67, 69n8
Derrida, Jacques 29–30, 44n1
Descartes's account of abstraction 84–5, 91n36

embodied self, Merleau-Ponty's notion of 63–4
empirical ego 52, 55
Encyclopaedia Britannica (Husserl and Heidegger) 59n27, 94, 102

Farber, Marvin 87n3
"Fifth Meditation" 22, 24, 25

givenness, notion of 5–8
Great Phenomenological Schism 92–5, 101, 103–5
Grenzprobleme der Phänomenologie (Husserl) 106
Gurwitsch, Aaron 89n17

Hartmann, Nicolai 100
Heffernan, George 2
Heidegger, Martin 2, 29, 44n2, 45n24, 92–4; *Being and Time* 92, 94–5, 100, 101, 104; corroborating evidence for 101–5; Dasein 35–6, 38, 40; "My Way Into Phenomenology" 95, 97, 100, 101, 106; *Rektoratsrede* (1933) 43; "Spiegel Interview" 95
Hopkins, Burt C. 2
Husserl, Edmund 4, 45n28, 56, 59n27; *Cartesian Meditations* 20–5, 49; concept of reflexion 11–12; contingency of reason 37–9; *Crisis of European Sciences and Transcendental Phenomenology, The* 72–3, 86; givenness and self-givenness 6–8, 15n21; Great Phenomenological Schism 92–5, 101, 103–5; *Grenzprobleme der Phänomenologie* 106; and Heidegger, Martin *see* Heidegger, Martin; *Idea of Phenomenology, The* 8, 15n20; *Ideas for a Pure Phenomenology and Phenomenological Philosophy* 92, 97, 98, 100; *Ideas I* 95, 97, 101, 104; *Ideas II* 2, 61–2; influence on Merleau-Ponty's work *see* Merleau-Ponty, Maurice; inner and outer perception 6–7; intuitive evidence 31; *Investigations into Phenomenology and Theory of Knowledge* 96; *Logical Investigations see Logical Investigations* (Husserl); metaphysics of presence 43; narrowing and cutting 10; phenomenological and eidetic reduction 15n22, 16n37; Phenomenological-Existential Schism 92–5, 101, 103–5; phenomenological subject and object 4–5, 8–10; phenomenology and transcendental idealism 92–3; "Philosophy as

121

INDEX

Rigorous Science" 105; *Philosophy of Arithmetic see Philosophy of Arithmetic* (Husserl); plurality of perspectives 12; principle of intentionality 49–52; "pure logic", idea of 5; "pure phenomenology" 97; on Sartre's philosophical development 49; theory of intuition 17; *Yearbook for Philosophy and Phenomenological Research* 94, 104

Idea of Phenomenology, The (Husserl) 8, 15n20, 93
Ideas for a Pure Phenomenology and Phenomenological Philosophy (Husserl) 92, 97, 98, 100
Ingarden, Roman 92, 93, 106
"Intentionality: A Fundamental Idea of Husserl's Phenomenology" (Sartre) 49, 50, 52, 57, 59n19
intentionality, notion of 18–19, 49–52
Investigations into Phenomenology and Theory of Knowledge (Husserl) 96

Kant, Immanuel 52–3, 55, 59n24; *Critique of Pure Reason* 52; transcendental ego 52–3
Klein, Jacob 2, 71, 87n1; 'intentional history', notion of 72, 88n6; "Phenomenology and the History of Science" 72, 85–6; relation to Husserlian phenomenology 72, 78–83; "sedimentation", concept of 72, 80, 85, 88n7; symbolic abstraction 84–6; Vieta's innovation 80–3
Koyré, Alexandre 73, 89n12, 89n17

Levinas, Emmanuel 17, 27n19, 28n26; on *Cartesian Meditations* 20–5; ethical debt 26; ethics and critique 19–20; intellectual debt 25; intentionality 18–19; relationship of teaching 26–7; *Totality and Infinity* 18, 19, 26–7
Levy, Lior 1
Logical Investigations (Husserl) 75, 83, 95–102, 108n27; consciousness in 54–5; ego as empirical object 6; empirical ego 55; intentionality in 51–2; performative contradiction 30–1; phenomenological subject and object 9; reflection in phenomenological project 57–8; relation of intention to fulfillment 31–3; Sartre's response to 49, 56; transcendental ego in 53

Majer, Ulrich 90n21
Mensch, James 1
Merleau-Ponty, Maurice: "Cézanne' Doubt" 70n25; embodied self, notion of 63–4; flesh, notion of 67, 70n26; Husserl's philosophical example 61–3; *Phenomenology of Perception* 63, 69n6; Philosopher and His Shadow, The 65, 69n7; "sort of reflection" 62, 65, 70n23;

"subject-object" 65–6, 68; unthought-of element 68–9, 70n28; *Visible and Invisible, The* 64, 70n26
Miller, J. Philip 88n10
Moran, Dermot 89n17
"My Way Into Phenomenology" (Heidegger) 95, 97, 100, 101, 106

Nagel, Ernst 85–6, 91n37
Natorp, Paul 55
Nietzsche, Friedrich 33, 34
nothingness, selfhood and 35–7
numbers, concept of 73–4; *see also Anzahlen*

On the Manifold Meaning of Being according to Aristotle (Brentano) 95

Patočka, Jan 83
performative contradiction 39–41; Husserlian response to 34; presence and 30–1
Pfänder, Alexander 92, 93, 106, 111n120
phenomenological and eidetic reduction 15n22, 16n37
Phenomenological-Existential Schism 92–5, 101, 103–5
phenomenological investigation, stages of 11
"phenomenological movement" 1
phenomenological subject and object 4–5, 8–10
"Phenomenology and the History of Science" (Klein) 72, 85–6
Phenomenology of Perception (Merleau-Ponty) 63, 69n6
Philosopher and His Shadow, The (Merleau-Ponty) 65, 69n7
Philosophical Essays in Memory of Edmund Husserl (Farber) 87n3
"Philosophy as Rigorous Science" (Husserl) 105
Philosophy of Arithmetic (Husserl) 49, 59n14, 72; cardinal numbers, concept of 77; "figural moments" 76; Klein's account of 78–83; "logical equivalence" 76; numbers, proper concept of 73–4; psychological abstraction 75; symbolic numbers, accounting for 76–7; universal arithmetic, definition of 78
post-Husserlian phenomenologies 13–14
presence: constitution and 31–3; performative contradiction and 30–1; transcendence and 41–3
Prior and Posterior Analytics (Aristotle) 81
psychological abstraction, notion of 75
pure ego, notion of 4, 53, 55
"pure logic", idea of 5
"pure phenomenology" 97

rationality, constituted presence with 33–4
Reinach, Adolf 92–4, 106

INDEX

Sartre, Jean-Paul 17, 37, 41, 43, 47, 51, 58; *Being and Nothingness* 37, 48, 57; on ego 52, 56; hodological space 39; Husserl's phenomenology and 48–50, 57; on intentionality 51–2; "Intentionality: A Fundamental Idea of Husserl's Phenomenology" 49, 50, 52, 57, 59n19; noema as unreal 32–3; *Transcendence of the Ego, The* 48, 49, 52, 55, 57; unity and individuality of consciousness 53–4
Scheler, Max 92, 93, 106
Schneider, Artur 96
Schuhmann, Karl 73, 87n2, 89n12
Schutz, Alfred 56
"sedimentation", concept of 72, 80, 85, 88n7
self-givenness, notion of 6–8, 15n21
selfhood and nothingness 35–7
self-temporalizing consciousness 54
Spiegelberg, Herbert 3, 14, 14n1
"spiritual ego" 7
Stawarska, Beata 47–9, 58n2, 59n18
Stein, Edith 92, 93, 106

Strauss, Leo 73
Ströker, Elisabeth 15n19
Stumpf, Carl 77
symbolic abstraction 84–6

Totality and Infinity (Levinas) 18, 19, 26–7
Transcendence of the Ego, The (Sartre) 48, 49, 52, 55, 57
transcendence, presence and 41–3
transcendental ego 48, 52–3, 55

universal arithmetic, definition of 78
"unthought-of element" 68–9, 70n28

Vietae, François 78, 80–3, 91n31
Visible and Invisible, The (Merleau-Ponty) 64, 70n26

Wilson, Curtis 89n16

Yearbook for Philosophy and Phenomenological Research (Husserl) 94, 104